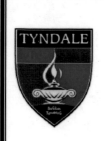
Brian—

Thanks for your interest in
helping the church in Canada
be strong in its wisdom of leadership.

— Brian C. Stiller

— June 1/05

FROM THE

TOWER OF BABEL

TO

PARLIAMENT HILL

HOW TO BE A CHRISTIAN IN CANADA TODAY

BRIAN C. STILLER

HarperCollins*PublishersLtd*

http://www.harpercollins.com/canada

First edition

Canadian Cataloguing in Publication Data

Stiller, Brian C.
From the Tower of Babel to Parliament Hill :
how to be a Christian in Canada today

Includes bibliographical references and index.
ISBN 0-00-255753-3
1. Christianity and politics.   2. Canada - Politics and
government - 1993- .   I. Title.

BR115.P7S74 1997   261.7'0971   C96-931885-5

97 98 99 ❖ HC 10 9 8 7 6 5 4 3 2 1

Printed and bound in the United States

In dedication to those who have encouraged me to understand and consider the relationship of faith to our surrounding culture.

The Honourable Jake Epp, colleague, friend, and Christian, who modelled the integration of faith with spiritual well-being in the most challenging of environments, the federal Parliament;

The Reverend Alvin C. Schindel, teacher and friend, whose reverence for the sacred and passion for spiritual integrity helped me see the relevance of the Gospel to all of life;

Mr. George Spaetzel (1931–1991), friend and businessman, who demonstrated an understanding of the Christian faith, lived out in the world of business.

In dedication to those who have encouraged me to understand and consider the relationship of faith to our surrounding culture.

The Honourable Jake Epp, colleague, friend, and Christian, who modelled the integration of faith with spiritual well-being in the most challenging of environments, the federal Parliament;

The Reverend Alvin C. Schindel, teacher and friend, whose reverence for the sacred and passion for spiritual integrity helped me see the relevance of the Gospel to all of life;

Mr. George Spaetzel (1931–1991), friend and businessman, who demonstrated an understanding of the Christian faith, lived out in the world of business.

Contents

Preface / vii

Contents

Preface / vii

Preface

The sea of faith
Was once, too, at the full, and round earth's shore
Lay like the folds of a bright girdle furl'd;
But now I only hear
Its melancholy, long, withdrawing roar,
Retreating to the breath
Of the night-wind, down the vast edges drear
And naked shingles of the world.

—Matthew Arnold, "Dover Beach"

In this, perhaps his best-known poem, Arnold saw clearly the state of faith in his own mid-Victorian England, and inadvertently, but accurately, foresaw Canada's for much of the twentieth century. During the early part of this century, while institutional Christianity was strong and had a considerable influence on society, there was some evidence of a weakening of spiritual life within the churches. In the latter part of this century, evidence of its frailty is conspicuous. Considered unworthy of serious consideration by our media, banished from our public schools, and viewed as quaint by our cultural gatekeepers, "the sea of faith," in social and political terms, is a small pool at best as we lurch towards the new millennium.

Christianity dwindled for a number of reasons. Secularization—an ideology as well as a process—trivialized matters of the transcendent, while certain forms of Christianity were susceptible to secularism, and at times scarcely distinguished from the surrounding culture.

Sectarianism, fostered by fear of the secular world-view, caused people of faith to withdraw from cultural engagement; in the process, intentionally or not, many became supporters of an almost mindless status quo. Christians between these poles felt discouraged and uncertain. Faith as a decisive factor in Canadian life became cloistered in the private fortresses of church and personal life.

However, there are signs of further change. The remarkable April 1993 cover story in *Maclean's*, "God Is Alive," broke the rules that had been keeping personal and vital Christianity out of our mainstream secular magazines. As well, sociologist Reginald Bibby, along with the Angus Reid group, the pollsters and pulse-takers of Canadian living, have documented the critical place Christian faith continues to have in the ethos of this nation. Even while it has been shunted out of sight, faith is reasserting itself in new ways and is re-emerging as an influence on our culture and people.

Some people wonder if this resurgence of faith is driven by the various agendas of American life, and particularly by the rise of the "Religious Right," those politically and religiously conservative Americans who, out of angst over the moral drift of their nation, want to bring about change. But while Canada's border is unprotected and the media overflow from the United States has, at times, an imperialistic influence, the late historian George Rawlyk reminds us that because of our "irenic" nature, that is, our tendency to promote peace, what goes on in Canada is more a matter of our own making than a reproduction of what preoccupies our neighbours to the south. Our history, our demographics, and the more moderate nature of our religious communities suggest that religious renewal will develop and manifest itself in peculiarly Canadian ways.

The reason for writing this book is to help Canadian Christians steer clear of the secular/sectarian polarization and, at the same time, avoid the midstream paralysis. To move into a new way of thinking, I've had to re-evaluate the assumptions of my own church heritage, which tended to view the world as either unimportant or unredeemable. Since taking part in public debate, be it on "The Hill" in Ottawa, in a Supreme Court intervention, or on radio or television, I've had to practise a language of public discourse in order to relate Christ's message to our social realities.

This book explores the evolution of that language. I've framed the discussion here with two biblical events: Babel and Pentecost. The story of Babel speaks of confusion, of a culture misunderstanding its role in creation: this is my place of departure. The Hebrew day of Pentecost is a fitting image of the Christian life: the barrier of different languages removed, people were able to hear the Gospel in their own language, and thereby to achieve a common understanding of the task ahead.

This book is divided into three parts: "Canadian Language," "Biblical Language," and "Kingdom Language." Part I examines the fragmentation of our country and the reasons for our loss of a Christian witness within the public square. Part II digs into the Old Testament to learn what the Hebrews, as people of faith, believed a nation should be. It then moves on to the New Testament to unwrap Christ's call to his Kingdom, and ends with an examination of what it really means to "think Christianly." Part III looks at the history of the church and politics, beginning at the time of Christ and ending with an overview of pluralism, which is at the heart of our modern culture. Finally, it undertakes a quest for a language of public discourse shaped by Jesus Christ.

The genesis of this book was when I saw our son, Murray, as he received his undergraduate degree from Trinity Western University. As he walked across the stage I wondered what could I put into his hands which would help him (and his generation) understand the call of Jesus Christ today. This, then, is my offering to Murray, our daughter, Muriel, and their respective spouses Catherine and Jesse. It is my attempt to understand the simple and yet complex message and life of our Lord to this world, in this age.

WITH THANKS

There are many who have greatly helped me in this process: Kathryn Dean, who in the early stages helped me with the primary structure and assumptions; Daryl Reed, who did research and writing on chapter 2; Bruce Gunther, who did considerable research and writing on chapters 2 and 3 and assisted me in many ways to think through our religious past; Debbie Fieguth, who helped research chapter 3; Audrey Dorsch, who gave special assistance at a critical point in the writing;

and those who carefully read the manuscript at various stages and offered pointed recommendations: Bruce Clemenger, Aileen Van Ginkel, John Kessler, Paul Marshall, Don Posterski, John Redekop, Ian Rennie, Gerald Vandezande, and John Vissers. A special thanks to Susan Travis for her loving assistance in helping with the manuscript. And, finally, to Carol Bonnett and Nicole Langlois of HarperCollins for their enthusiasm and outstanding editing.

In the end, what is written here, its style and perspectives, are mine. I do hope this material will provoke further research and writing, so that as Christians in Canada we will better understand our times and, in that understanding, know better the strategies to take (1 Chron. 12: 32).

PART I

CANADIAN LANGUAGE

CHAPTER 1

The Babel Syndrome:
A Country Fragmented

Every time I walk up from the flame to Centre Block on Parliament Hill and look up at the Peace Tower, I'm filled with a sense of history, destiny, and goodwill. The majestic buildings, rising from the high banks of the Ottawa River, seem so righteous and trustworthy. At Canada's inception, our Fathers of Confederation chose the designation "Dominion" from Psalm 72 ("He shall have dominion from sea to sea, and from the river to the ends of the earth"). Growing up in this country, it seemed to me that a biblical vision shaped our very soul.

But now, as we experience the transition to a new millennium, this country, symbolized by that biblical text, and in its earlier years shaped by an unabashed recognition of God, is going through a radical shift. We seem embarrassed to acknowledge our spiritual heritage unless the occasion demands it, such as a funeral of our political or cultural greats.

The span of time from the ancient Tower of Babel to the Peace Tower of today is long, but "progress" has barely separated the two.

The children had been well prepared for the school's annual Christmas program. Songs had been carefully selected from the various religions represented in this urban school. But little was the principal prepared for the outrage of a parent and the eventual disbanding of the celebration, both on account of the Christmas carol "Away in a Manger." Program plans could proceed only when the school removed any mention of "Jesus" from its celebration.

In 1985 the Supreme Court of Canada ruled that the Alberta law on Sunday closing of retail stores violated the Charter of Rights and Freedoms. The reason? The law was built on a religious rationale. That ruling, the *Big M Drug Mart* case, established the legal basis by which religious faith would be increasingly marginalized.

Subsequently our national newspaper, the *Globe and Mail*, decided it did not need a reporter on religion. Our national broadcaster, the CBC, decided the radio show *Morningside*, which offered panels dealing with children's books, politics, cooking, music, drama, regional reports, and so on, did not need to include an occasional panel to deal with matters of faith.

It is of interest to note the history of the *Globe and Mail* and of the host of *Morningside*, Peter Gzowski. The *Globe and Mail* was founded by George Brown, a Father of Confederation, who had come to Toronto with his father to establish a Presbyterian newspaper. Peter Gzowski's forebears included the great engineer Sir Casimir, who as an ardent Anglican Christian was active in the founding and ongoing work of Wycliffe College (the evangelical Anglican college on the University of Toronto campus) and whose son gave time and finances to numerous Christian organizations, including Toronto Bible College (now Ontario Bible College/Ontario Theological Seminary), where he was a member of the board for some years.

From sea to sea there has been a loss of public Christian presence and influence in the life and governing of this nation. Some Canadians call for Canada to return to its religious roots as a "Christian country." Believing that Christian symbols are being stripped from cultural events, and angry at courts, politicians, and educators for rejecting biblical values, they are unnerved by the moral degeneracy of life in general. On the opposite side of this call for Canada to return to its

Christian roots is unrelenting pressure to distance the church from the arena of social/moral influence and to strip our values of all distinctly Christian views.

These opposing currents of profound differences and antagonisms flow together in the same broad stream. Some Christians, in their desire for a return to a "Christian country," go so far as to support the imposition of their version of Christian faith on society. In contrast, people who operate with an explicitly secular agenda, though espousing liberal-individualism, often resist individuals who seek to express their faith in the public square.

Government is caught in the debate. Given the increased political influence of the courts—through the 1982 Charter of Rights and Freedoms—and the growing incursion of public policy in our lives—everything from what media we can access to what books can be on the shelves of school libraries—the role of government is enormous. In fact, any debate on the issue of religious liberty eventually broadens into a clash of views on the role of government. However, for many Christians the issue isn't so much the government's role as it is the question of whether or not Christian faith is to have a place in shaping and influencing government. Indeed, how do we, as Christians, view this relationship? Are we to oppose government? Take it over? Diminish it? Just ignore it? And is there anything particularly biblical about any one of these alternatives?

This search for an understanding of the role of Christians in government and public life must begin with a look at the current Canadian condition. Since the early 1970s, the English/French language debate has been a significant and contentious issue. But that is not the primary language confusion we face. (Even that debate is complicated by the many languages we speak: French or English, Ukrainian or Mandarin, to name four of the hundred languages heard each day in Canada.) The real confusion comes from seeking to define what we believe is true, be it in terms of secular materialism, individual liberalism, technology, conservatism, humanism, or Christianity, amid a cacophony of language.

To live as Christians in Canada, we must discover the Christian meaning of nationhood. That search takes us back to an earlier moment of political and social confusion.

The Spirit of Babel

In early biblical history, people living in what is now Iraq built a city with a tower "that reaches to the heavens" (Gen. 11: 4). On the surface, the project may have appeared to be a noble one—something of a large-scale urban-renewal project providing people with homes and places of work. However, the plan to build the tower sprang from less than dignified motives: the primary goal was to "make a name for ourselves" (11: 4).

Seeing their objective, God's response was: "If as one people speaking the same language they have begun to do this, then nothing they plan to do will be impossible for them" (11: 6). God then confused their speech, scattering them all over the world: "Come, let us go down and confuse their language so they will not understand each other. So the Lord scattered them from there over all the earth, and they stopped building the city" (11: 7–8).

And fragmentation began.

"That is why it was called Babel—because there the Lord confused the language of the whole world. From there the Lord scattered them over the face of the whole earth" (11: 9).

At Babel, the people contravened God's command "to be fruitful and multiply and populate the earth ... and multiply in it" (9: 7), choosing, instead, to remain together and accumulate power.

By confusing their language, God divided them. But for what purpose? To prevent the accumulative power of consensual evil. Lack of diversity would, by centripetal force (that is, by driving and focusing towards the centre), intensify evil and thus cause the community to self-destruct.

The confusion of language had the opposite effect: by centrifugal force, it drove people away from the centre, thus breaking up the convergence of evil. As a result, human existence was preserved. Confusion saved us. Later, at Pentecost, God again used diverse languages, this time to create an occasion of unity.

Looking for a Canadian Language

Babel is a fitting point of departure for our search for a Canadian language. While we seek to understand the role of the Christian faith in national life, Canadians face another challenge: what does it mean to be a Canadian? We desperately need a language that defines who we are, symbols we can share. We know we are not American. But who and what are we? We want an answer that's more definitive than a simple list of what we are not. Layer onto that quest the Christian guiding impulse for something grander and higher in its poetry of identity, and you can feel the longing for a nation whose sense of self is more than just a sum of its parts. A spiritually sensitized citizen longs for an overarching and integrative framework of life.

As we struggle with the issues of linguistic primacy and nationalistic self-definition, we have been trapped in a mind-set whereby the only appropriate language is one that describes life without God.

Babel is a version of Canada's story—not because Canada has tried to make a name for itself (we are, after all, a modest power on the world stage), but because our history and our country's guiding principles have brought us to a state of cultural, political, and spiritual confusion. From its early beginnings, Canada has been a loose-knit and diverse country that never developed the intense patriotism that unites other nations. Although it has produced a relatively open and varied society, our diversity is now degenerating into factionalism and disharmony. We enter the twenty-first century a divided nation in need of a unifying vision.

Divided by History

As we muddle through, attempting to define Canadianism, it is easy to forget the history that has shaped us. People are immigrating to Canada in growing numbers (in 1991, 23.5 per cent of people living in Ontario were born outside of Canada), and these different groups of citizens have different visions and versions of the past, which leads to more Babel confusion.

Canada was not founded, as was the United States, with a unique political philosophy or set of ideals. Central to our development were two European powers looking for ways to increase their colonial dominance. The hostilities and self-interest that characterized relations between France and Great Britain were transferred to the New World, and escalated into outright warfare.

The French presence in North America began in 1534. Jacques Cartier landed on the Gaspé on his way to another place, erected a thirty-foot wooden cross, and mused out loud (or so it is reported), "I'm rather inclined to believe that this is the land God gave to Cain [when he punished him]."[1] Later, British explorers sailed into Hudson Bay and began to trade in furs in competition with the French.

When the English finally gained precedence over the French after the Battle of the Plains of Abraham in 1759, hostilities between French and English Canada were entrenched. The Quebec Act of 1774 gave Quebec the right to retain the French language, French civil law, and a system of education directed by the church. While the Roman Catholic Church in Quebec did not have the privilege of the mother church in Europe, through its links with a powerful political machine it became a dominant ruling force in Quebec.

In 1864, George E. Cartier, George Brown, and John A. Macdonald, under the Great Coalition ministry, worked to bring about an alliance, resulting in the 1867 confederation of provinces called "Canada" under the British North America (BNA) Act. Today the creation of this confederation is the source of some debate: why was Canada formed? Was it an agreement bringing together "two founding nations" to resolve the English–French deadlock? Or was it a formula to unite many provinces into a non-American national unit?

This distinction is important. For, if Canada is at its heart a political enterprise primarily made up of "two founding nations," then efforts to reshape the Canadian construct will necessarily focus on that aspect. According to this view, Quebec, as one of Canada's "two founding nations," would have a stronger position than that of any other province. If the "equality-of-provinces" view is closer to the original intent, then Quebec becomes like any other province. (Of course, it is different historically, ethnically, and linguistically, and the province needs assurances that that distinctiveness will be preserved.) According to this interpretation, Quebec is large and influential, to be sure, but one-tenth, not one-half, of the federal formula.[2]

The notion that Quebec is only one of ten provinces plays stronger the farther west you go from central Canada. Ontario and the Maritimes have found it easier to live with the assumption that Confederation was really the amalgamation of two nations. That is not surprising, since they were at the table when Confederation was hatched.

The idea may make sense in Ontario and Prince Edward Island, but, if you are descended from immigrants who arrived later than 1867, and your first language is Swedish or Chinese, and you have invested your life in settling the resistant prairies or laying train track through the rugged regions of British Columbia, then it is difficult to sit around the kitchen table and be convinced that your contribution to the development and expansion of Canada is secondary to that made by those who were part of the original union. The same is true for Newfoundlanders, who were the last to join Confederation.

Add in Quebec's internal struggle, and you have the makings of intraprovincial conflict. Reacting against the hierarchical control by the Roman Catholic Church and the government of Premier Maurice Duplessis, Quebec underwent radical changes during the Quiet Revolution of the 1960s. Determined to escape the shackles of church–state control, Quebeckers focused their energies on building a strong self-identity and increasing their own control over linguistic, cultural, and ethnic issues. The result? Powerful groups in Quebec argue that the province cannot preserve its culture and identity within the bosom of the Canadian state unless it is given the right to define itself as a "distinct society." And the leaders of that would-be distinct society are able to press their agenda because of Quebec's very size: Quebeckers comprise almost one-quarter of the population of Canada.

But there is more than size involved. French Quebeckers have their roots in the dynamism of seventeenth-century France. The only people they can be compared with are the Americans, whose roots lie in seventeenth-century English Puritanism. Both believed themselves called by God to the New World, and from here to serve him. The call and the vision have been secularized, but both have a dynamic sense of identity and purpose.

Divided by Geography

Whether the national plant has two roots or many, any attempts to reconcile our divergent views are hindered by the very size of the place.

Look at a map of Canada. The land mass covers 9,841,000 square kilometres, stretching 7,314 kilometres from the Atlantic to the Pacific. Our more populated regions are divided by the sparsely inhabited Canadian Shield. It sits right in the middle and covers 4,600,000 square kilometres, or 47 per cent of all of Canada! Numbering fewer than 30 million, the population is scattered across our vast territory, and has no real geographical connection. Bound on three sides by the longest coastline in the world, 75 per cent of us live in a 160-kilometre corridor running along the American border. The great north exists, but most of our attention is drawn to the neighbour to the south. No wonder at heart we seem divided.

Geography has an immense influence on how a nation is defined. Because Canada's territory is so immense, the populated areas today were settled over a long period of time. As well, settlers of the different regions made Canada their home for very different reasons.

Many who first settled in what is now Ontario (apart from a few hardy French homesteaders who came in with the fur trade) did so because they rejected the populist democracy of the Thirteen Colonies during the American Revolution. They saw in Canada a haven in which they could retain their allegiance to the British Crown and stay close to their British roots, or, like the Mennonites and certain other Pennsylvania Dutch minorities, receive better protection from a monarchy for their distinctiveness than they would receive from an egalitarian American democracy loath to recognize any form of distinct society.

The prairies were settled by Europeans—Ukrainians, Jews, Swedes, Norwegians, Germans, Mennonites, Scots, Irish, and English. The English, Scots, and Irish, coming from Ontario and the United Kingdom, were seeking an opportunity to better themselves. They had no desire to be free from the restrictions of government; rather, they valued their governmental inheritance. Others such as the Ukrainians and Mennonites depended on the Canadian government to transport them to Canada, settle them, and protect their ways of living.

Still others, fleeing famine, war, and persecution, wanted to start a new life free from the restrictions of repressive governments. As settlers they learned to survive and thrive, far from the centres of political control. The lure of free land attracted many living in Ontario to try their hand on virgin land in the West. The challenge of taming the land was too much for some to resist. It is not surprising, then, that many Westerners are still known for their independent and entrepreneurial spirit.

As a family is enriched by the different temperaments and approaches to the life of its members, Canada's regions, each characterized by the uniqueness of its settlers, created a richer experience for all. But those differences have now become a source of conflict rather than unity. "Regional think" keeps us from understanding each other and from broadening our understanding of humanity.

Divided by Language

"Language" is a metaphor for the different approaches to culture and government that vie for attention. However, language, in its literal sense, has caused one of Canada's most publicized divisions. Having two official languages can potentially give Canada richness and diversity; it provides an opportunity for a breadth of understanding, greater than that which comes from living with only one language.

But having two languages also divides. The Canadian classic *Two Solitudes*, written by novelist Hugh MacLennan, describes the clash of franco- and anglophone families in Quebec and remains a quintessential diary of Canadian cultural conflict.

I was raised in Saskatchewan and lived in Montreal. The bipolar views on language I hear from French- and English-speaking communities remind me of the lack of understanding many English-speakers have for francophones and for their fierce loyalty to their own language and culture. The official bilingualism introduced by Prime Minister Trudeau was interpreted by many anglophones as what francophones in Quebec wanted, when in fact this policy served Trudeau's agenda more than it spoke for Quebec's interest. However, it ended up sparking a furious debate among English-speaking Canadians, who saw it as a jam-it-down-our-throats Quebec move. How wrong this view was. As English-speaking Canadians react, so do French-speaking Quebeckers when confronted with anglophones wanting to assimilate them into the English-speaking mass of North America.

This split in languages also affects the way we interpret events, as, every night, French Canadians watch one version of the news, and English Canadians another.

The Forgotten Dialect

Until fairly recent times, the majority of Canadians had forgotten or ignored another of our country's "languages" —Canada's first peoples. Their forgotten language has been waiting for years to be heard. Distanced by geography (until recently Canada's aboriginal peoples have lived in the North or on reserves) and by culture (most Natives in cities live outside the mainstream, and often in inner-city ghettos), we have forgotten they exist. When they launch protests, non-Natives resent them. When they show up in disproportionate numbers on prison lists, non-Natives dismiss them as being irresponsible. But these stereotypes are finally breaking down. As a people, they are no longer tolerating such attitudes, nor are they letting the rest of Canada get away with continuing the abuse and neglect of the past.

The sins of our ancestors will cost dearly. Our forebears took the Natives' land and their way of life, forcing many to assimilate and speak a new language. Although it would be equally wrong to view Canadian aboriginals romantically, as if their plight is only of others' making, we must recognize that Canadians of European descent have a collective debt to pay. Just as America continues to experience the entail of slavery in its social violence, so we suffer for having robbed, and then banished, our Native population, forcing them into a form of servitude. The quest for answers is difficult, but our attitudes to the particular needs of Canada's first peoples are critical in finding them.

Divided by Religion

Unlike state churches in Europe, which represented the established order (for example, the Swedish Lutheran Church or the Church of England), churches in North America had no privileged status with the government. In seventeenth-century Europe, there was a movement to disengage the church from the state. Radical evangelicals—Mennonites and Baptists—were among those who wanted to be free from the constraint of the state, promoting a church/state relationship whereby no church could be favoured or financed by government—in other words, the church would be "disestablished." Many immigrants who settled the New World brought with them this separationist view. In so far as their congregations were free to form and organize, they became a symbol of the free spirit of those building a new world. This was especially true in the United States.

In Canada, the notion of a disestablished church did not prevail at first. The Roman Catholic Church in Lower Canada represented the conservative élite as well as most of those who wanted to preserve European tradition. In Upper Canada, the Anglican Church served the same function. Although both churches stood against the common enemy of American political liberalism, the fact that they came out of two separate European political traditions kept them from together constructing a common Canadian identity. In fact, as the two staunchly defended their own traditions, they came into conflict.

Perhaps the most tragic example of this conflict occurred with the Riel Rebellion and the Northwest Rebellion as the two religious communities split over how to handle this rebellious leader. The English Protestants supported hanging Riel; the French—most of whom were Catholic—opposed it. In the end, Riel became a flashpoint for the smouldering feelings of the French towards the English. The enmity and distrust the French had for the English was set ablaze by the decision to hang Riel. The Protestants, in supporting this government action, and the Roman Catholics, in opposing it, helped to intensify the alienation of the two language groups. It also served as a rallying cry for late twentieth-century Quebec nationalism and the political drive towards separation. The Riel episode was too destructive for the religious glue of the Catholics (French) and Protestant (English) to hold the nation together. The seeds sown in the hanging of Riel are bearing fruit today.

Divided by the "Mosaic"

Given our historical, geographic, linguistic, and religious divisions, it is not surprising that Canada refers to itself as a mosaic. Unlike the American "melting pot," in which immigrants are assimilated into the country's prevailing culture, the Canadian "mosaic" allows—indeed encourages—ethnic groups to retain their individual cultural and linguistic identities. In fact, with the passage of the Canadian Multiculturalism Act in 1971 and the Canadian Charter of Rights and Freedoms in 1982, Canada has legislated and constitutionally entrenched the mosaic into permanent existence.

But what exactly is this Canadian mosaic?[3] With the best of intentions, Canada has glued together chips of different colours, in the hope that they will eventually make a picture. The problem is that, today, we are not sure what that picture is. Like the joke definition of "modern art," it is whatever a person imagines it to be. We each have our own interpretation.

While this mixture of many cultures is something to be celebrated, it can become divisive. Often we end up with something more like a kaleidoscope—the chips form a different pattern every time they are shaken.

In our desperate desire to be fair, we are caught between wanting to give equal place and recognition to each newly arrived group, and struggling to find an overarching national vision. We applaud the reputation for fairness and sense of fair play we have among nations. We call on our political overlords to sustain that reputation, but when we attempt to write a national constitution, we are not sure what our common denominators are and whether we have the solid foundation necessary to hold together the bits and pieces of our mosaic.

In our desire to be fair, caring, and supportive, we have devised a system which, in times of national crisis, seems less than reliable.

Divided by Politics

The Americans broke away from Britain to establish their own form of government. We Canadians didn't. At Confederation we retained the relationship with Mother Britain and imported her political structures. More than 125 years later, Ottawa works with a Senate and House of Commons that have been modified only slightly—a patch has been added here and there, but little reconstruction has taken place.

Living shoulder to shoulder with the Americans, from whom we receive a daily flood of information, we base our expectations of our political system on what is done in Washington. We assume that our politicians are chosen to express their constituents' views to the national body. They don't do so. Our caucus system calls members of the same party together (while in Ottawa, each Wednesday morning), to air their views and beefs. But once they walk out of the caucus, they must sing from the party songbook.

In 1996, John Nunziata, a Liberal MP, dared to voice his concern over his ruling party's failure to deal with the Goods and Services Tax (GST) as his party's leader had promised in the election campaign. When the budget failed to signal the government's will to fulfil their promise, Nunziata voted against his party's legislation. The result? He was kicked out of his party and forced to sit as an independent in the House of Commons.

This form of democracy is different from that in the United States. Our political traditions ensure that, when in Ottawa, our politicians have very little opportunity to press forward into policy what is being said at home.

The Senate is another imported tradition that may have worked in the British system but seems less than effective here. While it is different from the House of Lords and acts as a chamber of second thought, it too often seems powerless and without political legitimacy.

Our struggle to find a better parliamentary system is made more difficult by our general distrust of our political leaders. Cartoonists, columnists, open-line hosts, and commentators specialize in using politicians as scapegoats for all our ills. There is no easier way to gain approval from a Canadian audience than to flail at politicians. We make fun of their oddities, ridicule their frailties, point out their inconsistencies, and denounce their failures. Should we be surprised, then, when those who run for office may not be of the calibre we want? Do we have any reason to criticize them for spending to obtain what we asked for, when all along we knew we would end up paying the bill? Why do we snarl at those who have risked their reputations and future on the precarious block of political fortunes?

Caught between the American fondness for charismatic heroes and the European proclivity for the understated, we don't seem to know who we are or what we want.

Living with the Elephant

For hundreds of years Canadians have lived on the same continent with the proud, boastful, and now world-embracing Americans, all the time knowing that our internal divisions were serious enough that, under pressure from the giant to the south, we could give way. Our fears are well grounded, for even though Americans have given up their forebears' goal of gaining jurisdiction over all of North America, the country's very size makes it a formidable neighbour.

At a speaking engagement in Minneapolis, I was asked what it was like to live alongside the United States. I responded using Pierre Trudeau's analogy of the "elephant and the mouse."

"Yes," said my American friend, "that is a good comparison, but you must remember that, as Americans, we are a warm and friendly elephant. Why, just look at our border—the longest undefended border in the world!"

I nodded. "Yes, but remember, as the mouse in bed with the elephant, we have to keep our eyes open. Regardless of how friendly the elephant might be, when it rolls over in the night the mouse has to keep watch."

It is a challenge being a Canadian, especially if you consider retaining our cultural ways to be important. We are a nation physically larger than the United States with one-tenth its population, and to keep our nation intact we must build roads, railways, and airports, and maintain armed forces, in an environment of extreme cold and heat—all the while keeping up an American standard of living.

Not surprisingly, Canadians have a love/hate relationship with the United States. Although we have much in common, we have throughout our history made clear choices not to become Americans. Four times Canada made a clear decision not to join the United States, choosing instead to remain apart and distinct. In 1776, when the Thirteen Colonies broke from Great Britain, Canada did not. In 1812, Canada turned back the invading Americans. Twenty-five years later, in 1837, after rejecting American Jacksonian democracy, Canada chose British "Responsible Government." Then, in the founding of Canada in 1867, as the last remaining British colony in North America, Canada stopped the Americans from pushing north.

Our new founding documents show the difference. The American Constitutional fathers spelled out their goals: "life, liberty and the pursuit of happiness"—a focus on the well-being of the individual. The Canadian Confederation fathers saw the goals differently: "peace, order and good government"—a focus on the well-being of society.

Seymour Lipset gives us another view of the choice Canada made. The United States, he says, "was Whig and classically liberal or libertarian—[it subscribed to] doctrines that emphasize distrust of the state, egalitarianism, and populism—reinforced by a voluntaristic and congregational religious tradition." Canada, on the other hand, "was Tory and conservative in the British and European sense—accepting of the need for a strong state, for respect for authority, for deference—and endorsed by hierarchically organized religions that supported and were supported by the state."[4]

And yet we have not wholeheartedly embraced our position. As the American joke goes, Why did the Canadian cross the road? To get to the middle.

We are ever the compromisers, and over the past two centuries have looked to Europe with respect and to the United States with envy. Frequently I hear Canadians say, "I wish we had the patriotism the Americans do." Watch a crowd singing our Canadian national anthem. Too often, after the first few lines you will see tell-tale signs that the words have been forgotten. It is a challenge to be patriotic living alongside a mammoth nation when your sense of who you are is defined by who you are not.

Our ambivalence is especially clear in the realm of culture. We pay enormously for the protection of our culture, yet many Canadians watch American television almost exclusively—including American news. Recently, while staying at a hotel in southern Ontario, I went to a magazine shop in the hotel and asked for *Maclean's* or *Saturday Night*. The clerk said they stocked only American magazines.

That is less the case in Quebec. While Quebeckers' favourite holiday spots are in the United States, their ethnic/linguistic/cultural reality seems to give them a stronger sense of identity than Anglo-Canadians have.

Trapped by Our Narrow Focus

The troubles within Canada are surely much larger than all of these historic and current problems. Every country is called on to solve its past problems and face its immediate realities. What makes it difficult here is that too easily we fall prey to the notion that only scientific views, and those acceptable to the cultural élite, are legitimate. Increasingly we have been led to accept, by law, regulation, policy, and public conversation, that we speak only the secular language, which says that at the centre of existence is humankind and that the sum total of life's wisdom can be discovered only through human endeavour.

Our country, like so much of the Western world, has undergone a process of secularization: religious views can be held in private, but not voiced in the public square. Universities, publishers, radio and television media, human-rights commissions and other public regulators and policy-setters have contributed greatly to this process. (Canadian churches have also played a part in this process, as is shown in chapter 3.)

With secularism shouting at us from so many quarters, it is not easy for Christians to hear the voice of the Scriptures. But it is important we try. Otherwise, we will be browbeaten into focusing on our own self-interests and will forget the vastness, the diversity, and the enormous opportunities of this land. Trapped by our puny views, we will cut ourselves off from seeing life as part of an eternal reality that goes beyond an individual's life span. We will lose the vision that planet Earth is part of a greater creation and that, as people, we do not live alone. Secularism shuts out any understanding of life beyond our world; it discounts the ongoingness of life in its emphasis on our tiny time projections. And to lose that perspective is to lose the vastness of life itself. That is where an understanding of Christ's Kingdom can make the difference, as noted in chapter 5, on Jesus and politics.

Canadian Christians have too easily given in to the processes that relegate matters of faith to the emotional or religious realm, erecting barriers around the public square to keep faith out. Indeed, the tragedy is that churches have allowed another religion, secularism, to drive its stake so deep into our culture that attempts by a Christian community to address an issue outside the confines of their church are seen as intrusive. We have limited our attention to God's concerns to the interior sense of self and the future destination of the individual, and in doing so have obscured the wholeness of God's creation and concern.

The Christian church, the courier of the message of Jesus Christ, has had an enormous influence on this country's development. This body of faith has provided a common understanding of the nature of creation and the dignity of people. Central to the lives of many of Canada's pioneers, it gave direction to education, hospital care, public institutions, and government. Today, one out of four Canadians attends church weekly, but the real issue is not church attendance but the church's influence in society. While Canada has accepted the ideology of secularism, the church, in various ways, has lost its ability to speak and to be heard with integrity.

Part of the problem stems from failures of the three main Christian Canadian communities:

- The Roman Catholic Church, since the 1960s, has lost its dominant role in Quebec. Its religious orders are getting smaller and, though it maintains its own school system in many provinces, the strength it once had to shape our culture has been greatly diminished. As well, in the past few years it has further discredited itself in light of the revelations of sexual abuse in its boarding-schools.
- Among the old-line Protestant churches, there has been a dramatic loss in membership and attendance. In attempting to accommodate their changing view of the Bible to cultural shifts, they have lost not only members, but their role as spiritual leaders in the land. Even though they speak out on social issues, the churches' ability to shape cultural life is no longer apparent. Less and less are they able to mount a serious call and be heard.
- Evangelical Protestants have a mixed reputation. While maintaining their growth patterns and surprising many by their ability to attract Baby Boomers, their lack of involvement in the cultural mainstream has served to keep them from making a great deal of difference in the culture. Trapped for much of this century in a sectarian mode—a withdrawal from mainstream considerations and activities—evangelicals have only

recently become concerned with what is going on in the public sphere. But, in terms of cultural influence, they are still very much outsiders.

WHAT DO CANADIANS BELIEVE?

Though it is apparent we do not live in a Christian golden age, there is evidence that a spiritual memory exists. Public surveys show that 78 per cent of all Canadians continue to affiliate with a Christian denomination; 67 per cent believe that Jesus Christ was crucified, died, and was buried and resurrected to eternal life. In matters of Scripture and prayer, 32 per cent believe that the Bible is God's word, to be taken literally, and 49 per cent feel that God always answers their prayers. Regarding Christian activities, 23 per cent attend a religious service at least once a week, and 29 per cent pray daily.[5]

This brief picture is a reminder not to get trapped into assuming that Canada has turned its back on Christian faith. Just because the media ignores issues of faith, and the attendance and membership figures of old-line churches are dropping, that is no reason to assume that all is lost. In 1842, in Upper Canada (now Ontario), 17 per cent indicated they had "no religious preference." That figure fell to 1 per cent in 1871.[6] Shifts away from faith can be reversed.

However, even with a relatively strong base of belief, one does not have to look far to recognize that our nation is far from the Christian ideal. Examine the entertainment section, sports pages, business review, or social calendar of a daily newspaper, and it will be obvious that Christian faith is doing very little to influence popular culture. While occasionally one finds a religion story in the daily newspaper, it is usually about religion per se and seldom about a Christian view of an issue, be it business, sports, or politics. A review of current scholarly books and papers shows how little Christian faith is influencing our academic culture.

Canadians need a fresh vision of what it means to be part of God's creation. We have so turned in on ourselves that the big picture of what we might become seems lost. The benefits and incredible opportunities here—even with all the attendant irregularities and anomalies—are frequently forgotten. I do not intend here to minimize the stress caused by our conflicting languages or to underplay the need to define ourselves; rather, I am issuing a call to see the larger picture.

In searching for what Canada might become, it is historically naïve to concentrate on finding meaning in our national roots and ignore the Christian faith that is foundational to our national being. Attempting to secularize our nation's history and, by so doing, chronicle our nationhood without a consideration of the enormous impact of faith is to be factually incorrect and hopelessly biased. Because faith has been an integral part of our journey, it seems that we would be better off to examine that road and see what guideposts it might offer us.

Yes, Canada has much in common with Babel. Pushed out from the centre, we are scattered, divided by our many languages. Harangued by the preachers of rationalism and individualism, we are not sure what to believe. Hesitant about transcendent values, we poke around, looking for what works or is accommodating. In the end, we complain about life while living on the richest and most rewarding land mass in the world.

CHAPTER 2

Was Canada
Ever Christian?

A rumour has circulated that the United Nations had declared Canada was no longer "Christian." I was unsure of the basis for such a declaration, and so I called. After a search of their records, the U.N. spokesperson assured me they never had, nor would they ever, make such an assertion.

The point here is that this appraisal seemed right to so many. Statistics show Canadians to be "very Christian," but we sense the lack of a real Christian presence. And so the U.N. story was accepted because it sounded believable.

While the numbers of Canadians who believe in orthodox Christian faith are significant, the behaviour of the churches makes it seem as if their interests are narrowly focused, on themselves, and not on a grand spiritual vision. This inward focus, along with the increased secularizing of life in general, has left the impression that Canadians no longer regard Christian faith as central or critical to life.

My point is not that, by showing our Christian roots, we somehow have the right to return to what some might think of as those "golden years," but rather that the Kingdom of God invades, shapes, and brings health to a nation. Nations come and go, but the Kingdom of God is the central concern of Christ. Trying to make a nation "Christian" is both threatening to those who are afraid of religion and confusing to those who want the Gospel to make a difference. But by celebrating the reign of Christ's Kingdom, its vitality and rationale will spill over, bringing about civility and spiritual well-being.

Whether it is a matter for national pride or not ... there is no doubt that the history of Canada, as European peoples have made and known it during the past five centuries, is inextricably bound up with the expansion and expression—in politics and society and culture—of the Christian churches.

—William Kilbourn

The golden thread of faith is woven throughout the history of Canada from its earliest beginnings up to the present time. Faith was more important than commerce in the minds of the European explorers and settlers.

—Pierre Elliott Trudeau

The question "Was Canada ever Christian?" triggers sharp disagreements. Some worry about what they see as a collapse of discipline in schools, about the spread of pornography, and about strident voices attempting to change the definition of marriage; they contend Canada has lost its Christian core.

However, God remains in the national anthem and in the constitution, and many Canadians believe there was a time when our leaders took seriously our national motto, 'A mari usque ad mare,' from "He shall have dominion from sea to sea" (Ps. 72: 8).

Others simply dismiss the question as trivial and archaic. They treat the role of Christianity in Canada as a quaint footnote in history.

The question is not irrelevant, however. Christians have played a significant role in shaping Canada—in fact, Christianity is considered by many scholars to be the most formative influence on Canadian society.[1] Furthermore, historians have long known that how we regard the past shapes our view of both the present—who we are—and the future—who we will become. But to answer the question "Was Canada ever Christian?" we must first agree on a definition.

What Is a Christian Nation?
Three Definitions

First, "Christian" can be used in a weak sense to mean a country with some connection to the Judaeo-Christian heritage. Though almost every country in the West, from the late Roman Empire until 1800, was "Christian," many political and social realities were as far from New Testament Christianity as you can get.

Second, "Christian" can also refer to a nation in which there are many individuals who claim to be Christian. However, having a lot of Christians does not guarantee that what a culture does is Christian. For example, note the former racial policies of South Africa. Genuine Christians can get caught up in policies which are anything but Christian. So, in the end, the presence of Christians might paint a picture of a country that is religious but not necessarily Christian.

Third, the term "Christian" can refer to a society that reflects the ideals and principles of Scripture. In such a society, the people are not just talking about doing God's will, but are doing it. An American historian comments, "Although we would not expect perfection, we would expect that a 'Christian' society in this sense would generally distinguish itself from most other societies in the commendability of both its ideals and practices. Family, churches, and state would on the whole be properly formed. Justice and charity would normally be shown toward minorities and toward the poor and other unfortunate people. The society would be predominately [sic] peaceful and law-abiding. Proper moral standards would generally prevail. Cultural activities such as learning, business, or the subduing of nature would be pursued basically in accord with God's will. In short, such a society would be a proper model to imitate."[2]

Making these three distinctions helps us avoid equating our own political ideals with what we learn in Scripture. Getting caught up in assuming they are the same leads to idolatry and an irresistible temptation to national self-righteousness. These definitions call us to be careful in using the term "Christian nation." It is a fuzzy term that can make it difficult for Christians to be active, especially if it produces a distorted and overinflated view of any one country as being distinctively or uniquely Christian.

Are any or all of these definitions evident in Canada's history?

CORPORATE AND INDIVIDUAL CHRISTIANITY: TWO VIEWS

Two major ideas have guided Christians in acting on Christ's call to "be in the world but not of it." On one side, there is "corporate" Christianity—the Christendom model—and on the other side, "individual" Christianity.

Corporate Christianity's first expression occurred in the fourth century, when Emperor Constantine made it the state religion. Christianity changed over several centuries, from an obscure sect worshipping a Jewish rebel, to a major world religion that sought to apply Christ's teachings to the political structure of the world's then greatest power. For the next 1,200 years, this approach was used and, even when the church was divided by the Reformation, this Christendom model was included in the Protestant Church through the teachings of the early reformers; Luther in Germany, Zwingli in Zurich, and Calvin in Geneva.

It was also introduced to Canada by the English Anglicans, the Scottish State Church Presbyterians, and, to a lesser extent, the New England Puritans. The Catholic version found its way to Canada via the Roman Catholic Church of France. In the nineteenth century, most Canadian Protestants, while denying the establishing of a state church, recognized dominant Protestantism as a most-favoured religion. This was true even in the United States, where there was a purported separation of church and state.

At the heart of the Christendom model is the belief that God deals not only with individuals, but also with nations. Based on the dealings of God with the children of Israel, it sees beyond the salvation of individuals to the formation of a godly society. Salvation is viewed as more than an individual matter; it extends to include families, communities, and ultimately the state. This model holds that nations which, through their rulers, seek to obey God will be blessed in this life, and nations which disobey will be judged.

To accomplish the task of constructing a godly society, the church and civil magistrates worked out various kinds of alliances. Ideally this relationship was to be reciprocal: the rulers had responsibility for ensuring the economic strength of the church, for passing godly legislation, and for restraining evil within society so that the church's teaching would have its intended impact. The church, for its part, was responsible for pointing the way of salvation, instructing people in their duties towards God, and supporting those whom God had placed in authority over them. The result, then, was to be a society that was Christian in its beliefs and godly in its life.

Inwardly, the aim was to bring all its members to the knowledge and worship of God; outwardly, despite the fact that not all its individual members would become good Christians, it was hoped that at least they would display a godly character in the world.

Even with such worthy ideals, such a system needed power to ensure that people conformed. Despite the imperfections of the Christendom model, those who supported it believed that it was based on Scripture and that, in the end, it would ensure Christian patterns for living.

The opposing view to corporate Christianity is "individual" or "Believer Church" Christianity. In this model it is not assumed that people will be socialized into a church. Church affiliation is a matter of personal choice. While reformers were reworking the old corporate model, the Anabaptist movement of the sixteenth century was a major force in shaping North American Christianity. Menno Simons, best known for leading the Anabaptists (better known in North America as Mennonites), emphasized that a person needed to be old enough to make a conscious choice to follow Jesus Christ (and thus to be baptized), which eliminated infant baptism as a means of salvation.

At its heart, individual Christianity sees the relationship of the individual to God as being the context in which the most important expressions of Christian experience take place. This relationship is to be sought through Scripture reading, prayer, and living a Christ-like life.

Anabaptists accused Christendom of confusing works—which cannot earn salvation—with God's grace, and of not being serious in living the Christian life. This confusion, they argued, resulted in an emphasis on good citizenship that effectively lifted the requirements the Gospel places upon individuals themselves. Anabaptists argued that society could never become Christian: society can only comprise redeemed individuals.

It should be noted that these two views, though often in opposition, are never completely distinct. The aim of corporate Christianity is the regeneration of society. Individual Christianity does not reject the broader societal implications of the faith. Indeed, Anabaptist groups who attacked the Reformed societies of sixteenth-century Europe built in Russia, for example, alternative Christian communities. These two views within our Canadian experience have had a transforming effect upon each other.

With that background, we turn our attention to the enormous influence the Christian Gospel has had on shaping and defining the Canadian experience.

NEW FRANCE: "NONE BUT FRENCH CATHOLICS"

On a drive through the villages and towns of Quebec's St. Lawrence Valley, one can see the historical influence of the church. In the middle of each settlement is a tall, dramatic piece of architecture—the local Roman Catholic church. This influence began in Quebec on July 20, 1534, when Jacques Cartier raised a cross on the shore of the Gaspé to explain to the watching Iroquois the message of salvation. Cartier urged Francis I of France to support missionary work to win these "savage peoples living without a knowledge of God" to the Catholic Church.

Almost a century later, Samuel de Champlain—called the "Father of New France"—brought the same sense of mission to the shores of New France with Recollect priests. Two decades later, the larger and more famous Jesuit missions to the Hurons began. Of his efforts to bring missionaries to the New World, Champlain later writes that, "having observed on my previous voyages that in some places there were settled tribes with a taste for tillage of the soil, but without faith or law, living without God and without religion like brute beasts, I thereupon concluded in my private judgment that I should be committing a great sin if I did not make it my business to devise some means of bringing them to the knowledge of God."[3]

These devout French explorers believed that God had a great design for New France. Along with many of their fellow countrymen, they were convinced that their discoveries were part of God's plan to spread salvation around the world and that their new nation was responsible for both civilizing and Christianizing the inhabitants of this discovered territory.

This missionary drive was powerfully influenced by the Catholic Reformation, a spiritual renewal that pulsated through many countries in Europe during the sixteenth and seventeenth centuries. It not only reasserted Catholic doctrine, but nourished a spirit of deep piety and promoted sacrificial missionary enterprise through new orders. Nowhere was this revival felt more strongly than in France. It in turn became a powerful force in developing the North American colony.

The missionary drive was also fuelled by a rather popular interpretation of the time that North American Indians were descendants of the ten lost tribes of Israel, and, further, that the discovery of the New World announced the arrival of a new age. This rapid conversion of North American Indians, it was thought, would restore the church to its apostolic purity preceding the second coming of Christ.

France, more than any other country, was the prime example of corporate Christianity. As the harsh realities of frontier life and the slow rate of progress gradually tempered the enthusiasm for missions, religious orders gave more attention to the struggling settlements on the banks of the St. Lawrence. New France was seen as a God-given opportunity to create a truly Christian and Catholic society as a light to the world.

At first, the church in New France had great influence without holding political office. In 1647 this changed as the church was given a share in administrative power with the creation of a two-man council made up of the governor of the colony and the superior of the House of the Jesuits. Though the church's political influence rose and fell with the political intrigues of the day, one highlight was the leadership of François de Laval as Vicar Apostolic of New France. His arrival in 1659 gave a breadth and intensity to the church's efforts to produce a Christian society. He opened a seminary for Canadian clergy. Then he established a system of parishes intended both to meet the spiritual needs of the habitants and to provide funds for the training of the clergy. The manor house served as the centre for both the religious and the social life of those new communities. Laval was out to build in the New World a garden of the Lord where all would have access to Christian teaching.

Despite the church's failure to fulfil its greater vision for building a Christian society, it did establish an ongoing presence in the religious, social, and administrative life of the colony. Even the conquest by the British in 1759 did not subdue the influence of the church. In fact, the Catholic Church probably benefited from the event. In order to secure Québécois loyalty in the face of the impending American Revolution, the British, in the Quebec Act of 1774, gave the Roman Catholic Church the right to act as a quasi-state. The church could then take credit for preserving the French language and culture in the face of serious and persistent threats of anglophone assimilation. Until the twentieth century, the Catholic Church helped create a society with control over education, politics, and life-in-the-village, which formed a dam to hold back the cultural tide of the powerful North American civilization. This "Christian" character survived until well into the second half of the twentieth century, when the secularizing influences of the Quiet Revolution broke the bond between Quebeckers and the Roman Catholic Church, and when the corporate Christian vision would die.

EIGHTEENTH-CENTURY NOVA SCOTIA: RELIGION AND REVOLUTION

The French Catholics were not the only ones to use the Christendom, or the corporate Christian model, to create a Christian society in the New World. In 1749 the British in Nova Scotia built a military base at Halifax from which they could attack the French stronghold at Louisbourg. Accompanying these military plans were settlers from a variety of Protestant groups, but at the centre was the Church of England, which assumed that its privileged status in Great Britain would be duplicated in the New World.

In addition to the tough and gruelling problems of settling this demanding land, Nova Scotians were troubled by the noise of revolutionary trouble brewing against the British in the American colonies. Though many sympathized with the aims of the American Revolution, to support it meant jeopardizing their relationship with the local government. They were trapped. Supporting the American Revolution and taking up arms against New England would mean shooting family and friends. And yet refusing to sympathize openly with the American colonies made Nova Scotians vulnerable to

American privateers' attacks, as Nova Scotia was the closest British colony. This period of enormous uncertainty and political turmoil coincided with a remarkable series of religious revivals which came to be known as Nova Scotia's Great Awakening.

The revivalist at the centre of this awakening was Henry Alline, a tanner from Falmouth who, in 1775, at age twenty-seven, underwent a dramatic conversion. He spent the next eight years preaching back and forth across what is now Nova Scotia, Prince Edward Island, and New Brunswick. He used unconventional methods—open-air preaching, public singing processions, informal sermons, and intense emotionalism. As he was a skilful public debater, his preaching convinced many to turn to Christ. His courage earned him considerable respect among his contemporaries. He was dubbed the George Whitefield of Nova Scotia. (George Whitefield [1714-1770] was the famous Methodist evangelist whose large open-air meetings stirred communities in North America.) After Alline's death in 1784, revival again swept through many of the Yankee settlements, and some of the English ones in Nova Scotia, this time due largely to the tireless efforts of Methodists William Black and Freeborn Garrettson.

These itinerant evangelists transformed entire communities. Although their preaching centred on an individual's relationship to God and focused on the experience of the Holy Spirit in the "new birth," the impact went far beyond an individual's spiritual life. In addition to "leading many people to Christ," Nova Scotia's Great Awakening had social and political implications. Alline challenged the New England colonies for their sinful and illegal activities, such as war, and Britain for general corruptness. Far from being an isolated backwater of the British Empire, Nova Scotia was, as Alline saw it, a central player in God's will for the world.

The message of these itinerant evangelists triggered a mass social movement. The élite no longer held sway. Central religious power was diffused through evangelism. The individual was no longer just a member in the religious community. This new-found individual self-expression challenged and displaced the power and control of the established church.

The objections raised by the Anglicans against Alline's movement, the New Lights, show what was at stake for the Anglican Church.

Bishop Charles Inglis describes the view of the new religious movement: "Fanatics are impatient under civil restraint & run into the democratic system. They are for levelling everything both sacred and civil; & this is peculiarly the case of our New Lights who are, as far as I can learn, Democrats to a man."[4]

Inglis saw the New Lights as a serious threat to the control of the Anglican Church. The Maritime élite saw the revivalism as a challenge to the social and political status quo. Inglis voiced a common fear when he said that "their [New Lights'] political principles are equally dangerous with their religions. It is believed that the conductors of these people are engaged in a general plan of a total revolution in religious and civil government."[5]

Inglis knew that Alline and his followers were not involved in political espionage that might incite a revolt or mob rule. Rather, he feared that the spiritual power of individual converts might produce a generation that would begin to assert democratic ideals. Inglis's vision was that of a corporate Christianity, with his church, of course, at the helm. Alline and his message of individuals freely receiving God's grace apart from the mediating role of the church only upset Inglis's plans for Anglican leadership and control.

Such opposition did little to discourage Alline and his co-workers. If anything, it increased their prestige among the people as God's special messengers. The evangelical emphasis that each individual must take responsibility for his or her own spiritual welfare generated ideas of equality, liberty, and freedom, all of which had enormous political implications. There was a definite link between the freedom of religious expression and political ideas. It can be argued that this evangelical presence made a powerful contribution to the democratizing of Canada.

But even with this revival fervour, the Great Awakening in Nova Scotia and New Brunswick did not bring about a Christian colony. In fact, Alline's preaching and community revivals often ended in bitter religious conflict. The emotional excesses led to the real story in Alline's movement—namely, the consolidation into a more orderly, Baptist Nova Scotia and New Brunswick. This consolidation took place because the emotional excesses could not be sustained, and those influenced by the revival needed a more orderly place in which to live out their newly acquired faith. Many Maritimers today who hardly practise Christianity at all still call themselves Baptist. "Radical evangelicalism" (historian George Rawlyk's term) was thus permanently stamped on Maritime culture.

NINETEENTH-CENTURY ONTARIO: COLLISION OF TWO RELIGIOUS IDEAS

The American Revolution (1776) had an enormous impact on Canadian history, breaking up Britain's North American colonial empire and forcing the creation of what eventually became known as Canada.

After the Treaty of Paris in 1783, in which the Thirteen Colonies became the United States of America, a large number of United Empire Loyalists left the American colonies and immigrated as settlers to Upper Canada (Ontario). This large group of settlers gave the region its first substantial population and led to the creation of a separate province in 1791. Soon after the first migration, others came, more interested in land than in political or social ideology. These arrivals brought with them a variety of religious beliefs and traditions, which triggered a debate that dominated Canadian Christian life for almost fifty years.

Though no one questioned that Ontario should be a Christian society, what was at stake was which Protestant denomination would receive official recognition and status. On one side were the Anglicans—and, to a lesser extent, the Presbyterians—organized under a strong corporate tradition with the assumption that they should be accorded the same privileged status in Canada that they had held in Great Britain. Although they did not get all they wanted, in the Constitutional Act of 1791 they came very close to having the Church of England made the official Canadian state church.

On the other side of the debate were the more individualistic Methodists and Baptists. They wanted a deal that would acknowledge the existence of various Christian groups and ensure equal and fair treatment by the state. The outcome of this debate had a direct bearing on church/state relations and public education during the nineteenth century. The most prominent spokesmen for the two sides were John Strachan, Anglican archdeacon of York (later Toronto), and the young Egerton Ryerson, a zealous and articulate Methodist. The clash between the two was set off over a sermon published by Strachan in 1825. Although their quarrels became personal, they were really a clash between the worlds of corporate Christianity and individual Christianity.

The dispute took place on several fronts. In addition to public clashes between Strachan and Ryerson over what they believed made up "proper" Christianity, politicians wrestled with the issue of whether public funds should support church activities and, if so, which churches. This issue came to be known as the Clergy Reserves Controversy. The church's role in both university and public elementary education was also a divisive issue. In each case decisive victories were won by those who wanted a society that embraced many faiths rather than a single denomination.

Strachan's corporate Christian vision came from the long-established traditions of the Church of England. Under this corporate model, Christianity offered salvation as the means to redeem people from sin, to reconcile God and humanity, and to draw earth and heaven together. The redemption of the human race would be slow and gradual. This process would be helped by the church through daily worship, the sacraments, and education by an informed clergy. This regeneration of society could come about only through the careful pooling of the resources of religion and government, seen as the twin pillars of society: the state would uphold order, restrain evil, and create an environment in which humanity's fallen nature was held in check; the church would teach Christians to live virtuous lives, in turn transforming citizens into useful and productive subjects of the state by ensuring public order and unity of belief.

This vision of the role of an established religion called for the careful collaboration of church and state in building a Christian nation, and thereby an ordered society whose citizens would be faithful subjects and serve the state and its institutions. Without the steadying influence of the Church of England, Strachan wrote, the country was "certain to become a moral waste and a hotbed of sedition and discontent."[6]

What upset Strachan's vision of a corporate Christian culture were a number of Methodist itinerant preachers who attracted Ontarians in high numbers. The Methodists had well-organized circuits and a good supply of tireless, inexpensive preachers and lay exhorters. This system allowed Methodism to grow in sparsely settled frontiers. By 1812

Methodism had become the largest Protestant denomination in Upper Canada. These unruly Methodists represented all that Strachan did not want to see happen in the new colony. Strachan viewed these itinerant ministers as lazy men who left their jobs, setting out, without any preparation or training, "to teach what they do not know, and which from pride, they disdain to learn."[7] But Strachan's view did little to intimidate these out-to-take-the-world Methodists.

They soon found a champion in young Egerton Ryerson, who rose to the challenge, mounting a spirited defence and attack upon the religious-establishment views of Strachan. Ryerson accused Strachan of mistaking his own political and denominational prejudices for the call of Christ to the individual. Writing in the *Upper Canada Herald*, he asked, "Do you think that the Lord of Hosts assumed our nature, lived in poverty, died as a malefactor, and ascended as a conqueror, to reveal and give efficacy to a code of doctrines and precepts, that should be a stepping-stone to the accomplishments of your selfish system, your highly exceptionable measures, your ... heartless policy?"[8]

These hot-blooded Methodists were not interested in spouting learned phrases with a view to gradually changing society. They worked in the emotional turmoil of camp meetings, where sinners, tormented by guilt and urged to seek God, wrestled with their Creator and found assurance of salvation. For Ryerson and his colleagues, the kind of Christianity advocated by Strachan denied the work of true, heart-felt religion. For them, the church was to persuade by preaching rather than to coerce with political power. For the Christian faith to influence society while staying true to its character, it had to stay away from unholy alliances or compromises with the state. Ryerson's arguments became the focus of opposition against the Church of England's attempts to hold on to its privileged status.

Although there was never a formal separation of church and state, as occurred in the United States, the dissolution of the Clergy Reserves in 1854 and the break-up of Anglican domination meant that all churches became financially dependent on their members, and not on the state. This separation of the church and state—which, ironically, had been achieved not because of the secularization of society, but because of the public fight among Christians—marked the last serious attempt to impose a model of corporate Christianity on Canada.

By the turn of the century, the "individual Christianity" world-view assumed that Christianizing society had to be done outside the political arena; that is, conversion of the population was a necessary first step for affecting public life. They were wrong. In focusing only on the salvation of the individual, to the exclusion of the means whereby society is managed, they lost the opportunity to ensure that Christian principles prevailed.

In the end, there were two losses: corporate Christianity could not impose Christian faith on Canada, and individual Christianity gave up the means to influence political life.

AN AGE OF COOPERATION

During the nineteenth century, corporate Christianity and individual Christianity found a new synthesis. As Anglicans were stripped of the support of the state, their plans to Christianize society forced them to become more evangelistic. Methodists were fundamentally changed by their rising wealth, education, and social status. After Confederation in 1867, Protestants became more cooperative and developed a vision that led to a collaboration to ensure that this growing country would become "a genuinely Christian nation."[9]

Towards the end of the century, both groups were confronted by the intellectual challenges of Darwinism and biblical Higher Criticism (a more "scientific" means of understanding the Bible). Any differences between Anglicans and Methodists over how best to make Canadian society Christian were overcome in this rising tide of unbelief. As a result, they had to look for ways to address their similar concerns. Out of this came a new spirit of cooperation among the Protestants. Each group retained their long-held beliefs but became more willing to redefine their relationships by a new spirit of cooperation.

This joining produced a synergy which, in turn, redefined the religious character of Ontario during the late nineteenth century. This character was essentially Protestant in doctrine and moralistic in tone. Although it failed to convert Catholics in Quebec, it had a strong influence in Ontario and the West. The foundation of this collaboration was an "evangelical creed" that was biblical and activist, not metaphysical and speculative. It was based on the single truth that God's will, as revealed in the Bible, could sanctify and transform the human soul, human knowledge, and the community. Though not adopted by every member of society, this evangelical creed represented, as perhaps at no other time in Canada's history, the spiritual, intellectual, and moral tenor of the times.

Another integral part of this Protestant cooperation was a nationalistic vision of Canada as "His Dominion." Its message was to establish the Kingdom of God in Canada. Now that the nation of Canada had been formed, the task was to make its citizens Christian. This optimistic goal of creating a distinctively Christian character was unifying and created a sense of destiny, and it was the force behind a variety of social-reform movements, educational institutions, missionary activities at home and overseas, and voluntary societies.

An Age of Mission

Protestants saw missionary activities as essential to the call of Christ. Increased mission work and the raising of money for missions to reach Canadian aboriginals were emblematic of the growing confidence Canadian Christians had about achieving the goal to Christianize Canada.

For many today, the era of missions to aboriginals is an embarrassment. In part, such a view is justified. To the Europeans who explored and settled in North America, embracing the Christian faith was equivalent to becoming a European citizen. To be civilized was to believe in Jesus Christ, to follow the practices of a particular denomination, and to accept the norms of a European society. To "Christianize" was not only to convert to faith in Jesus Christ, but to accept an Anglo-Saxon/Protestant or French/Roman Catholic way of life. The unhappy link between Christianity and European civilization was strengthened by the churches' connection with the Canadian government, which was seemingly intent on changing the way of life of the aboriginal peoples. And so Christianity at times was a willing partner of political and social forces that interfered in the Native way of life, bringing smallpox, alcoholism, and social dislocation. Confronted with the lasting evidence of the depth of this cultural crime, many Christians now feel a justifiable burden of guilt.

This, however, is not the complete story. While horrific accounts of life in the residential schools dominate the public press and suggest there is only one history to be heard, it would be wrong to assume that aboriginal peoples were only passive recipients of an aggressive and domineering religious assault by overzealous missionaries. Historian John W. Grant says that historians assumed missionaries were always insensitive, while idealizing the state of the aboriginal society. He writes: "The myth of the noble missionary seeking to reclaim degraded barbarians has been replaced, in many quarters, by the myth of the noble savage spoiled by meddlesome missionaries. A closer examination even of the recent literature of Indian protest, however, turns up a surprising number of exceptions to the general indictment."[10]

Today, while the media give much attention to the upsurge of traditional Native spirituality, the vast majority of Canada's Native peoples continue to claim Christian faith and affiliation.[11] In some cases, these affiliations have been part of Native culture for four centuries. This enduring attraction of Christian belief suggests that more than the forces of cultural imperialism have been at work. While Christian faith has too often been presented in European garb and without sensitivity to the receiving culture, it is my experience that Christian faith translated into existing ways of worship and life profoundly meets a culture's spiritual needs.

During this period of growing influence by an evangelically based Protestantism, many individuals were active in social leadership through the "voluntary societies." These groups were involved with evangelistic, philanthropic, moral, and social issues. Literally thousands of Protestants committed themselves and their resources to these organized activities, believing it would help make Canada more Christian.

William Holmes Howland is a model of this combination of personal faith and social concern. In the late nineteenth century, Howland rose to prominence in the public life of Toronto. His ability to combine a strong faith, untiring activism, social concern, business success, civic responsibility, and political savvy indicates what a thoughtful Christian leader could accomplish.

The son of Ontario's first lieutenant-governor, Howland was well connected in the Ontario establishment. By age twenty-five he was a rising star in the Toronto business community. Converted at age thirty-two,

Howland turned his energies to Christian and charitable efforts. Through his business enterprises and Christian endeavours, he became part of a network of Christians, people like himself, concerned with spreading the Gospel and influencing society. Deeply disturbed about declining standards in public morality and the spread of crime, gambling, and prostitution, in 1885 Howland ran as "the people's candidate," and won.

Right from the beginning, Howland made no apologies for his personal faith or his reformist policies. He mounted on his office wall a twelve-foot reproduction of a Bible verse which read: "Except the Lord keep the City, the watchman waketh but in vain" (Ps. 127: 11). During his first term he undertook to reform public sanitation, suppress pornography, and strengthen Toronto's police forces to deal with an assortment of moral vices: cruelty to women, children, and animals; gambling; houses of prostitution; desecration of the Sabbath; indecent exposure; and unlicensed liquor dens. In addition he prosecuted several city officials caught in acts of dishonesty.

Returned to office for a second term in 1887, Howland devoted his energies to the clean-up of municipal business affairs, suppression of the liquor trade and prostitution, and getting tough on crime. It was under Howland's administration that the city acquired the nickname "Toronto the Good." He later returned to an assortment of Christian and business enterprises. What is striking about the public career of W.H. Howland is the apparently seamless way in which the aims of a modified corporate and individual Christianity worked together. His concern for individual salvation and for living conditions led him to a broader concern for shaping public policy. Howland's mayoralty represented an attempt to effect many of the reforms proposed by Christians during that time.

Despite attempts by Howland and others, Christian coalitions that tried to persuade society to live more righteously were frustrated by a sense of powerlessness. Eventually they asked government to help them by enforcing a Christian code of conduct and passing laws. They needed more than moral persuasion; they needed the strong hand of the law.

Church Union:
The Creation of a "National" Church

As W.H. Howland modelled the linking of individual Christianity to Canada, the movement to create the United Church (church union occurred in 1925) reshaped corporate Christianity. When government made it clear they would not support the idea of an established church, this divisive issue, which had separated Protestants, was removed; Protestant denominational tensions relaxed; and merger, or church union, became a possibility.

But other factors also led to merger. Denominations lost financial support from the old country. As clergy were trained in Canada, the doctrinal fights in Europe mattered less and less. Presbyterians and Methodists collaborated in interdenominational efforts, in the build-up to a growing consensus that transdenominational union was a real possibility. A church historian of the time, C.E. Silcox, wrote, "Canada is our parish. It is the vision of Dominion-wide service that inspires the new Union. ... There will be not a hamlet or a rural community in the whole land where the United Church will not serve."[12] A united church could be a real broker in Canadian political life and could serve as the mechanism to exert a religious and political influence.

This church union in Canada was unique, and did not take place in the United States. Church historian John Webster Grant identifies several reasons. First, because of the country's huge expanse, and relatively sparse and scattered population, Canadians placed a premium on cooperation in its confederation, already a model for church union. Second, the nineteenth-century evangelical movement still retained the dual emphasis on individual and social salvation.

"Unlike the United States, which imbibed a tradition of secularism from its founding fathers, Canada grew up under the tutelage of its churches. The pulpit, the school and the press were the leading forces in moulding the Canadian character. Almost all the well-known educators of the period were clergymen, and many leading newspapers were in effect organs of particular religious groups. ... By preaching, editorializing, and founding universities, they sought on the one hand to lay the moral and spiritual foundations of nationhood, and on the other, to act as a conscience to the state."[13]

Underneath this influence was a desire not only to uphold values, but also to correct them and create new ones. Protestant activism was energized by Confederation and its accompanying nationalism and spirit of cooperation. Church union provided a broad mobilization of forces for the spread of the Gospel in a rapidly developing frontier of the country.

At the turn of the twentieth century, Christians were confronted, as were all Canadians, with new realities. One was the opening up of the West and the government's aggressive immigration policy to settle it with farmers, many of whom were non-British and non-Protestant. Churches became more vigorous in trying to meet the immigrants and integrate them into Canadian society. In this changing society, church union appeared to be a practical way of using limited resources to meet social needs. It promised to cut down on the waste of administration and competition among fellow Christians. As well, those pressing for church union saw it as a means of providing a consolidated front for competing more effectively with the Roman Catholics.

For Canadian Protestants, like their American counterparts, this was a period of great optimism. Before the major conflicts of the twentieth century and the religious upheavals that would shatter communities of faith in the 1920s and 1930s, Canadians saw the possibility of building in their land a Christian world. Historian Grant writes, "Only let the Churches unite, it was often urged, and their influence for reconciliation and righteousness would be irresistible."[14]

Looking back, this optimism seems misplaced. In a century of two world wars and one world economic depression, the movement towards church union was never what its founders hoped it would be. Although the union of all the Methodist churches, almost all of the Congregationalists, and two-thirds of the Presbyterians was eventually achieved (into the United Church), it was tarnished by bitter controversy as one-third of the Presbyterian community chose to retain their identity and churches.

TOWARDS THE SECULAR SOCIETY?
THE RISE OF THE SOCIAL GOSPEL

Although the Social Gospel—as it came to be known in North America—has a number of roots, some of which are quite different from the evangelical world-view of the mid-nineteenth century, it is acknowledged that evangelical Protestant faith played an essential role in its beginnings. Methodism, with its concerns for salvation, sanctification, and victorious Christian living, nourished the growth of Social Gospel thought. Methodists were less concerned about theological debates than with the need for forgiveness. Once this had been received through repentance, God's grace would flow, enabling the believers to live sanctified lives. Yet, sanctification could never be a static thing; as sanctified believers responded to God's love in a world that was radically fallen and sinful, they became soldiers in a battle of cosmic proportions. It was thus warfare against the effects of the Fall that led many evangelicals to emphasize social action.

As with evangelical faith throughout most of the nineteenth century, the Social Gospel sprang from the emphasis on claiming the land for "scriptural holiness." This led many into spearheading a number of social-reform movements, including the temperance, Sabbatarian, and anti-slavery movements of England and America. Methodist preachers were sometimes involved in the early trade-union movement, and the slogan "Saved for Service" became important.

The Social Gospel decidedly made a shift from its evangelical roots. It emphasized Christianity as primarily a social religion, concerned with human relations and not so much with the individual's relation to God. Put in more dramatic terms, it was a call for people to seek the Kingdom of God within the very fabric of society, and not in personal conversion. Turning from a focus on God's revelation in Jesus Christ (as recorded in the Bible and impressed on sinners saved by the Holy Spirit), it moved to an emphasis on God, who was actively present in all social and cultural forms, helping people of goodwill to make the world more expressive of the spirit of Jesus.

Increasingly influenced by philosophies that emphasized God's work within history rather than transcendence, Social Gospellers came to downplay the concept of individual and personal salvation. Towards the turn of the century, as the social needs of an immigrant population became more obvious, along with the rise of an industrial complex that was often harsh on its workers, church leaders opted for a call to social salvation.

By the end of beginning of the First World War, leading Social Gospel thinkers in Canada such as J.S. Woodsworth and Salem Bland came to equate the cause of social justice, and the political means of achieving it, with the essence of the Christian message. This equation would lead Social Gospel radicals into the causes of Canadian labour, social welfare, democratic socialism, and, occasionally, communism. Although the Social Gospel as a movement would begin to fracture with the development of such radicalism, there was significant agreement among many Canadian Christians that the Gospel of Christ needed to challenge the social structures of the day and condemn the great inequities thrown up by unbridled capitalism. This broad consensus played a significant part in the expansion of Canada's social-welfare mechanism during the twentieth century.

But by the end of the First World War, Canada was rapidly becoming a secular society, and any claims for Canada's being a Christian society were receding. The evangelical consensus of the mid-nineteenth century was breaking down. Causes for this rapid transformation remain the subject of debate, which we return to in chapter 3.

In looking at these individuals and groups who significantly influenced the shape of Canadian culture, the question remains: was Canada ever Christian? The answer depends on the definition. One can say that, at an early point, the country was very much influenced by a corporate Christianity and, from time to time, there have been strong outbreaks of individual Christianity. But to say that Canada was substantially Christian is to deny our history. Those working to bring about either a society that was thoroughly Christian or a society of Christian individuals did so with an awareness of their enormous task. Given the consistency of their calls to righteousness and the urgency with which they went about their tasks, it seems that none would have called Canada "Christian." They all strove for the victory of Christian belief in their society. But this victory, which required the submission to Christ in each heart, seemed beyond their grasp.

Historian John Stackhouse observes that, despite the process of Christianization in Canada (which on some occasions brought substantial numbers of unchurched people into the church), Canadian culture never became thoroughly and exemplarily Christian. This is not to say that Christianity did not have a significant impact on Canadian culture. Even today one can see "contemporary Canadian culture as residually Christian in many respects."[15]

Perhaps then, the better question is "Was Canada once more Christian than it is now?" Although the population of Canada has never been uniformly Christian, the influence of Christianity has always been present, informing society of Jesus Christ. At times this Christian call resonated less effectively with Canadian culture than it did at others. But it is clear that Christian belief, in calling Canadians to be a holy people, has had a significant effect upon Canada and the way in which its people see the world.

The remarkable way in which Christian belief occupied minds and hearts during the early and mid-nineteenth century, and the resulting impact it has had upon Canada's educational, social-welfare, and political structures, suggest that, while never being "Christian" in its entirety, Canada may have been more nearly Christian during this period than at any other time. It is not without considerable justification that historian Michael Gauvreau, in a book by the same name, calls the nineteenth century Canada's "evangelical century."

However, even the most obvious Canadian Christian success stories have their own ironies and ambivalences. During the "evangelical century," rigorous church discipline virtually disappeared as church culture became less distinguishable from that of the broader society. Church leaders were inclined to leave aside the prophetic call to rigorous discipleship, opting for a cosy relationship with an emerging middle class. And the period was hardly a model of biblical justice in its treatment of non-Anglo-Saxon immigrants, women, and Native peoples. One could even say that some of Canada's social policies are more biblical today, largely because they have been informed by a biblical vision. So we cannot look back to any one time in Canada's history as some kind of Christian golden age. However, we can, and should, look back with careful appreciation for what considerable good was accomplished in these and other contexts, and then turn to face the challenges of our own time, informed by the Christian experiences of our past.

CHAPTER 3

How Did We Lose
a Biblical Centre?

The question I'm often asked is, how did we lose our Christian foundation in Canada? It's an important question. Many Christians assume the loss was occasioned by secular forces pushing faith out of the public square. But, while the forces of secularization have had an enormous influence, to isolate that as the cause is to grossly misunderstand the impact of Christian privatization: that is, Christians walking away from cultural engagement and practising their faith within the privacy of their own lives, homes, and churches.

This chapter is critical for our long-term strategies. To capture a sense of what we can be as (what Christ calls us) "salt" and "light," we examine here what happened to Bible-based communities during the twentieth century as Canada became increasingly shaped by a secular vision.

Even though Christianity in 1967 was still part of the Canadian establishment, by 1987 it had become little more than a memory.[1]

—John W. Grant

As the ink on the 1867 Confederation papers was drying, church leaders viewed Canadian western expansion as an enormous opportunity to reach into the new hinterlands, ensuring that the newly enlarged Canada would be "a genuinely Christian nation."

Why did Canada lose that Christian heritage in such a short time? Did society reject the claims of its Christian majority? Or did church leaders fail to transmit successfully the Christian message to the expanding and changing culture?

THE CHURCH AT CONFEDERATION: 1867

As politicians hammered together the deal which led to this new federation, it did not take long for Protestants to see Confederation as a grand new opportunity. Robert Murray, the young, outspoken editor of the *Presbyterian Witness*, hailed the new nation as "the Canaan we are invited to occupy."[2]

In the late 1800s, the church in Ontario was at the centre of community life: in 1871 the three largest Protestant denominations—Methodists, Presbyterians, and Anglicans—made up 70 per cent of the population. Ministers had influence. Most Ontarians attended church, including politicians. The church spoke to and for the people. Sunday was a day for reading religious books or periodicals, and newspapers carried devotional columns. Underlying these practices was a profound belief in God's order: church life shaped not only belief, but the way people lived.

But it did not end there. Churches played an important role in education, health care, and social-reform movements, for Christian faith was the basis for social order. "Family life, educational institutions, many philanthropic and voluntary organizations, the drive for moral and social reform, and the understanding of civilization and human nature were all somehow dependent on Christianity," observes historian David Marshall.[3] Canadian sociologist S.D. Clark said that "there are few countries in the western world in which religion exerted as great an influence" in shaping the social and cultural life as in Canada.[4]

The Church Loses Influence

At the close of the nineteenth century, Canadians saw their country as a "Christian" nation. But, as the new century dawned, dramatic changes shattered this idea.

The false assumption is that Christian influence was eradicated by the winds of radical thought that appeared in the post-1960s: feminism, relativism, same-sex politics, and secular humanism. While it is true that these factors have had an enormous impact, the church has always had to contend with forces opposed to biblical faith. So what happened in Canada? There are two primary factors, at least as seen from a Protestant point of view: mainline Protestants lost focus and spiritual vitality, and the evangelical Protestant community lacked influence and presence within the societal mainstream.

At the heart of these factors was the powerful and absorbing current of secularization. In this process, Christian values and a Christian world-view slowly receded, and churches came to play less and less of a role in public life. Not that Christian institutions disappeared, nor that people no longer believed in Jesus Christ, nor that people stopped attending church. Even though, in the post-1960s, the mainline Protestant and Roman Catholic churches saw a decrease in attendance, and the evangelical churches saw an increase, Canadians continued to affirm their faith in the Bible, in Jesus Christ, and in spiritual values. In a secularized society, the Christian message continues to change people personally and to influence human social movements. But as a public reality, secularization pushed faith from public life with the result that it no longer was a primary force shaping the fabric of intellectual, social, and cultural life.

Indeed, the seeds of secularization were sown before the twentieth century. One seed was "disestablishmentism." It disconnected the state and the church so that no church would have constitutional preference or special powers granted to it by the government. Whereas the U.S. constitution categorically states that church and state are to be separate, in Canada the process of separation was more gradual and not as clearly defined. Today the state and church work together in many ways, such as in education and the care of seniors.

During the 1830s and 1850s, the battle to disconnect the powerful Church of England from the Canadian government was fought on several fronts. The government had set aside a million hectares (2.5 million acres) to support the Protestant clergy. (The Church of England monopolized this land.)

On one side of this battle for control of the land was the Family Compact, led by John Strachan, Church of England bishop of Toronto. He argued that the church—he meant the Church of England—should be protected and financially supported by the state. In turn, the church would ensure the loyalty of citizens by accepting responsibility for religion, education, and charity.

On the other side were evangelical "voluntarists" led by the young Methodist itinerant preacher Egerton Ryerson. He opposed Strachan. For him, the state should be neutral in its treatment of denominations. The sole duty of the civil magistrate, he contended, is to protect religious liberty: to ensure that all groups would be equal before the law; to encourage churches to be funded by the voluntary support of their members; to see to it that churches use persuasion rather than coercion in expressing their views and recruiting members. Only in this way, he argued, could true Christian faith flourish, as it would entail no compromises with the state.

The dissolution of the Clergy Reserves in 1854 and the loss of Anglican dominance opened the way for other Protestant groups to grow and expand. After many years of wrangling, Strachan was isolated by other churches who agreed it was time to dissolve the Reserves. And so the task fell to John A. Macdonald's administration to deal the death blow. From this point on, no church would have a favoured or protected status with the government. As well, the churches' sole means of financial support was now their members.

This important change meant that, for churches to Christianize society, they had to act from outside the political arena. Likewise, no longer could the state rely on churches to support it with their agenda.

Not surprisingly the state became more secular as it turned to material progress—as the means to ensure social and political stability—for the core of its belief system. "Progress was to replace religion as the new opiate of the masses," writes Canadian historian William Westfall.[5]

"His Dominion": Cooperation for Reform

Although Protestant denominations—Methodists, Baptists, Congregationalists, and Presbyterians—continued to compete with one another after Confederation, by the end of the nineteenth century they began cooperating and saw the need to work together to ensure that Canada would be more Christian. Through social-reform movements, education, missionary activities at home and overseas, and the formation of many voluntary societies aimed at improving society, such as the Young Men's Christian Association (YMCA), Protestants strove to effect social change. The involvement of churches in these enterprises was more by way of volunteer association and funding than directly through church establishments. The new spirit of cooperation also produced two powerful reform crusades: the anti-alcohol crusade (temperance) and the protection of Sunday (Sabbatarianism).

It is hard for us to understand today, despite the carnage on the highways, the devastating impact alcohol was having on personal and social life in a growing, frontier colonial society. The human cost was enormous. In these early communities, drinking was not so much a social activity as a way to get drunk. Many drank because they could not see any way out of subsistent living. The effect on the social, physical, and spiritual life of many settlers was disastrous, women and children often paying the greatest price in physical abuse and food deprivation. And who can estimate the extent of the tragic consequences from the exchange of liquor between fur traders and Indians?

Although the temperance movement started in Montreal in 1828 (and within a decade almost 400 temperance societies had been formed), by mid-century it was obvious these volunteer societies were no longer reaching their intended audience. During the early years of the twentieth century, they gradually shifted their emphasis from moderation to the evils of drinking, to teetotalling, and finally to political intervention, in their effort to abolish the liquor trade. This final phase marked a transition from local church involvement to the formation of large, national organizations.

Despite the 1898 national referendum favouring prohibition, the Laurier government ignored the issue. It was not until the First World War that prohibition legislation was finally passed. Patriotism, swelled by wartime conditions, along with the support of French Canadians and the trade unions, helped push the argument for prohibition. By 1919, every province in Canada was dry. Although prohibition was repealed in 1926, anti-drink sentiments remained strong for decades to come: lasting evidence of the influence of church-directed concern over a plaguing social issue.

Keeping the Sabbath was very much a part of the British tradition. The coming of railways clashed with this tradition and forced the federal government into the fray. Trains, canals, and post offices operating on Sundays were particularly offensive to churches, as they were run by the government of a supposedly Christian nation. In 1853, 20,000 Canadians petitioned Parliament for the Sunday closing of all public works and offices, but failed. Even though George Brown presented this bill to the government almost every year, it never got a majority vote.

It probably would have remained that way if it were not for the Reverend J.G. Shearer, founder and first general secretary of the Lord's Day Alliance of Canada (1895), editor of the *Lord's Day Advocate*, and later the secretary of the Moral and Social Reform Department of the Presbyterian Church. He led a broad coalition—including union leaders, all Protestant groups, and the Catholic hierarchy—with a shared purpose: arguing that continuous work was brutalizing, they called for one day off per week, reasoning that citizens needed time for leisure and for cultivating spiritual life. After a long battle, they finally won. The Dominion Lord's Day Act was made law and became part of the Criminal Code of Canada on July 13, 1906. It allowed for "works of necessity or mercy" and gave concessions to industries that needed to maintain equipment. However, it did not pass easily. Opposition from newspapers and others charged that Sabbath legislation violated the principle of separation of church and state. While church leaders argued that the debate was over labour legislation, the religious language in the debate and the active involvement of so many churches showed it was something more.

Businesses, including railway companies, opposed the law. They feared it would interfere with their earning power and that freight competitors to the south would take advantage. So they simply refused to obey the law. Sabbatarian legislation eventually died the death of a thousand qualifications.

It is important to note here the voluntary and interdenominational societies that emerged. Christians saw that their task was to educate and lobby a world influenced by an industrial and capitalistic society. For Protestant churches, this marked a major change in strategy. The church which had determined Christian standards was being pressed in on by the power of business, industry, travel, and recreational activities, including sports. And so temperance and Sabbatarianism were not promoted as puritanical attempts to foist a particular morality upon the country, but rather as a means of bringing a sense of order and humanity to the depersonalizing effect of an industrial economy. Living years away from that moment, and unable to accept the notion of social movements campaigning against alcohol or promoting the keeping of the Sabbath, we are inclined to forget the important service they provided in trying to ennoble society and protect it from self-destructive forces.

These newly developed Christian groups tried to persuade society to live more righteously. But they faced the frustration of being politically powerless. And so they made a profound and historically defining shift: they moved from fighting for separation of church and state to lobbying governments to legislate standards of behaviour that matched their vision of Canada as a Christian nation. Even though they were unable to achieve a lasting victory by these two campaigns, and while they needed the help of non-church groups like labour unions to pass legislation, they showed how secular Canadian society was becoming even at the turn of this century. Through this experience of religious groups pressing for their own agendas, politicians learned that giving concessions to one group inevitably led to demands from another, and that the safest course of action was to stay clear of any religious issues.

CHURCHES AND EDUCATION

Public education is another arena in which the church and state had serious conflict. Indeed, some decisions rising out of these tensions later had a direct impact on secularization in education.

But first some background. In British North America, after Britain's defeat of France on the Plains of Abraham, education was the responsibility of the churches. Settlers took for granted that Christian faith was integral to learning. For them, "religion and education were inseparable and ... the state had a responsibility to foster, wherever possible, a harmonious relationship between the two."[6] For Protestants, literacy was important because it helped people read the Bible. The Roman Catholic Church in Lower Canada (Quebec) incorporated schools into their parish system.

A key figure in the early development of education in Upper Canada was John Strachan. In 1816 he introduced the Common School Act to even out the quality of elementary schools; made education more accessible; and curbed the influence of American books and teachers, many of whom were Methodists, thought by Strachan to be far below the acceptable standards. In 1823 he proposed a centralized board of education, made up entirely of Anglicans, to oversee a system of improved schools. For a decade, this church-controlled board managed all school lands and finances, regulated teacher appointments, and selected textbooks.

During the 1830s, the Church of England's domination of public education broke up. The rebellions of 1837–38 unleashed anti-American sentiment and led the people to demand a more centralized, government-funded system, thus lessening the grip of the churches' control on education.

In 1844, Methodist Egerton Ryerson became chief superintendent of education for the Province of Canada (Ontario). As architect of the public-school system, he emphasized the "essential elements and truths and morals of Christianity" as the best way to safeguard the spiritual foundation of society. This system, which became the model for many other provinces, was to be non-sectarian, accessible to all, and one in which the "essential principles of religion and morality" were taught instead of "the dogma of a sect."[7] Though the Bible was no longer used as a textbook, the Scriptures were read, and the Ten Commandments and the Lord's Prayer recited. Legislation also stipulated that no student should be required "to read or study from any religious book or join in any exercise of devotion or religion objected to."[8]

It is important to recognize that, even though the foundation and motivation of Ryerson's educational system was clearly Christian, he did set up a dividing line which in the end served to support powerful forces already at work in the secularization of the system. For example, while the clergy had earlier played a prominent role in Canadian schools, this situation changed. As teaching became more professionalized, clergy were moved out of the classroom. After 1871 inspectors, superintendents, and senior administrators were drawn from the teaching profession, not from the clergy. Schools by then had come under the exclusive control of the state bureaucracy.

Historian David Marshall points out that this separation of the school system from the churches and its incorporation into the state was not at that time a victory of the secular over the sacred. Even with this change, few expected that the school system would become wholly secular and without a religious foundation. In fact, Christian faith remained a significant influence in public-school curricula up to the 1950s. At an annual convention in 1875, Ontario teachers failed in an attempt to eliminate the subject of Christian morals. During the 1930s and 1940s, there was a resurgence of the role of Christian faith in education. The rise of fascism, and the impact of two world wars and the Great Depression, reinforced in people's minds the need for a sure understanding of life. Most provinces required two half-hour periods of religious instruction per week (attendance was subject to the formal right of withdrawal on the grounds of conscience). During the 1950s, these regulations were relaxed, allowing religious-education classes during the school day without dictating what they should be. Even the report of Ontario's MacKay Commission, *Religious Information and Moral Development* (1969), concluded that all religious views and value systems should be recognized by the schools.

But as the Christian consensus weakened, the separation of moral education from religious education increased. At first the motivation was not to exclude religious values from the public-school curricula; rather, it was to avoid imposing one particular religious system of beliefs on students. However well intentioned, it led to further elimination of Christian thought from the curricula and policies of education, under the pretext of making the system "neutral." Some provinces eventually struck down policies which had made the Lord's Prayer a part of the daily program. Many school boards have banned the distribution of New Testaments by Gideons, and in some school districts teachers are not permitted to make direct references to Christianity at Christmas celebrations. A major court case, the 1988 *Zylberberg* case in Sudbury, ruled that the reading of the Bible and a Christian prayer was in violation of the Charter of Rights and Freedoms. Two years later, the Ontario Court of Appeal struck down a regulation that required students to participate in two periods of religious instruction per week on the basis that the curriculum provided by the Elgin County Board of Education—the board being charged—denied non-Christian students freedom of conscience and religion. Some schools have gone so far as to ban all forms of religious activity on school property, including voluntary Bible studies during lunch-hour.

Moreover, governments are unable to reach a consensus on which "morals" or "values" should be taught. The effort to provide a religiously neutral environment has created curricula and programs that try to teach ethical principles without reference to the philosophical framework that undergirds our Western society. These attempts to teach "values" within an ideologically or religiously neutral vacuum stems from an assumption that religion is irrelevant to public life.

The Roman Catholic experience with education varied, depending on the province. In Ontario, the separate-school system, provided by constitutional agreement, allowed the Catholic Church to operate its own schools, fully funded by the public purse. In other provinces where public funding is not provided, the Catholic Church continued to operate its own schools. Early Roman Catholic leaders understood the critical place primary and secondary education has in the life of the student, and ultimately in the church and society. Their insistence that they control their own educational program was strategic and has served to support the long-term life and presence of the church in society.

Canadian educator Harro Van Brummelen, a professor at Trinity Western University, has documented the distorted picture of Christian faith presented in school texts. These texts ignore stories of the contributions made by religious leaders, major churches, and religious-based schools, and do not acknowledge their influence on society. These omissions stand in sharp contrast to the prominence given to the portrayal of Canadian Native culture (and that of other groups) in the very same textbooks. Many parents object to these educational materials, seeing them as part of an effort to impose secularistic humanism on their children. Writers of school texts surmised that excluding Christian faith from our understanding of history and culture creates the perception by students—and future generations—that Christianity was either a negative or a non-existent factor in the development and shaping of our land.

Churches and Higher Education

Higher education also raised questions about the appropriate role of religion, specifically the domination of the Anglicans.

In 1788, Bishop Charles Inglis had established King's College in Windsor, Nova Scotia, with the proviso that all faculty were to be Anglican and all students were to subscribe to the Thirty-nine Articles, the doctrine that defines what it means to be Anglican and is at the very heart of that faith.

In 1827, John Strachan secured a royal charter for a university in York called King's College; the college did not require religious tests, except for divinity students and for professors who sat on the university's governing council. Eventually, in 1847, the Anglicans lost control when the college was turned over to the "godless" University of Toronto, at which time religious tests for students and teachers were abolished. As well, the chair of theology was dropped; clergy could not become president or chancellor; and the provincial university endowment was placed under a government-appointed board.

Other denominations challenged the Anglican monopoly and opened their own colleges: the Presbyterians, with Pictou College in 1816 and Dalhousie College in 1818; the Baptists, with Horton Academy in 1829 (now Acadia University); and the Methodists, with Victoria University in 1842 (now a part of the University of Toronto), which required no religious tests and was financed by money collected by itinerant Methodist preachers. The Catholics did the same in Kingston in 1837, with Regiopolis College, and the Presbyterians opened Queen's University in Kingston in 1842. Nine more denominational colleges were founded in Ontario before 1860. This period appropriately became known as the "golden age" of church colleges.

The Protestant colleges, controlled mostly by evangelicals, pointed the way in the development of the modern Canadian university system. Public universities were generally not associated with a church, but the church-started colleges gradually dropped their denominational connections, affiliating with public universities as it became increasingly difficult to operate without government funding.

During the two world wars, governments needed specialized help in the war effort and turned to universities for skilled professionals, researchers, and technicians. Universities that provided this pool of talent received financial support from government, and thus later became dependent on government subsidies. Church-related colleges, struggling for survival, affiliated with these universities in order to have access to government grants. By the 1970s, only three older church-related colleges—Acadia (Baptist), Bishop's (Anglican), and Mount Allison (United Church)—continued to be independent of university affiliation.

New ideas spawned during the nineteenth century slowly gained a foothold in the early twentieth century and profoundly changed the way people viewed the world. Charles Darwin's theory of evolution—documented in his *On the Origin of Species* (1859) and *The Descent of Man* (1871)—was a critical idea that contributed to the churches' loss of influence in Canadian life. At first the impact was gradual as Protestant clergy saw the theory, not so much as a threat to faith, but as an opportunity to broaden the sway of the church. But, in the end, Darwin's theory would resonate beyond discussions of a contrarian view of human origins.

Darwin's theory of evolution attempted to give evidence that living things had emerged from a single, primitive form of life over a long period of time within an unthinking physical process—meaning God was not in control. His evolution model posited change as resulting, not from the intent of the Creator, but from random selection. The attendant notion of "survival of the fittest" saw the process of creation as ongoing and concluded that millions of beings are born only to die, for no other apparent purpose than for survival of the species. Darwin's ideas held that, instead of creation existing for human benefit, it is a matter of natural law and thus has no regard for human value.

The Darwin debate was not simply a conflict between science and religion; in fact, many scientists argued that evidence from geology and biology disputed Darwin's theories. Rather, it was a debate between those who wanted belief in God accounted for within scientific explanations and those who argued that faith had no place in discussion of the origin of creation. William Dawson, a Canadian Presbyterian reputed to be anti-Darwinian, warned the church of coming implications: "If God's role as an immediate, if occasional, adjuster of the material world was whittled away, He would also be displaced as a governor of its inhabitants."[9]

Underlying the debate was a growing belief in scientific methods. Operating with a rationalistic and materialistic approach in the search for knowledge, science excluded belief in the supernatural and ridiculed the miraculous. In the early 1800s, church leaders believed that obtaining knowledge about the world was a good way to learn more about the Creator and his creation. But, by the end of the century, this view had experienced a reversal: Christian faith no longer shaped science. Religion, although interesting, and even helpful, was seen as being neither true nor essential in the search for truth. In fact, religion was increasingly viewed as standing in opposition to reason. The seed planted a hundred years earlier was now in full bloom. As philosopher David Hume wrote, "Religion has lost all specificity and authority; it is no more than a dim, meaningless and unwelcome shadow on the face of reason."[10]

As the twentieth century dawned, few mainline Protestants resisted Darwinian ideas. Though their leaders considered Darwin's theories troubling, they did not see them as destructive. Instead, they tried to harmonize their faith with this new and respectable science. To this end, they sought to minimize Darwin's view that evolution explained the origin of humanity and they emphasized that evolution described how God improved the creation. Reverend E.H. Dewart, editor of the *Christian Guardian* and a prime voice in Canadian Methodism, wrote in 1870: "No one can deny that evolution is one of the methods of nature. The world did not spring at one bound from nothing into its present state of completeness. ... Every intelligent Christian will candidly admit that evolution is one of God's modes of working in the universe."[11] The editor of the *Presbyterian Witness* wrote in 1880: "The derivation of man from inferior species need give the student of the Bible no trouble of mind provided in connection with it, a divine act is admitted to have been present, both physically and spiritually in the new creation."[12] This accommodation reassured church members that the theory gave greater strength to the Bible.

Church leaders assumed an affinity between the Bible and science. To oppose this seemingly irrefutable scientific "fact" was, in their view, to be out of step with a rational and reasonable faith. Universities, many with roots in nineteenth-century evangelical Protestantism, seemed to have little interest in jettisoning Christian faith. Instead, there was a growing conviction that, in the light of new thought and discoveries, a reappraisal of faith and fundamental assumptions was needed. This need to harmonize modern science and faith left mainline Protestant churches vulnerable to an even greater intellectual force that threatened to further secularize them from within.

HIGHER CRITICISM OF THE BIBLE

Of all the ideas of the 1800s that influenced Protestant churches in Canada, the most significant—even more so than Darwinism—was the loss of confidence in the Scriptures as God's Word. At the heart of this shift was Higher Criticism, a critical study of the literary methods and sources used by the authors of the Old and New Testaments. By using modern or "scientific" methods of historical, textual, and literary analysis, this approach to the Bible generated scepticism about whether or not the Scriptures were trustworthy and authentic. The life and teachings of Jesus were challenged, and seminary professors and ministers ended up excluding portions of the Bible deemed not to be authoritative and believable. This means of studying the Scriptures led many of the mainline Protestant churches into adopting a theology that, in turn, radically shaped the Canadian church during the twentieth century.

Although Protestant leaders at first worked out an accommodation with these new intellectual trends, the acceptance of the underlying assumptions of Higher Criticism eventually eroded confidence in the Bible. Though this approach inspired some new methods of study and uncovered some important insights such as a better understanding of the historical context and the personality and style of biblical writers, it inevitably led to the conclusion that the Bible was not a divine revelation but, instead, a product of its culture, just like any other book of history or literature.

Canadians of all Protestant denominations debated the meaning of Higher Criticism in journals, the popular press, and religious periodicals. In several instances, it led to heresy trials and the dismissal of faculty members from theological colleges in Canada. Most Protestant leaders handled this controversy much as they did Darwinism: they sought to harmonize the tensions between traditional evangelical theology and newer ideas. Presbyterians such as Donald H. MacVicar and John Mark King, prominent figures in Presbyterian theological education, agreed with William Caven, Principal of Knox College, who said, "Theology is the same now that it has been in every age of the Christian era, so far as its great central truths are concerned, but continually changing by the growth of new truths, which an increasing knowledge of the Bible has furnished."[13]

Methodists, led by Samuel Nelles, President of Victoria College, looked for a balance between reason and faith, criticism and certainty, stability and progress. Nathanael Burwash, Dean of the Faculty of Theology at Victoria College, made a distinction between "reverent criticism," by which the text would be studied, and even criticized, but with an overall trust in the Scriptures as God-given, and the destructive approach, which he associated with rationalistic critics who did not affirm the Bible's essential character and its value for Christian living.

Higher Criticism became a way for theologians and ministers to explain away morally repugnant stories and doctrines, such as God's commands to wipe out entire communities, or the story of Jonah. It also opened the way for Jesus to be reinterpreted. Instead of viewing Christ through such doctrines as the atonement and resurrection, Higher Criticism turned attention to his moral example and social teachings. Sin need no longer be seen as a radical break between God and humanity, but could be interpreted as a matter of ignorance, and thus able to be corrected by education. This shift away from an evangelical doctrine is, in part, what helped drive the process of the secularization of Protestantism. Canadian church historian David Marshall describes the struggle: "Rather than trying to understand God being outside history and beyond human comprehension, those struggling with faith, in a sense, wrestled God down to earth, making him understandable in human terms and conformable to the needs and demands of society ... Conceptions of God were being based, in part, on what people would like God to be."[14] Thus, Marshall reduces the process of secularization to its essential tenet: God can be tamed. As God was being tamed, and as the Bible lost its credibility, Protestantism became vulnerable to other radical shifts of the time, its churches ministering to a society in spiritual bankruptcy and failing to give strong moral leadership to the nation.

While most Canadian Protestant clergy were not aware of the destructive conclusions of Higher Criticism, gradually the Scriptures were robbed of their power. Sermons concerned with the most recent biblical theories or social commentaries created an impression that the Bible was difficult and inaccessible. And so, at the end of a sermon, the congregants would have heard a message about a book for scholars, but not about a book describing God's message of life and salvation.

Scientific methods not only gave credibility to evolutionary theories and biblical criticism, but also fit with the Victorian optimism about "progress." Science was evidence that, with this "natural" ability to reason, along with a greater understanding of the universe, the human condition would get better. The material, social, moral, and spiritual advance of humanity appeared inevitable.

Optimism among Protestants converged with post-millennial notions that the Kingdom of God would be established after a long period of progress. Many were convinced that the material, moral, and spiritual improvements brought about by the recent enlightened developments in human thought and action signalled the installation of Christ's Kingdom on earth. It seemed that the human race—at least in the Western world—was on the verge of being in full control of its destiny. Reminders of sin and evil were masked by the emphasis on the improvement of humanity. For example, the transportation system of roads, railways, and canals was constantly expanding. Newspapers, the telegraph, and eventually the telephone facilitated rapid communication.

Mechanization found new ways to ease tedious and back-breaking tasks. Industrialization provided unprecedented opportunities for wealth.

As years of this century came and went, it became obvious Canada was not on the edge of the millennium. While holocausts and war undermined human optimism, there was such an overriding trust in human potential that faith in God—as a means of explaining life—was shunted aside.

CHRISTIANITY—JUST ANOTHER RELIGION

The study of Christianity as just one religion, nothing more than one of many, helped to undermine still further the belief in the uniqueness of Christ. Protestants had a firm view of foreign missions as the ultimate act of dedication. But as early-twentieth-century missionaries reported on the work of Christ in saving people from other religions, they did so to a growing number of parishioners who were being pressed by their ministers to question whether the Bible was true, whether Christ was divine, and whether he was the only means of salvation. Not only did interest in missionary enterprise drop off, the missionary focus turned to a concern for moral and social reform.

In this context, the view of Christianity as unique and distinct from other religions was minimized, replaced by religious relativism, which saw Christianity as one of many faiths, one more product of Western civilization. Conversion to Christ was no longer considered a necessary part of the missionary message. Not surprisingly, enthusiasm for missions declined among groups influenced by a liberal theology.

THE SOCIAL GOSPEL MOVEMENT

"[I]t is the business of the Church to set up on earth the Kingdom of God as a social organization based on the Golden Rule of Christ,"[15] decreed the Board of Social Service and Evangelism of the Methodist Church in 1914. As the new century rolled on, the Western world began feeling the full impact of unrestrained capitalism. Gross inequities in income, poverty created by high levels of unemployment, erratic cycles of economic depression, rapid urbanization, the unpredictable religious make-up of massive numbers of foreign immigrants, and eventually the drought on the prairies during the 1930s, gave impetus to a movement to address social ills and pushed church leaders to think about what the Gospel had to say about the way these societal forces affected people.

The Methodists, and to a lesser extent the Presbyterians and Baptists, played an important role in giving leadership and official church support to this movement. Though it was not a uniquely Canadian movement, it was first translated here into a ruling political party—the Co-operative Commonwealth Federation (CCF) under Tommy Douglas in Saskatchewan in 1944. It pressed its agenda by applying its ideas to political policy and legislation. Walter Rauschenbusch, a German-Baptist pastor in Rochester, New York, and Salem G. Bland, a Methodist minister in Canada, were two of the most prominent Social Gospel thinkers; J.S. Woodsworth, in Winnipeg, was its most outstanding practitioner.

Canadian Protestants had generally argued for free enterprise, laissez-faire economics (opposing government interference in the economy), and individual freedom. For example, in 1872, Presbyterians, Anglicans, and Methodists together opposed the strike of the Toronto Printers' Union. This kind of hands-off view prevailed until almost the end of the century. In 1887, when news of Henry George's Anti-Poverty Society reached Toronto, the *Christian Guardian* responded by stating, "We have no faith in the abolition of poverty by any laws that can be made in legislatures. ... The best anti-poverty society is an association of men who would adopt as their governing principles in life, industry, sobriety, economy and intelligence."[16] Up until the 1890s, conventional wisdom attributed all forms of social ills to moral failure.

By the end of the century, it became obvious that this marketplace view was inadequate in the face of desperate social conditions. While the principle of good works gave some relief, it did not address underlying causes. In a sense Protestants determined to bring about change were trapped: the underlying assumption of Darwin's theories was "survival of the fittest." If one agreed with that in natural history, did one not have to apply it to economic history? The growth of capitalism was given encouragement in this Darwinian context.

But some church leaders—such as Rauschenbusch in New York and Woodsworth in Winnipeg—saw how human misery increased as capital took the upper hand. When education proved inadequate as a strategy for coping with changing conditions, the churches turned to government to set the moral standards.

By placing emphasis on achieving Christ's Kingdom on earth, Protestant leaders replaced theological explanations for evil and suffering with secular explanations. Nineteenth-century ideas reinforced one another in laying the base of the Social Gospel Movement: an optimistic view of progress; the potential of humanity; the influence of Darwinism; and the radical reformation of biblical understanding by Higher Criticism.

God as transcendent and intervening was replaced by God in nature and history. Distinctions between the supernatural and natural, church and world, were replaced with the secular. Liberal theology contended that experience and feeling were needed more than creeds and doctrines. A social definition of Christ's Kingdom replaced doctrines of sin, salvation, and redemption. Truth was defined by its moral impact on individuals and society, and not by a biblical word. Concern for this world overshadowed interest in the afterlife. Jesus' death was not seen as the sacrifice for the sins of the world, but rather as the expression of the supreme power of love. The "mission" of the church was reinterpreted to mean bringing home the Kingdom of God, and by religious education and social reform.

At first, only a few ministers from the mainline churches supported the Social Gospel message. But, by the early 1900s, it was appearing in sermons and editorials. In 1906, a coalition of church and labour groups secured passage of the Lord's Day Act and formed the Moral and Social Reform Council of Canada which, in 1913, became the Social Services Council of Canada. In addition, the Social Gospel influence was felt in such organizations as the YMCA, Epworth Leagues of Methodist young people, and the Ecumenical Methodist Conference in Toronto in 1911. Its most long-term influence came by way of denominational boards of evangelism and social service.

In the beginning, their programs were quite modest: they called for conversion of industrial leaders, redistributing wealth, and influencing society with Jesus' teachings. Theology reinterpreted Jesus' teachings to apply to an ethical program of social regeneration, with less emphasis on individual salvation.

The bloody events of the First World War were a wake-up call for the Social Gospel Movement: its vision of progress was shattered. The Social Gospel's identification with the state robbed the church of its prophetic role by reducing God's activity to social reform and political activity, while minimizing personal conversion. In addition, Social Gospel theology was challenged by those who clung to a dispensational understanding of the Kingdom: they believed the world was about to witness the physical return of Jesus Christ.

Themes and causes of the Social Gospel were adopted by the CCF, the forerunner of the New Democratic Party, and it brought together former Social Gospel leaders J.S. Woodsworth, T.C. Douglas, William Irvine, and Stanley Knowles. While there is no dispute that the Social Gospel Movement had an enormous impact on churches at the time, and on Canadian social policy throughout the twentieth century, still, as J.W. Grant argues, it never went beyond the clergy and the service professions. In so far as it depended on a naïvely optimistic faith and a belief in the perfectibility of humanity, in the end it was a substitute gospel.

Leaders in the Social Gospel Movement considered their vision to be more than a response to changing social conditions: they believed that, if their churches failed to find economic and social solutions, the church would lose the working classes to secular materialism. However, in its attempt to renew the church by making its message more "relevant," it ended up secularizing mainline Protestant churches from within. For historian Ramsay Cook, it ended up replacing "theology, the science of religion, with sociology, the science of society." Social Gospel leaders thought they were making room for a more religious Canada, but instead they paved the way for Canadians to become less religious.

Political Liberalism

At the end of the twentieth century, political liberalism was playing an enormous role in making religion private. Liberalism as a social and political theory does not mean being generous or broad-minded. Neither does it have anything to do with a particular political party. It is a life view that freedom and autonomy of the individual are of primary importance to society. Canadian philosopher George Grant defines it as "a set of beliefs which proceed from the central assumption that man's essence is his freedom and therefore that which chiefly concerns man in this life is to shape the world as we want it."[17]

The roots of liberalism can be traced to the French Revolution, which was foundational to the American political experiment: independence of individuals and family through urbanization, the market economy, and industrialization; building a political system (which is non-religious) to solve problems often created by religious wars; and philosophies that encourage belief in human progress through reason.

Liberalism stresses individuality, freedom, individual autonomy and rights, the separation of religion and politics, reason, tolerance and the non-imposition of belief. It asserts that a neutral political system provides a place of tolerance for many views. In theory, its creed is that it has no creed: its objective is to provide a framework within which each person can pursue his or her own freely chosen life, in which each tolerates the other; each view is accorded equal respect, and no view is imposed upon another; and the state is neutral. Individual freedom is vital to the workings of a democratic state—it is an idea found in the ministry of Jesus and expressed throughout the Gospels, although always within the framework of putting the interests of others ahead of one's own.

But liberalism is not neutral towards conflicting theories of the human good. By promoting human autonomy as the ultimate good, it undermines distinctive and traditional communities and replaces them with a uniform regime of individual choices. In forming public policy, liberalism is forced to take sides. In that sense, it is not neutral. While the legitimacy of the government to rule rises from the vote of each elector, the government must rule on a broader basis than individual rights. For example, a public ban on smoking in public places overrides the rights of the individual in order to serve the greater good. Regardless of their intended benefits, such bans are not neutral in their view of what constitutes that good.

The issue of public funding of alternative (Christian, Jewish, Muslim, etc.) schools points out the trap a government falls into. In Ontario (which constitutionally is required to fund Roman Catholic primary and secondary education from the public purse), the government refuses to provide funds for other religiously based schools. (Note: Most other provinces, apart from Nova Scotia, Prince Edward Island, and New Brunswick, do fund, to various levels, religiously based schools.) Parents who want their children trained in a school shaped by their religious world-view have only one choice: send them to a school of their choice and end up paying double tuition—that is, the tuition for the chosen school and their school taxes, which go only to the public system. In this case, in Ontario, the courts have agreed with the government. The argument is that the public system is needed to serve the whole community, which requires that the liberal doctrine, which is to serve individual rights, be set aside.

But in other situations, the reverse is true. The most important Supreme Court case on religious-liberty issues to date is the *Big M Drug Mart* case in 1985. The issue in this case was whether a drug store in Calgary could be open on Sunday, which was a violation of the federal Lord's Day Act. The company applied to the court for permission to stay open on the basis of the freedom-of-religion clause in the Charter. In this case, the historical tradition of reserving one day for religious observance and for relief from work was set aside in favour of individual liberties. It ended up wiping out what was of interest to large numbers of Canadians. As Justice Dickson said in his ruling, because it rose out of "religious values rooted in Christian morality," the law was therefore illegitimate. In this case the rights of the community were set aside in favour of the rights of the individual.

This creates a problem for Christians: the Charter is predicated on the notion that, if a law rises out of a Christian ideal, it therefore is unacceptable in a multicultural community. One by one, we are seeing the values that characterize a Christian understanding of life set aside. Recent attempts by gay-rights advocates to restructure the traditional definition of marriage—as being between two people of the opposite sex—as a way of receiving benefits tears at the fabric of marriage and family. In this instance, again the individual-freedom argument is imposed.

As individual freedom is made the highest good, and the human will is exalted, then that which is beyond the human will is made to appear irrelevant. Freedom as the highest good cannot live alongside any other good, for any other good—if it is genuinely universal—would limit its autonomy. This world-view is imposed upon Canadian society, often through the dominating power of the state, be it through the parliaments or the courts. The underlying assumption is that individualism is to be imposed. But this ends up replacing a genuinely pluralistic society with an enforced homogeneous society ruled by individualism.

Canada as a liberal democracy gives the individual the right to choose who will govern. But, since the introduction of the 1982 Charter of Rights and Freedoms, liberalism has gone beyond merely defending and providing for individual freedom. Although the Charter does retain certain groups' rights (e.g., the rights of dissentient schools, language rights, rights of aboriginal peoples), what receives court action are special-interest groups, who are reshaping our culture by appealing to individual rights. This, of course, provides an opportunity for any group to make a case against what, in their view, is a violation of personal rights. The Committee for Freedom in Education in Ontario—an evangelical group—has put to the courts a complaint against the provincial government for failing to provide the opportunity for parents to have their children given instruction in the faith of their choice.

However, the Charter shifts power from legislators to judges by imposing new limitations on the former and conferring new powers on the latter. Before 1982, Parliament set the rules, and the courts refereed compliance with the rules. Today, the courts can also set the rules. In doing so, the courts have created opportunities for interest groups to advance their ideological agendas, even though they have not been able to sway public opinion sufficiently to get the federal government to pass a bill favouring their concerns. Supreme Court Justice John Sopinka, in a speech given at Concordia University, on October 27, 1993, criticized special-interest groups who "have extended their demands so far that they threaten freedom of others. They not only criticize the expression of views that do not accord with their own but demand that contrary views be suppressed." He added, "This movement has had its effect on the judiciary."

In effect, we have created a perception of society as a collection of individuals. Pushed to its logical conclusion, even the state—not to mention a social unit like the family—is seen as artificial, designed only to serve the interests of individuals. This prevailing emphasis undercuts certain features that have distinguished Canada and is having a direct impact on Christian communities. By treating religion as strictly a "private" matter, liberalism contributes directly to the secularization of Canadian society.

An example is the 1985 *Equality for All* report of the Parliamentary Committee on Equality Rights—a committee dominated by members of the Progressive Conservative party. Its mandate was to examine Canadian laws to see if changes needed to be made to come into line with section 15, subsection 1, of the Constitution, which states: "Every individual is equal before and under the law and has the right to the equal protection and benefit of the law without discrimination and, in particular, without discrimination based on race, national or ethnic origin, colour, religion, sex, age or mental or physical disability."

The report depicts Canada as a collection of individuals. Each individual has his or her own particular characteristics and personal traits—religion, age, gender, and so on—but these are private and irrelevant matters that should be left at home when people enter the social, political, and economic world. The report openly suggests that religion is not "relevant to a person's fitness to compete for a given job or reside in particular accommodations."[18] It ignores the fact that religious beliefs shape the private and public life patterns of millions of Canadians. As a result, these characteristics are of utmost public significance as factors that inform social interaction. Nonetheless, the influence of liberal-individualism continues to create conflict between Christians who believe it is our faith that informs all of life and those who view faith as irrelevant in social, legal, and political contexts.

This struggle is clearly seen in public-school classrooms. For many educators, liberalism is the ideal form of pedagogy. Its purported aim is to expose each child to a fair and balanced view of options from which to make a serious choice. However, there are two attendant problems: A so-called liberal education omits the faith perspective from these studies, as though faith has no business in the understanding of such disciplines as politics, ethics, and history. As well, subjects such as physics or math are seen completely outside any reference to creation and faith, and instead are viewed solely within a mechanical and closed universe. The underlying message for a student is that no one religion can be true; that faith is important only as it relates to an individual's choice; and, more important, that faith is not essential to the understanding of life.

The Emergence of Evangelical Protestant Groups

Up to now my examination of the impact of secularization has focused primarily on "old-line" Protestants who, prior to the early twentieth century, held evangelical theology as their base, including Presbyterians, Methodists, and Baptists. This situation changed dramatically in the early 1900s, when much of Protestantism was reshaped by theological liberalism. In reaction to this change (especially of the Methodists), theological conservatism rushed in, birthing new evangelical Protestant groups such as various Baptist denominations, the Associated Gospel Churches, new formations of Mennonites, Pentecostals, the Evangelical Free Church, the Church of the Nazarene, the Christian and Missionary Alliance—to name just a few—and, in more recent years, various charismatic groups. But it would be wrong to assume that these groups did not themselves play a part in the process of secularization.

Canada Becoming Secularized

Most twentieth-century evangelical movements, prior to the early 1960s, allowed themselves to be ghettoized within their own subculture groupings, often out of concern about being contaminated by "the world." By default, they relied on old-line Protestant and Catholic communities to be the nation's religious and cultural gatekeepers and to influence society with Christian morality.

Four factors encouraged this ghettoization.

First, the fundamentalist-modernist conflict during the early part of the century convinced many evangelicals to have nothing to do with any group other than their own. The growing influence of a liberal theology and the Social Gospel convinced many evangelical Protestants (sometimes called "fundamentalists" or "conservative Protestants") that old-line Protestants were too uncritical of new ideas. Evangelicals emphasized personal sin and conversion, and viewed Social Gospel ideas as a sell-out to worldly thinking. Biblical inerrancy—that is, the belief that the Bible was absolutely without error in any respect—became a major preoccupation. Energy and finances poured into evangelistic efforts and missions. Social or political involvement was left for others to worry about.

Second, the influence of premillennialism (a belief that Jesus would return before God brings in the thousand-year reign) painted a gloomy view of the world, teaching that social conditions would get worse and worse in the lead-up to the second coming of Christ. These ideas were popularized by prophetic Bible conferences and the Scofield Bible, the King James Version that Bible teacher Charles Scofield published with his notes, and with many written by John Darby, who had developed the theory of Dispensationalism. The belief that those living in Christ would be taken away from the earth—"raptured"—provided a biblical rationale for Christians to keep apart from the world, and made evangelism and missions more important than social activism. In this paradigm, the winning of converts was seen as the most important of all activities.

Premillennialism not only served as a catalyst for aggressive evangelism and missions, but became a means of confronting postmillennialism (a view that Christ would return after the thousand-year reign), which old-line Protestants seemed to prefer. It challenged the thinking that the Kingdom of God was brought closer by the moral and spiritual improvements resulting from so-called enlightened ideas of social reform. The newer churches simply had to point to the atrocities of the early 1900s to show how barbaric humanity was in contrast with the vaunted notion of progress. Although premillennialism nurtured a distinct subculture, it did provide the church with an important alternative way of seeing God at work.

Third, hanging on to European culture and language kept some evangelical groups from being absorbed into Canadian culture. A prime example were the Mennonites, who tried to maintain their distinctiveness by living together in Mennonite communities, speaking their own language, and practising their own culture. With the exception of Swiss Mennonites, who settled in Ontario during the late 1700s and 1800s, most Mennonites arrived in Canada in several migrations between 1870 and 1930. Although the government had guaranteed them the right to operate their own private elementary schools, most Mennonites had no choice but to send their children to "English" schools. To compensate for this loss, they established networks of institutions between 1913 and 1950, including schools (elementary, secondary, and Bible schools) and other inter-Mennonite groups such as the Mennonite Central Committee to preserve their culture and theology and to facilitate their interests in relief and development. Even so, the subsequent generation gave up speaking German for English, which made it easier for them to access Canadian culture.

A fourth reason why evangelicals were culturally marginalized was because of socio-economic differences. Most were not well educated, preferring training offered at Bible institutes (which nurtured a suspicion of higher education—"if theological liberalism came from seminaries and universities, then best avoid them" was the logic) over education offered at universities. As well, many evangelical Protestant churches tended to attract fewer professionals than did their mainline counterparts.

Some twentieth-century evangelical groups developed out of a reaction to theological liberalism. Others began out of the Pentecostal experience, springing from a spiritual awakening at a meeting on Azuza Street in Los Angeles. Others were started by missionaries such as the Sudan Interior Mission under Canadian Rowland Bingham, or because of a distinct ethnic immigrant focus, such as the Swedes who formed the Baptist General Conference, and the Germans in the North American Baptist denomination.

In the early part of the century, these evangelical groups made up a relatively small minority among Protestants, but, over the next decades, many showed impressive gains. In the 1911 census, only 515 people claimed to be Pentecostals. By 1991, that number had increased to more than 436,000 (1.6 per cent of the Canadian population), making it the sixth-largest Protestant group in Canada. Even during the 1930s, the Pentecostal Assemblies of Canada managed to increase the number of their churches from 65 to 300. The Christian and Missionary Alliance also experienced phenomenal growth. Researchers note that, since the 1980s, the cumulative number of Canadians actively involved in evangelical Protestant groups exceeds the combined total of those involved in the United Church, the Anglican Church, and the Presbyterian Church. It is estimated today that about 1 per cent of Canadians are evangelical by faith and practice.

By the 1960s, many evangelical groups were on their way out of cultural isolation. In addition to the numerical growth that helped them become cumulatively the largest and most robust religious community within Canadian Protestantism, still more surprising has been the manner in which they became integrated into Canadian life. Despite being seen by the press as narrow-minded, unsophisticated, belligerent, and rural sectarians, they have created a vast interlocking network of institutions and organizations in areas including theological education, campus youth ministries, missionary work, publishing, and broadcasting.

This confluence took place as Canadian culture steadily became less influenced by traditional Christianity. Instead of seeing themselves as outsiders, evangelicals called for a change, pressing for cultural participation.

A "Quiet Revolution"

Quebec is the one place in which secularization has most radically and quickly occurred. Long the bastion of Roman Catholicism, and for centuries controlled by the church, Quebec underwent radical changes during the "Quiet Revolution" of the 1960s.

Throughout its history, the Catholic Church has consistently been the central player in Quebec's social and political life. Following the British Conquest in 1763, the Catholic Church was offered certain rights if it promised to keep Quebec loyal during the American Revolution. This guaranteed the church enormous influence within Quebec: politicians and churchmen were drawn together by the common goal of survival. The church's central role and influence was further strengthened during the nineteenth century as Quebec resisted the threat of assimilation by the Americans after the rebellions of 1837–38. At the same time, Catholicism experienced a "devotional revolution" that renewed spiritual life, and in turn resulted in the church's having more influence in education and welfare.

In the nineteenth century, the more aggressive ultramontane Catholicism ("ultramontane" literally means "over the mountain," and refers to the world domination of papal power) pressed the view that the state should defer to the church in education and legislation of a moral character. This movement gave the church the ability to continue to assert itself "as the spiritual and cultural force that defined, with ever increasing intensity, the social reality of French Canada. This Catholicism was the religious cement that enabled French Canadians to resist assimilation and decline."[19] In the twentieth century, it joined in a marriage of convenience with Maurice Duplessis, premier of Quebec from the mid-1930s to the end of the 1950s. The church gave him its support, and in exchange Duplessis's political philosophy of anti-statism permitted the church to continue its control of education, health services, and welfare. Although social conditions changed dramatically, the church stayed at the heart of the province's public thinking. Out of its religious nationalism, the church helped Quebeckers to see themselves as "a chosen people, a faithful remnant, the bearers of a Catholic civilization in Protestant/secular North America."[20] It defined for Quebeckers who they were, and why they should not assimilate into Anglo North American culture.

After 1960, this situation changed radically. The new provincial Liberal government regarded itself, not the Catholic Church, as the principal agent responsible for defining Quebec society. It began a process of "political modernization," taking control of social institutions formerly under the church's control. As well, a new and secular view of self-determination focused on modernization and an attempt to catch up with other societies that had become industrialized. This, along with the felt need to preserve Quebec's culture and identity, served to create an environment for a new and revitalized French presence in North America. These changes were immensely popular and gave Quebeckers a new pride in being French Canadian.

At the same time that the church was being pushed out of the public sphere, it began losing members at an unprecedented rate. Quebeckers, particularly those in urban areas, suddenly stopped going to church. In a single decade, the church lost at least 50 per cent of its members. In rural communities, 70 per cent remained practising Catholics, but, in urban communities, religious participation dropped to as low as 7 per cent. In a dramatic way, Quebec Catholics rejected the authoritarian attitude of the church and argued that the church's archaic emphasis on a classical religious curriculum instead of on science and technology had kept them behind the rest of Western society.

The Second Vatican Council, held in 1962–65, had been called by Pope John XXIII out of what he described as a sudden inspiration of the Holy Spirit. The council's task was to review the life of the church and bring its teachings, disciplines, and organizations up to date, with the unity of all Christians being its ultimate goal. In part, it helped the church avoid a cultural split, offering a compromise in education that preserved the church's presence within the public-school system. But the exodus of members continued. In 1992 the Laroche Report, prepared by a commission appointed by the Quebec Catholic bishops, made the radical suggestion that the church turn its back on "cultural Catholicism" and begin functioning as a "voluntaristic religion based on spiritual experience and profound conviction."[21] In this age in which Baby Boomers turn from the support of institutions, opting instead for spiritual ideas and experience which relate to their own needs, such a move by the Catholic Church will connect with the spiritual hunger of emerging generations.

CONSUMERISM

Perhaps far more powerful in dulling the cutting edge of Christian faith than the combined influences of Darwinian evolution, scientific progress, higher criticism of the Bible, and liberal theology was the gradual bestowing of a sanction to consumerism, which applauded the values of material well-being, instant gratification, and the pursuit of pleasure and self-fulfilment.

In 1878, E.H. Dewart, editor of the *Christian Guardian*, warned that the "accumulation of wealth promotes irreligion and worldliness."[22] Despite such warnings, Protestants enthusiastically promoted economic growth and technological development as being fundamentally good. Though it can be argued that the pursuit of industrial activity was motivated by the desire to make Canada an economically viable country, this incentive was eventually replaced by the crass pursuit of wealth.

As well, British immigrants were motivated more by the opportunity to improve their standard of living than they were by the need to find a sanctuary to practise their religion or build the Kingdom of God. The ever-increasing drive for wealth alarmed W.A. Foster, the leader of the Canada First movement, who in 1871 appealed for a "bond more uniting than a shiftless expediency; some lodestar more potent than a mere community of profit."[23]

As more wealth was distributed into the hands of people through a regular weekly wage, a growing middle class emerged. Higher levels of disposable income created a demand for consumer goods and more leisure activities. Shopping became a recreational pastime. Churches faced growing competition from newly organized sports organizations, trade unions, social clubs, libraries, theatres, music halls, and amusement parks. These took over some of the social functions that churches had traditionally provided, and by so doing contributed to the marginalization of the churches and the privatization of faith.

After the two world wars, manufacturers focused on producing a vast array of new consumer items. Indoor plumbing and electricity created still more "needs." If families had not saved a sufficient amount of money, purchases could be made on credit, on an instalment plan. Driven by the advertising industry, the "consumptive principle based on self-indulgence" transformed the values within Canadian society so that, in an effort to attain a sense of well-being, people focused more and more on material comfort or prosperity in this world instead of salvation in the next. David Marshall observes that "the emergence of consumer culture was central to the secularization of Canadian life, for the path to a sense of well-being was now clearly defined in material terms rather than spiritual or ethical ones."[24]

Throughout the twentieth century, churches have increasingly been forced to compete for the attention of adherents. As Canadians felt less inclined or pressured to go to church, churches entered into a conscious campaign to attract people into the fold, speaking to their felt needs, including personal meaning and significance; how to live in marriage and raise a family; and the issues of guilt, love, and life after death. Even so, Canadians are increasingly selective in the religious practices they will adopt and the beliefs they will accept. Churches that are attracting the Baby Boomers and Busters offer a range of options, allowing people to pick and choose what best satisfies their needs. As sociologist Reginald Bibby reminds us, potential congregants are customers in search of a product.

At the turn of the millennium, although many Canadians are showing continuing interest in Christian faith, public institutions remain entrenched in a secular view of life, with little expressed inclination in opening their doors to the influence of faith. If those doors are even to inch open, bold initiatives must be undertaken by Christians to reshape those institutions to accommodate a larger vision of God in life.

With this overview in place, we now move on to consider, as Christians, what Canada might look like within a more biblical construct.

PART II

BIBLICAL LANGUAGE

CHAPTER 4

Windows on
Nation Building

As we search for an understanding of what God might expect a nation to be, the first place we must look is the Old Testament. There we see how a nation should be constructed under God's direct counsel and presence. Although we must be careful not to overuse this historical and unique example, it offers us clues as to what a nation under God might look like.

❧

The Old Testament is an obvious place to begin in our search for a biblical model for a nation, but how should this material be treated? There are three ways to interpret Old Testament material so as to preserve its integrity.[1] These provide windows through which we can view the stories, promises, and histories of the Scriptures as emblematic of how God interacts with his people.

The first window shows us God at work among his people. At this level of interpretation, the stories are seen as historical, but the lessons (the key factor) emerge from the principles.

For example, God's call to Abraham to raise up a people to live in accordance with the covenant is a picture of God calling out a people. The principle here is that God calls people who will follow.

The second window offers a vision of the future, when life will be ruled by God. According to this level of interpretation, even though a text may refer to the present, it also may be speaking of the future. Zechariah's vision is an example. He writes that the Lord said to him, "I will return to Zion and will dwell in Jerusalem. Then Jerusalem will be called the City of Truth, and the mountain of Lord Almighty will be called the Holy Mountain" (Zech. 8: 3). While Zechariah is describing a contemporary event, he is also writing of a future time, when God will rule the nation absolutely.

The third window presents the New Testament church as the inheritor of God's workings with the Hebrews. Take, for example, the Year of Jubilee. This celebration was to be a time when debt would be forgiven. The people and their land were to be given breathing time to start again: "There should be no poor among you, for in the land the Lord your God is giving you to possess as your inheritance, he will richly bless you" (Deut. 15: 4). This idea was picked up by the early church, which incorporated into its fellowship the premise that "there was no needy person among them" (Acts 4: 34).

The Old Testament is the story of God and the chosen tribes. We are not meant to link it to today, holus-bolus, and imitate Israel. Instead, we are to see it as a growing, moving, unfolding drama of God and human life. In looking for nation-building principles, rather than templates, we avoid the trap of assuming that promises to Israel apply to, say, Canada, the United States, or Western Samoa. They do not.

But it is appropriate that we learn from Israel, called to be a light to the nations: "I will keep you and will make you to be a covenant for the people and a light for the Gentiles" (Isa. 42: 6). Again: "I will also make you a light for the Gentiles, that you may bring my salvation to the ends of the earth" (49: 6). Thus, Israel was an example to other nations, and it points us to vital lessons.

Israel provides us with a picture, a paradigm; a way of seeing a people in relation to their God. This pattern of God's will for a called-out people is surely of interest to us thousands of years later. It is helpful to read the "Maker's instructions" when attempting to construct a nation.

To get at the essentials of nation building, we can identify six periods in which God interfaced with his people: Creation; the Fall; the Abrahamic covenant; the laws of Moses; the kingly reign of David; and the message of the prophets. These give us a framework to construct an understanding of God's relationship to his creation.

The study of Creation helps us see political and social life on God's broad stage. The Fall brings us face to face with our individual failings and failed relationships: having turned away from its Creator, society is broken and the creation is alienated. Abraham learns of God's covenant, on the basis of which a sociopolitical community can be sustained. The laws given to Moses lead us further into the covenant; now society has laws and ethical mandates that specify how people should live together. King David's reign provides a particular political setting in which this covenant is worked out in detail. The prophets' stinging rebukes and powerful ethical challenges provide a counterpoint to the building of an understanding of what God has in mind for his people as they live out their lives in the nations of this planet.

CREATION

From the outset we are overwhelmed with the reality that the earth is the Lord's, owner of all. Everything is subordinate to God's ownership. Stewardship is a moral obligation from which we draw the four ethical principles that guide how we should live: shared resources, work, growth, and accountability.

The first principle is that resources are to be shared. The bounty of the earth is given to humans only in a trustee relationship. The Genesis story of creation disproves the view held by Canadians who believe they have prior claim to this land because their ancestors were among the first immigrants. All of creation is God's and is a gift. The created man and woman who inherit God's image are given the task of caring for creation. As legitimate as private land ownership is to Israel, it is subsumed under the overarching principle of the lands being of benefit to all.

The second principle is that work is a gift from God, instituted before the Fall. "Be fruitful and increase in number; fill the earth and subdue it" (Gen. 1: 28). God as a worker passes it on to human creation. "The Lord God took the man and put him in the Garden of Eden to work it and take care of it" (2: 15). As we are called to tend the environment, we are also called to work.

Third, growth is a result of our labour: "Be fruitful and increase" (1: 28). Growth is a principle inherent in creation. The cycles of plant life manifest the inner nature of creation—to grow and reproduce. But growth requires tending. A field left to itself will choke with weeds. A fruit tree left alone will produce scrawny fruit. At the heart of creation is the balance of growth and control. To cultivate the land or prune the tree is to aid creation. Within the earth there is sufficient food-growing ability to satisfy the needs of all. However, greed, the drive to produce more and more without regard for the shared-resources principle, abuses creation.

Fourth, while we are at the centre of creation, tending and overseeing, humankind is accountable, for we are linked to other elements of creation. "Let us make man in our image, in our likeness, and let them rule over the fish of the sea and the birds of the air, over the livestock, over all the earth, and over all the creatures that move along the ground" (1: 26). To understand Yahweh (a Hebrew word for God) is to recognize the integrity of creation: life forms are interconnected.

Each part of creation has the right to its own existence. But human leadership has a moral obligation to set limits to ensure the rights of all. Hoarding or private ownership without regard for the rights and needs of others simply does not figure in the scene of creation. "Dominion" does not mean "domination." "What is mine is mine" does not fit with creation.

The Creation account provides us with operating principles that enable us to construct a model for God's will as we live in our nation/state.

The Fall: The Impact of Human Sin

The devastation of sin broke the harmony of creation and humanity, pitting one against the other, and changed the relationship of God to creation. Living in that "fallen" world, we strain and peer through a clouded window as we struggle to make sense of our relationship to God.

Living on this side of that cataclysmic break, it is hard to grasp its vastness. The turning of the human will from the Creator was enabled by one of God's former leading angels, Lucifer. (One-third of the angels had followed Lucifer [Lucifer was senior along with Michael and Gabriel] who led an attack against God and encouraged both the woman and the man to disobey Yahweh.)[2] Human beings entered a different phase when they disobeyed, losing their purity and intimacy with the divine. "Then the eyes of both were opened, and they realized they were naked; so they sewed fig leaves together and made covering for themselves" (Gen. 3: 7). What was natural became an embarrassment. They not only hid from each other behind the covering of leaves, but tried to hide from God in the trees. The resulting impact was global. The relationship between Creator and created disjoined, and the man and the woman were set at odds with creation.

The Fall violated the principles established under Creation. The principle of shared resources was turned upside down. Resources became the object of greed and envy. The powerful hoarded rather than shared. Instead of care for the environment, abuse and pollution become the accepted standards. God's human creation became a means of oppression and of subjection.

Within this paradigm of failure and fallenness, the call to work is not abrogated. Indeed, it is affirmed. God, while forcing human creation out of the Garden of Eden, made an accompanying stipulation: "By the sweat of your brow you will eat your food" (3: 19). Whereas the responsibility of work was predicated before the Fall on the idea that caring for God's world was a joy, after the Fall it became an obligation. But along with this requirement came a promise. God always gives creation a means of going on. Implicit in the call to eat by the sweat of one's brow is the promise that there will be opportunity to work. Thus, there are now two work-related principles: work is an obligation, not only a joy; but, further, work is assured. Corrupted, however, work, like the Creation, is distorted, abused, "a commodity to be bought and sold, with little care or responsibility for the working human being. Work becomes a slave of greed, a tool of oppression, a means of replacing God with one's own ambition, even an idol in itself for some."[3]

The principle of healthy economic growth in which the creation is served is violated; creation is used rather than being served. That which was created for the good of others becomes that which is worshipped. This worshipping of growth loads an unbearable burden on those called to do the carrying. That which was seen by the Creator as a gift becomes the goal.

Economics then becomes the measuring stick of success instead of an expression of blessing. The principle of using resources for the good of all is turned into a tool of greed. The too-late-wise Solomon reflected on this unquenchable thirst for more: "Whoever loves money never has enough money; whoever loves wealth is never satisfied with his income. This too is meaningless. As goods increase, so do those who consume them. And what benefit are they to the owner except to feast his eyes on them?" (Eccl. 5: 10f.; cf. 5: 13f.; 6: 1f). Hosea the prophet points out the damage of violating creation: "Because of this the land mourns, and all who live in it waste away; the beasts of the field and the birds of the air and the fish of the sea are no more" (Hos. 4: 3).

Worship drifts away from Yahweh to the gods of the earth. This shift tends to be discounted in our technically sophisticated world, dismissed as archaic or melodramatic. Nevertheless, we ignore this power struggle at our own peril. We fumble in our attempt to find God's rules for nation building if we ignore these obvious signs of our fallen creation.

Yahweh's demands to defend those who are trapped by the power brokers of economic domination run at cross-purposes to greed and self-interest. To follow in obedience to this God was as inconvenient then as today. There are clearly opposing sides. God's call is that creation is to enhance all. Fallen human impulses are reduced to self-serving concerns.

The building of a nation requires one to be realistic about human nature. Romanticizing our nature leads to seeing human failing not so much as the result of individual fallenness as having a societal cause. To ignore the nature of individual sin is to discount the obvious: "The heart is deceitful above all things and beyond cure" (Jer. 17: 9). This is a good reminder for nation builders. Philosopher Immanuel Kant wrote, "From such warped wood as man is made, nothing straight can be fashioned."

The story of God and the Hebrew tribes culminates at the time of Noah, when punishment almost ended the human race. God saved Noah's family, and from this small family another civilization grows. It, too, however, runs into trouble, ending with the confusion of language at Babel. Meaning "the on-earth entrance into the heavenly or celestial," Babel was built for the god Marduke.[4] The word has come to mean the confusion of tongues, or "babbling."

In violation of God's call to populate the earth, humanity concentrated in one location; only one language was spoken. To break up the human race into different linguistic groups was to minimize the power of colossal evil of one large, unified group. God's intention in doing so was to preserve humanity. In the story, as Wright comments, "one can see the mercy and grace of God which uses that very effect of sin as a dyke to save the human race from being totally engulfed in the self-destruction of unified evil."[5] Because of Babel and the resulting confusion, civilization can continue.

THE COVENANT: A REDEMPTIVE MOVE IN FORMING A NATION

The Genesis record then turns to a plan and solution. It would take centuries to fulfil, but it would address the plaguing problem of human sin. The story now revolves around Abraham and Yahweh's covenant, and leads us to understand God's intentions for the people of the covenant.

Out of its simple beginnings, this ragtag assortment of Semitic tribes became a nation of substance and importance. It was not some mythical or prehistoric world. It was a world of various languages, nations, peoples, and ways of thinking.

Yahweh's choice of the Hebrew people was not a matter of selecting from among many groups. It was, instead, the making of a new people. Beginning with one family, God started a new tribal entity. Abraham's homeland was Ur, in Babylon, a sophisticated and culturally advanced community. With outstanding architecture and complicated religions, Ur was famous for its economics and political influence.

Leaving home, Abraham began his wanderings with a promise: "Leave your country, your people and your father's household and go to the land I will show you" (Jer. 12: 1).

The building of a new people called for a special progenitor. God saw in Abraham a person who would listen and trust. This was remarkable, for the people of Ur worshipped a number of gods. From a civilization of many gods, Abraham made an abrupt turn to a belief in one God.

Then came the Word: "I will make you a great nation and I will bless you; I will make your name great and you will be a blessing. And I will bless those who bless you, and whoever curses you I will curse; and all peoples on earth will be blessed through you" (Gen. 12: 1–3). This was the covenant, the promise. On the strength of this, Abraham proceeded. We watch as the idea of covenant becomes reality.

Nation building is tough. It calls for people with determination, vision, and competence. For a country in its early stages, or when renewal is needed, risk-taking leadership is vital. Movements inevitably centre on visionaries. It took an audacious Abraham to move his people across unknown and dangerous territory on the basis of a promise from an unseen God. Two principles are at work here: (1) a nation will founder without capable, vision-driven leaders; (2) Abraham operated with a deep conviction that the God to whom he spoke was real and could be trusted. Vision, in a national sense, is more than a dream for mining the potential of a nation; it sees the nation within the global community.

The word "covenant," as it is used here, means an agreement between two parties in which there is both a promise and a responsibility for each to fulfil his or her side of the agreement.

At its heart, it is a conversation. God called and Abraham heard. He raised objections with God about the promise of a vast progeny. It seemed hollow, as Abraham had no children and, given that he was already an old man, the likelihood of his having children was slim (15: 2; 17: 17). When promised a land, Abraham wanted to know how he would recognize it (15: 8). Lot, his nephew, was living in Sodom, a city God said would be destroyed. Abraham actually entered into negotiations with God, attempting to preserve the city (18: 23–33). Following God's instructions, he took Isaac, his only son born to

Sarah, to the mountain for sacrifice (22: 1–14). Through the working-out of the covenant, God allowed Abraham to ask questions, to press for greater consideration of Sodom, to be faithless in the promise of a son by Sarah, and to lie to a foreign king about his attractive wife.

By promise of the covenant, God would make of them a "great nation" (12: 2), great by virtue of its inherent goodness. Goodness attracts. The law of sowing and reaping is at play here. Israel would be great, measured not by power and military might, but by a different standard.

But there was another side to the covenant: Abraham had a duty to perform, a promise to keep. First, to trust in this deity. "Abraham believed the Lord, and He credited it to him as righteousness" (15: 6). It was out of this deep and all-encompassing belief that God made the promise: "On that day the Lord made a covenant with Abram and said, 'To your descendants I give this land, from the river of Egypt to the great river, the Euphrates'" (15: 18). God made the promise, but also required a response of obedience: "Walk before me, and be blameless" (17: 1). Out of this would come the more immediate reality of the promise of a specific land. But out on the far horizon was the promise that "in you all the families of the earth will be blessed" (12: 3).

Part of the story of the spectacular rise of Abraham is tragic, showing the damage unbelief brings. Abraham was doubtful about his and Sarah's ability, in their old age, to have a child. Sarah suggested that he impregnate one of her maids, Hagar, to ensure a child. But Hagar's pregnancy infuriated Sarah. Abraham gave in to Sarah's anger, and Hagar was driven into the wilderness with her young son. Even with Abraham's weakness and the lack of faith he showed in substituting something for God's promise, the plan moved ahead. But a woman was badly treated and another people (the Arabs) was raised up, eventually ending up in conflict with the children of Abraham and Sarah.[6] This is a classic story of human interference in God's agenda.

To Christians, this history is very important. It describes the making of a covenant between the Creator and the created. Abraham is dignified: he is able to question God, negotiate, and fail, and still God is faithful. Thus, the cosmos, the Creator, and the created are integrally related.

Moses, Mt. Sinai, and the Decalogue

The exodus of the Jews from Egypt was extraordinary. It was an act of liberation for the descendants of Abraham, who for 400 years had laboured, at times as slaves, in Egypt. During that time, the memory of God's promise to their father, Abraham, was kept alive. They retained that identity, even under the cruel heel of their taskmasters. But it was in the exodus that they became a nation, albeit without a land or constitution. Against the backdrop of being delivered from Egypt and spending forty years wandering the wilderness in search of the promised land, they received specific laws for living.

Now that they were on their own, not ruled by the laws and rulers of Egypt, they needed guidelines, those understood requisites a culture needs to survive. This undertaking, as was Abraham's, was a covenant, a promise from God. But it was not detached from God's actions. It followed the mighty act of God in the exodus. It was action and speech; God acts and speaks, and the two are linked. This bedrock to their national constitution was law, but at its heart was a covenant from God to his people: "Now if you obey me fully and keep my covenant, then out of all nations you will be my treasured possession. Although the whole earth is mine, you shall be to me a kingdom of priests and a holy nation" (Exod. 19: 5, 6). What an extraordinary promise. But it also called for sacrifice on the part of this priestly nation to live up to the requirements of their calling.

The law had two parts. First was the Ten Commandments, which in concise terms described the requirements. They were the broad, ethical considerations which set the groundwork for the nation. The second part laid out the specific details that covered everyday living.

The Decalogue

As Yahweh had made a covenant with Abraham as the father of Israel, so one was made with Moses. In the Ten Commandments, or Decalogue, Yahweh made commitments to Israel, and, in return, obligations were imposed. God clearly lists what is critical to sustain a people living together. As basic as they were to Israel, these laws are also viewed by modern societies as essential for a working community. No code of any other society is so explicit, succinct, and all-encompassing an outline for societal living.

The details are many, yet the essence of the covenant is found in ten specific and precise calls that form the basis for all Hebrew law. These ten principles were intended to define the perimeters within which the people would find the fullness of life and develop a rich, rewarding relationship with their God and Creator. "Hear, O Israel, and be careful to obey so that it may go well with you and that you may increase greatly in a land flowing with milk and honey, just as the Lord, the God of your fathers, promised you" (Deut. 6: 3).

These commandments were not only a moral code, designed to assist people in developing their ideas about life, but specific commands, related to how people actually lived. They were directives by the God of the nation. Thus, to disobey a commandment was not just to fly in the face of the nation, but to defy God. The breaking of a law would not only threaten the stability of the nation, but impair the covenant or agreement with God.

To the Jews, the giver of this covenant is more than a lawgiver. He is the God of the exodus—the liberator, the one who freed them from slavery and bondage. The order is important. The one who rescues sets up the code for living. Liberation is always on the lips of the giver of the law. Although the commands are prohibitive in nature, at their heart is the principle of love: "Love the Lord your God with all your heart, and with all your soul, and with all your strength" (Deut. 6: 5).

The Land

A people cannot live without land. For the Hebrew tribes, the conquering of Canaan was seen as God's fulfilling the promise. Today, as then, in the Middle East the essential point of conflict is land. Nothing triggers passion more than dispute over land. The Old Testament notion of land promised to Abraham, renewed in promise to Moses, and finally received by Joshua, was that it was *given* to them. This is unique to Israel. What land they received was bestowed by God's election and promise. They could not take credit for acquiring it themselves.

The principle at work here, apart from the specific promise to Abraham, is that all land is indeed a gift from God. That people, be they wandering Semitic tribes or modern, technological peoples, possess their land by way of a gift: "It is not because of your righteousness or your integrity that you are going in to take possession of their land; but on account of the wickedness of these nations, the Lord your God will drive them out before you, to accomplish what he swore to your fathers" (Exod. 9: 5).

Understanding that the land is God's gift kept the Jews from regarding it as their neighbours did. For the Jews, Yahweh was the reason for the land: the land came from God. This view was in contrast to the popular Baal notion of a god rising out of the land. Baal, the most prominent Canaanite deity, was believed to live in the netherworld. To raise Baal, and thus to ensure a fertile rainy season, Canaanites engaged in orgiastic worship, which included human sacrifice, sexual rites, and the use of "sacred" prostitutes. God strictly forbade such worship (Judg. 2: 12–14; 3: 7, 8). In sharp contrast, the Hebrew God was sovereign, above the land and nation.

THE DAVIDIC KINGDOM

Nation building was to reach its zenith under David, son of Jesse. The journey had been long and treacherous. By failure, trial and error, and direct instruction, the Israelites were learning about God's intention and rule over their lives. They were to be a different people, separate from their pagan neighbours, and, most of all, to live in constant remembrance of their allegiance and dependence. King David's rule is the most complete snapshot of what a nation under God is to be and do. It is here we see the sum of what the Children of Israel had learned cemented into political reality. Looking back from our vantage point, we see how Abraham's vision and his covenant with God developed into the defined laws of Moses as the people left their nomadic existence for permanent settlement under their revered king.

The development of a state came slowly. In its early days, the Israelites were nomadic, living as a group of clans. Each clan had its own authority, but there was no class distinction. Central to the

Hebrew nomads was the Ark of the Covenant, constructed by Moses after fleeing Egypt. It was carefully preserved, and there, once a year, the high priest made a sacrifice for the sins of the people.

During the times when judges ruled the twelve Hebrew tribes, from time to time a strong charismatic person would rise up and lead. But a judge had no government and operated with no central authority. He or she had no army or administration by which to rule. Only when Israel was threatened by an enemy would the people rally in support of the leadership and coordination role of the judge.

The pattern of development of the Hebrews was different from the city life of the people already in Canaan. In the beginning, as the Hebrews began possessing the land of Palestine, they developed farms rather than building cities. For 200 years after winning the promised land, they continued as a network of tribes, identified by their racial and religious heritage but without a single political or geographic home state.

The Hebrews acquired a king when Israel was confronted not just by the Bedouin raiders, but by the organized and disciplined armies of the Philistines from the north. When the famous and powerful judge Samson was killed, the Hebrews were thrown into chaos. After being pressured by the people, Samuel the priest anointed Saul as king. But there seemed little Saul could do to cobble a strong army out of this tribal community.

That task was left to David, a young, brave and charismatic shepherd who replaced the terrible system of a frightened assembly of clans with what was the beginning of a nation. The people of Israel sang, "Saul has slain his thousands, and David his tens of thousands" (1 Sam. 18: 7). David had no lineage to argue for a legitimacy to rule. His authority came from the people. They made him their hero. He raised a strong private army in his defence against King Saul, and then a standing army. He married Saul's daughter and, through an election of sorts (2 Sam. 5: 1–4), was proclaimed king.

David took steps to create a united nation to defend the people against the Philistines, and he selected a site on which was built "the city of David" (2 Sam. 5: 9). He eventually defeated surrounding states and ruled from the Gulf of Aqaba, in the south, to Syria, in the north.

As David wrote his poetry and songs, and ruled as king, his framework was God. To David, Yahweh was king, not only of Israel, its priests and leaders, but over all kings of the earth (Ps. 97: 6). The entire construct of life, including earthly kingdoms (2: 6–9) and the physical creation is under the rulership of God (47: 3; 89: 9–19; 93: 1, 2). As ruler and Creator, the strategy for liberation and national rule falls within God's cosmic plan. All histories of all people are set within that plan, including those of Israel, Egypt, Assyria, and Babylon (48: 4–6; 96: 10–13).

David, as king of Israel, was regarded as the best example of what a king and ruler should be. Under his kingship, Israel reached her highest level as a civilization. David is remembered for honesty, humanness, and a deep regard for the creation. Today, Jerusalem, in his honour, is called the "City of David." Though King David's life was not spared from failure, his vision for his nation guided him in construction and management.

The song (Ps. 72) is a reflection on the nature of nationhood and a prayer for Solomon, David's son, who will rule after his death. There are four cornerstones that structured this vision for Israel. From this we get a picture of the essential elements of what is required in a nation in which godly values reign.

A Nation Built on Justice and Righteousness

Justice and righteousness are used throughout the Old Testament as primary elements of godly rule. David prayed, "Endow the king with your justice, O God, the royal son with your righteousness. He will judge your people in righteousness, your afflicted ones with justice" (Ps. 72: 1–3).

"Justice" refers to the activity of a lawgiver in carrying out the legal consequences of a verdict of law. "Righteousness" comes from a Hebrew root word which speaks of something "straight." It literally refers to accurate weights and measures used in everyday commerce. "Righteousness" means "rightness," that is, what will measure up to the standard.

Under David's administration, the laws were to be clear for people to understand and were to be made public so that no one could claim he or she was unaware of them. They were to reflect what the nation, as a people, believes is true. Only then does law become a standard against which behaviour can be measured. The standard will not vary from trial to trial; nor will it be interpreted to suit the self-interest of the judge. The rightness of the case will be judged with fairness.

A Nation Built on Effective Rule

In David's understanding, a nation was to provide its people with security and peace in which there was "rule from sea to sea" (Ps. 72: 8). Citizens and outsiders would recognize it as a *bona fide* nation with political integrity, not one ready for the pickings of some exploitive raider. Within the country, the people could expect their rulers to lead and to contain violence: "He will rescue them from oppression and violence, for precious is their blood in his sight"(Ps. 72: 14).

A Nation Built on Economic Well-Being

Regardless of the form of its economic activity, be it agricultural, technological, or world trade, a country needs a healthy economy. The problem is, for Canada and other nations, that economics has become an idol. But that does not deny that, for a nation to operate under God's mandate, economic well-being is God's will.

David's vision was of a prosperous nation: "Let grain abound throughout the land; on the tops of the hills may it sway. Let its fruit flourish like Lebanon." The basis of his economic vision is economic responsibility: "For he will deliver the needy who cry out, the afflicted who have no one to help" (Ps. 72: 12–14). Economic blessings are linked to justice and righteousness, which by direct implication reminds us that economic well-being is not only for the few. A nation that does not fulfil the economic calling of God could hardly be called a "light to the nations."

A Nation Built on Caring for Those in Need

David places strong emphasis on caring for those in need: "He will defend the afflicted among the people and save the children of the needy" (Ps. 72: 4). This theme is in line with God's constant reminder: those in charge are to be mindful of those who are in need, weakened, or unable to help themselves. Though this might sound like the social agenda of some political party, it is intrinsic to the theme and message of the Bible. Indeed, God evaluates nations on how they deal with the marginalized.

Psalm 82 reminds us, "Defend the cause of the weak and fatherless; maintain the rights of the poor and oppressed. Rescue the weak and needy; deliver them from the hand of the wicked."

David is not advocating a particular socio-economic plan. The glaring tragedy is that, under various systems, too often defence of the poor and the hurting is lacking.

David's leadership was built on a vision that God's rule over Israel required the nation to follow certain principles. His success in ruling demonstrates that his ideas were more than theoretical. From this we learn what is essential to Godly rule and, from that, we can extrapolate to our own national situation.

PROPHETIC RULE

After the rule of David, the nation was divided between Israel in the north and Judah in the south. This division served only to weaken the struggle to maintain national identity and governance against the onslaught of foreign nations. In a nation held for ransom, taken captive, and internally disarranged by its own political and social anarchy, prophets were called on to encourage, scold, and remind the people of God's will. It is to this group of people we turn to hear the clear word of God's call for nation building.

Israel as a nation had been called to break with ancient paganism. Central to their faith was their God, who controlled events in history. In this, worship of Yahweh contrasted sharply with surrounding pagan religions, which were polytheistic, with dozens of gods, housed in pantheons. These gods, having no moral character, represented nature or parts of the cosmos. As well, they could be manipulated in rituals, as they were a re-enactment of myth. Thus, they could be made to bestow on the worshipper whatever he or she wanted. The gods made no moral interpretation of physical events.

Yahweh is different. All of life comes from God the Creator, and all events are under his control. Yahweh is not to be linked to nature, and therefore cannot be appeased by any ritual.

The high vision of the kingdom slipped downhill following David's rule. His son Solomon ruled in wealth and splendour, but increasingly out of line with his father's vision. Nepotism, not calling or character, had decided Solomon would follow. The privilege and wealth of the newly developed aristocracy divided the people into the powerful and the powerless. Solomon and the kings who followed him assumed that people were to be ruled and owned as subjects, an idea foreign to David. As well, the lavish lifestyles of the kings had to be paid for by someone. That meant taxes.

The kingdom eventually ran into serious trouble. With the division into Israel and Judea, it was not long before other nations raided and plundered both kingdoms. During this time, the role and presence of the prophets increased. They encouraged and chastised, always attempting to remind the people of God's faithfulness.

Even during times of pervasive religiosity, when the community needed a type of self-examination that the established religion could not deliver, it took someone outside the religious establishment to speak.

Prophets antagonized rulers as they proclaimed their visions of justice and righteousness. Their blazing pronouncements of God's rule and glory cut deeply into the mind-set of a people who too quickly slipped into the worship of other gods. It was, however, the prophets' understanding of God's rule that pulled them back to faithfulness. Their bold and rousing rhetoric stirred the people's hearts and fanned the flame of obedience. From their righteous anger came the words that foretold disaster and God's faithful care.

While the prophets served the Jewish nation, their soundings were inspired by more than immediate circumstance: their rhetoric was about an all-encompassing reign of God. That reign was not to be confined to Israel. The call of Jonah to go to a Gentile city is an explicit reminder that God's rule is not only Israel-centred.

The Rule of God

Running through the messages of the prophets are a number of themes that help us understand their vision of God's Kingdom rule.

God's rule in Israel is redemptive. It has at its core a fourfold plan: politically, to free them from foreign tyranny; socially, to provide protection for family and community; economically, to free them from forced slavery and injustice; and, spiritually, to call them to remove themselves from foreign gods.

The Political Plan

Micah sees that, in the last days, "the Lord's temple will be established as chief among the mountains. ... Many nations will come and say, 'Come let us go up to the mountain of the Lord, to the house of the God of Jacob.' ... The law will go out from Zion, the word of the Lord from Jerusalem. God will judge between many peoples and will settle disputes for strong nations far and wide. They will beat their swords into ploughshares and their spears into pruning hooks. Nation will not take up sword against nation, nor will they train for war anymore" (Mic. 4: 1–5).

The themes of a Kingdom ruled by God weave their way through this famous passage. Yahweh will rule over all and will teach us wisdom and truth. The down-trodden will receive justice, and war will be no more. Fear will be neutralized, and all nations will walk in his ways.

Isaiah looks forward to a Messianic age, when, under a descendant of David, righteousness will rule and the people will be freed from oppression. There is no greater song of national unity and strength than that of the coming Messiah: "And he shall be called Wonderful Counsellor, Mighty God, Everlasting Father, Prince of Peace. Of the increase of his government and peace there will be no end. He will reign on David's throne and over his kingdom, establishing and upholding it with justice and righteousness from that time on and forever" (Isa. 9: 6–7).

The Social Plan

This God of Israel and Judah not only reigns over the earth, but protects the life of the people. Even in the difficult times, "I will be with you; and when you pass through the rivers, they will not sweep over you.

When you walk though the fire, you will not be burned; the flames will not set you ablaze. For I am the Lord your God, the Holy One of Israel, your Saviour" (Isa. 43: 1, 2).

The concern of the ruler is for their welfare; they will be led again into the promised land. The words are reminiscent of the exodus from Egypt: "I will bring your children from the east and gather you from the west. I will say to the north, 'Give them up!' and to the south, 'Do not hold them back.' ... Everyone who is called by my name, whom I created for my glory, whom I formed and made" (43: 5–7).

They see the nation healed by God's presence, a time and place in which the king will bring unity. As a result, the nation will be "a light for the Gentiles" (42: 6) and will attract Gentile nations: "See, I have made him a witness to the peoples. Surely you will summon nations you know not, and nations that do not know you will hasten to you, because of the Lord your God, the Holy One of Israel, for he has endowed you with splendour" (55: 3–5).

Central to social harmony is justice. Amos calls out, "For I know how many are your offenses and how great your sins. You oppress the righteous and take bribes and you deprive the poor of justice in the courts. ... Seek good, not evil, that you may live. ... Hate evil, love good; maintain justice in the courts" (Amos 5: 12–15).

The Economic Plan

Zechariah paints a vivid picture of the reign of God: "Before that time there were no wages for man or beast. ... But now I will not deal with the remnant ... as I did in the past. ... The seed will grow well, the vine will yield its fruit, the ground will produce its crops, and the heavens will drop their dew" (Zech. 8: 10–12).

Along with the promise of economic well-being, there is a constant reminder of God's care and special love for people in need. Amos combines a promise and rebuke: to the poor, they will be remembered; to the powerful and wealthy, they are to understand their unfairness will be judged: "Hear this, you who trample the needy and do away with the poor of the land, saying, 'When will the new moon be over that we may sell grain, and the Sabbath be ended that we may market wheat?'... The Lord has sworn by the pride of Jacob: 'I will never forget anything they have done.'"

The Spiritual Plan

While God's reign is political, social, and economic, it does not end there. For the prophets, renewal is at the heart of Yahweh's rule. Even though the people are faithless, God will put laws in their minds and write it on their hearts (Jer. 31: 31–33). To the people, God will continue to be faithful, even after long, hard years of struggle.

Jeremiah's resilient theme is that a time is coming when the kingdoms will be ruled by a righteous king: "In those days and at that time I will make a righteous Branch sprout from David's line; he will do what is just and right in the land. In those days Judah will be saved and Jerusalem will live in safety. This is the name by which it will be called: The Lord Our Righteousness" (Jer. 33: 15, 16).

Amos's call was to bring the people back to faith and worship. The problem wasn't that they were not religious. Indeed, they were. The problem was that they were religious in the wrong way. Religious ritual was just not enough. Living right and being just was needed to give their ritual any value: "I hate. I despise your religious feats; I cannot stand your assemblies. Even though you bring me burnt offerings and grain offerings, I will not accept them. Though you bring choice fellowship offerings, I will have no regard for them. Away with the noise of your songs! I will not listen to the music of your harps. But let justice roll on like a river, righteousness like a never-failing stream" (Amos 5: 21–24).

The Universal Reign of God

Beyond the borders of Palestine, some prophets saw the reign of God as universal. Ezekiel describes this worldwide rule of God in the life of all humankind. He opens with a powerful statement: "In the thirtieth year, in the fourth month on the fifth day, while I was among the exiles by the Kebar River, the heavens were opened and I saw visions of God" (Ezek. 1: 1).

Ezekiel reminds us that, at all times, in all places, "the Lord is there," a phrase on which he ends. Even though Ezekiel is a priest, he understands that God's domain is not limited to the sanctuary of the temple in Jerusalem but traverses the world, even to the exiled children in Babylon. Daniel, while in Babylon, was called on to interpret the king's dreams, which had baffled the king's magicians and sorcerers. Ringing through Daniel's interpretations is the residual hope of God's Kingdom, alive for ever. Even though he was living in a pagan land, Daniel envisions this Kingdom rule as applying not just to the Jewish world, but universally. Most prophets lived in Palestine; thus, their hopes were centred in that region, and with the Jewish people. However, since Daniel and Ezekiel lived in Babylon, they saw the future through a different lens. They envisioned a broader rule of God, extending beyond the borders of the promised land and including others besides the chosen people.

LESSONS FROM THE OLD TESTAMENT

The importance of reviewing some of the prophets is to hear their heart-cry for God's righteousness and justice in the way the nation is ruled. They defend the poor and widows. Their sharp cry cuts into the self-centred living of those with power and wealth. Living within a society pervaded by the idolatry of the Mediterranean community, God's people are called to renounce their spiritual wanderings and return to worship the one true God.

Through the series of windows through which we can see God at work in the life of his people, we can interpret these scenes and apply them to how we live as disciples in Canada. Going back to the three ways we can interpret the Old Testament—the paradigmatic window, in which we look for the principles of the story; the eschatological, by which we understand the text is looking forward to God's full and final Kingdom; and the typological, in that we see the church inheriting the essential truths for its well-being—we construct a vision of a nation.

Remember, we must not use the Old Testament to mean what it does not mean. With that caution in mind, we see God's intention to raise a people and nation, which in turn serves us as we structure a nation today. A nation founded on those principles produces a healthy society reflecting the psalmist's belief that a nation is enhanced when the Lord's values reign: "Blessed is the nation whose God is the Lord."

The Old Testament helps us see God in four ways: concern for the creation, God's rule over all of life, God's covenants and promises, and God's expectation of obedience.

Out of this time/space cradle, the Messiah, Jesus of Nazareth, comes. The seeds of the Messiah's rule are evident in the rule of Yahweh in Palestine. We now move into the time of Christ's earthly ministry to see how the actual working of the Kingdom moves beyond a nation and a particular people to a more integrated heart/mind reality.

Reflection on the Hebrew/Palestine experience is very important. Within this framework, we can work out a particular vision for a nation, applying what we learn, seeking to properly integrate that which God has shown in the Hebrew tribal model. From there, we proceed to the next stage to learn what Jesus of Nazareth had to say about being citizens and people of a nation.

CHAPTER 5

Jesus and Politics

Did Jesus ever expect his followers to deal with Rome? If we wish to influence a country to adopt biblical values, is there any evidence that Christ called on us to express our concern? In a stressful environment, rife with anger against Rome and intense expectations that the Messiah would rout their oppressors, Jesus had a surprising response to this cauldron of nationalism.

><

"My kingdom is not of this world. If it were, my servants would fight to prevent my arrest by the Jews. But now my kingdom is from another place."

—John 18: 36

Did Jesus preach a Gospel that was to affect political theory or governmental management? Or, to put it another way, did the political ordering of a nation matter to Jesus and the Kingdom? I argue that Jesus was a political force in that day: his message struck deep at the existing ruling assumptions. However, Jesus was not announcing another political theory. His message goes deeper into our self-serving interests than human theories are able to. Rising above political theories—be it democracy, of the Enlightenment; fascism, of dictatorship; or socialism, of Marxism—Jesus speaks to all people, regardless of their political and social systems.

I also argue that Christ's Gospel calls for Christian disciples to care for today's society, be it governments or major sectors of our public interest such as education, the media, the justice system, science, industry, and the arts. In Christ's Kingdom, all of life is subsumed under God's creation.

British Anglican Church leader and scholar John Stott comments that Jesus' "whole ministry was political."[1] "Politics" refers to people as citizens living together in society. (The Greek word "polis" means "city," and "polites" means "citizen.") In speaking about Jesus and politics, I am not limiting my discussion to the science of government and the election of politicians or appointment of officials. Instead, through an understanding of Jesus and politics, we can see how we relate as citizens living in Canada.

It is true that, while Jesus did not participate in political ruling, he did influence and speak to those who had a role in governance. And neither did Christ form a political party or contest the rulership of Pilate or Caesar. But he did effect change. Jesus spoke a new message, upsetting the status quo by setting forth a challenge to old and self-serving assumptions and values, both those of the Romans and those of the ruling religious leaders.

First, as we examine Jesus' relationship to politics, we cannot apply faith to life until we are familiar with what Jesus intended his life and the lives of the disciples to accomplish. Second, the coming of Jesus cuts across the grain of our religious expectations by not being what we expect.

As noted in chapter 4, running through Hebrew history is a belief that God would forever establish his rule. It was the hope of each Hebrew citizen to live to see this rule set in place during his or her lifetime. Even though hope was frustrated, a deep conviction remained that the Son of David would someday rule with justice and power.

THE SETTING

Because context means everything to the understanding of Jesus' words and ways, we need first to look at the social/political realities that cradled this advent.

Just prior to Jesus' coming, a Jewish revolt had been led by a Jewish family, the Maccabees. In 63 B.C., the Roman general Pompey annexed Palestine, bringing it under Rome's rule. Rome, while directly ruling Judea, gave much of its political oversight to the Sanhedrin, the Jerusalem city council. Thus, whatever Jesus said to the Jewish rulers implied commentary on Rome as well. In the north, the Jews were governed by a half-Jewish family, the Herodians. Divided up under different rulers and different forms of rulership, they were deeply embittered, fuelled by their deep desire for self-rule.

When Jesus arrived, the deep river of messianic hope was fed by two powerful currents, both wanting to secure national independence and stability. The Zealots, a Jewish party trumpeting a radical nationalism, were ready for war and were game to try to overthrow the Romans. Their deepening anger against the Romans was fuelled by what they regarded as an unholy alliance between religious leaders and Rome.

The Pharisees represented a movement begun more than a century earlier, in part to protect Hebrew nationalism from the powerful cultural forces of the Greek (Hellenistic) forces. Rejecting the Zealots' agenda, they believed that God would send the Messiah only when the people strictly observed the law.

It is not surprising that Jesus' announcement of a Kingdom met the people's expectations. Oppressed by foreign rulers and grieving over the treachery caused by the invaders, they rejoiced at Mary's (Jesus' mother's) words: "He has performed mighty deeds with his arm; he has scattered those who are proud in their inmost thoughts. He has brought down rulers from their thrones but has lifted up the humble. He has filled the hungry with good things but has sent the rich away empty" (Luke 1: 51–53).

Even though it had been 600 years since they had returned from exile in Babylon, they still considered themselves in exile as long as they were under occupation by a foreign power. Jesus' Kingdom announcement connected with their deepest aspirations.

THE COMING OF THE KING

Into history God came, and life would never be the same again. God had come to assert rule over all of life. Though we might regard the Kingdom in terms of what it brings—salvation, justice, and healing—Jesus' coming is more radical. At the very centre of it is the right to rule, and power and authority to effect that rule.

By "Kingdom" I mean that which is the rule and reign of the king: wherever the king is, that is the king's domain; whatever concerns the king, that, too, is the king's domain.

The Kingdom's message was to save the sinner, not the righteous. The message presupposes that we are unable to correct our ways. "Blindness" is the appropriate metaphor. Not only can't we see, but we don't know we can't. All human attempts to right our wrongs have failed and will continue to fail. God takes the task alone. Yahweh did not come because Israel was successful in creating a more just community or constructing a better political system, but because it could not. Simeon and Anna (Luke 2: 25–38), who prayed for the coming of the Messiah, knew that the religious leaders, political insurgents, or pious faithful could not build this Kingdom. It must be achieved by God's initiative. Even as the Earth is the Lord's, so was the need to take back what was rightfully God's.

But does Christ's Kingdom also include political life? At first glance,

Jesus gives the impression it did not extend to political concerns. However, a closer look shows that the opposite is true. What makes it unclear at first is that Jesus' analysis and prescription went deeper than what the people expected. Jesus not only followed Old Testament thought that God's rule included all aspects of life, but went further and announced a new provision—people could personally experience a rebirth.

But this was not what was expected. The home-town folk in Nazareth were shocked at the description of the coming Kingdom. When Jesus spoke of the less important members of society, those without power or influence, the townsfolk were scandalized. Jesus said, "The Spirit of the Lord is upon me, because he has anointed me to preach good news to the poor. He has sent me to proclaim freedom for the prisoners and recovery of sight for the blind, to release the oppressed, to proclaim the year of the Lord's favour" (Luke 4: 18, 19).

They were not only surprised by what Jesus did, but also disappointed. Jesus did not pick up the sword to drive out the Romans, nor accept the public celebration on Palm Sunday and take possession of David's throne. The talk about power and authority concerned itself with the rule of one's own spirit. They were confused. There was no announcement of the overthrow of Rome. Jesus made it clear they should give to God what was God's. But what was God's? Everything (Rom. 11: 36). And what was the meaning of the Kingdom? Peter, frustrated by the seeming undoing of what the disciples believed was a new order, tried to defend Christ in the final hours before death. Instead, the death pushed them into fear and despair.

Even the disciples, after three years of living with Jesus, asked, "Lord, are you at this time going to restore the kingdom to Israel?" (Acts 1: 6). I suppose that if they thought Jesus' Kingdom was going to throw out the Romans, it is not surprising that people today are confused by what Jesus had in mind about the relationship of the Kingdom to a nation. They would not see the nature of the Kingdom because they were looking for an immediate solution. It didn't occur to them that Christ's Kingdom was to rule, first and foremost, over the heart.

Jesus radically changed their understanding of the Kingdom. He redefined authority and power, and introduced symbols that were the opposite of what they expected. At the Last Supper, while the disciples talked about who would be greatest in the coming Kingdom, Jesus picked up a towel and washed their feet. In a society layered with power, ritual, and rank—among both the Jewish religious community and the ruling Romans—taking on the role of servant was both drastic and political, because it challenged agreed-upon societal rules. In the end, that is political. It may not organize itself into a political party, but it is a protest and an alternative way of life. And it is a strong protest, given that it is delivered by Jesus, a respected and increasingly influential rabbi.

The symbol of Christ's reign is not the sword of a conquerer, but the towel of a servant. This simple and yet powerful symbol of Christ is usually neglected. We cannot envision a towel as the grand emblem of a ruling Kingdom.

Neither was Jesus what the religious leaders expected. Keeping the law had become the icon, the fetish, the idol of the religion of legalism. Moses had brought the first law—the Ten Commandments; Jesus, who said he had come to fulfil the law, was different from Moses. He wrote nothing. Instead, he announced that the law would be written on their hearts. Kingdom behaviour was to work out of the spirit of the law and not to be bound by the letter of the law, as religious leaders supposed. For Jesus, hating a person was every bit as much a violation of the law as was killing.

At the deepest part of their misunderstanding was the Kingdom's role in affecting life. Instead of a sword, Jesus offered forgiveness; pushing aside legalism, Jesus offered reconciliation; stepping aside as the conquering hero, Jesus rode on a foal of a donkey; rather than denounce Rome, Jesus allowed soldiers to kill him. Seeming anything but a king, he was the suffering Saviour. It was this suffering Saviour who would ultimately deal a death blow to the assumption that political influence comes by the power of the sword.

THE ENCOUNTER WITH SATAN

There is no more explicit example of the mistaken hopes people had for the Messiah than the encounter Jesus had with Satan in the wilderness.

Early in Jesus' earthly ministry, and in preparation for what lay ahead, he went into the wilderness for forty days of prayer and fasting. At the end of this fast, as Jesus was in the weakest of condition, Satan appeared and challenged Jesus on three grounds, each representing a primary hope of messiahship. He called Jesus to turn stones into bread. What are most people looking for in a national leader but to be an economic miracle-worker? This has become the high-water mark against which we rate our political leaders.

Second, he promised Jesus all the kingdoms of the world if Jesus would bow down and worship him. Power is essential to the world's view of ruling.

Finally, Satan took Jesus to the top of the Temple tower in Jerusalem, tempting him to jump. The seduction of this temptation was that, by making such a public display, Jesus would verify that indeed he was the Messiah.

Jesus turned down all three, not only to refuse this co-opting by Satan, but to establish the essence of the Kingdom.

Those who expected the Kingdom of God to burst from the heavens, eradicate the Romans, eliminate hunger, restore justice, and care for the fatherless were bewildered by Jesus' seeming incapacity to deal forcefully with the power brokers. They failed to understand that the Kingdom's work was deeper and farther-reaching than any immediate political solution. Yes, political solutions are important, but at the centre of the human dilemma is self-interest, power, and ego. It was to that concern that Jesus' analysis was addressed.

KINGDOM TRUTH SPEAKS TO SOCIAL/POLITICAL REALITIES

In connecting Jesus' life and ministry to what we should do about political life, we often make the mistake of assuming that we should do only what he did. But that would fail to take into account an important difference: Christ's work was to inaugurate and set loose the Kingdom; our calling is to interpret and implement. He pushed beyond the ruling expectations of Messiah rule and underscored that ruling one's spirit was a greater victory than ruling a nation. But he was not saying that the ruling of a nation is not important. It is just that he dug deep into the soil of life and exposed what is deeper and more fundamental, pointing us beyond penultimate values to ultimate ones. By so doing, the Kingdom is inclusive and all-encompassing.

Christ's Kingdom speaks to our social and political situation in five ways:

1. It is linked to the lessons of Israel's experience.
2. It holds all of life within God's rule.
3. It is transformational.
4. It upsets the assumption of political power.
5. It speaks to the heart of a nation.

1. The message of the Kingdom and the suffering Saviour is linked to the lessons of Israel's experience.

Although the Old Testament did not use the specific term "Kingdom," the idea was common among the Hebrew people. Theologian John Bright says it would be clearly understood by the people of Jesus' day: "The Kingdom of God lay within the vocabulary of every Jew. It was something they understood and longed for desperately. ... While it underwent ... a radical mutation on the lips of Jesus, it had a long history and is, in one form or another, ubiquitous in both Old Testament and New. It involves the whole notion of the rule of God over His people, and particularly the vindication of that rule and people in glory at the end of history. That was the Kingdom which the Jews awaited."[2]

Isaiah described that expectation: "For to us a child is born, to us a son is given, and the government will be on his shoulders. And he will be called Wonderful Counsellor, Mighty God, Everlasting Father, Prince of Peace. Of the increase of his government and peace there will be no end. He will reign on David's throne and over his kingdom, establishing and upholding it with justice and righteousness from that time on and forever. The zeal of the Lord will accomplish it" (9: 6, 7).

Throughout the Scriptures there is the constant theme of a Lord who will suffer. While Jesus left no doubt of ultimate authority (he said to Pilate, "Do you think I cannot call on my Father, and he will at once put at my disposal more than twelve legions of angels?" (Matt. 26: 53, 54), he recognized the place of suffering (Mark 8: 31; 9: 12, 31; 10: 33, 45).

This suffering and death are in concert with Old Testament references, the most focused being Isaiah 53. The Jewish community understood the suffering Saviour (Isaiah 40–66) to be referring to the nation of Israel, not an individual. Jesus turned this around and accepted Isaiah's vision as speaking of himself.

However, suffering and death were not to be associated with failure. And on that turns the central notion of the Kingdom. Success is defined in terms different from those of Rome, and of the Temple administrators.

Speaking to the request of James and John to be seated in power with Christ in glory, they were reminded that "even the Son of Man did not come to be served, but to serve, and to give his life as a ransom for many" (Mark 10: 45). In Paul's commentary on Isaiah 45: 23, the reference to being a servant was not just an idea but a reality: "But made himself nothing, taking the very nature of a servant, being made in human likeness. And being found in appearance as a man, he humbled himself and became obedient to death—even death on a cross" (Phil. 2: 7, 8).

For Israel, the idea of a nation had begun with God's call of Abraham. Even though the shift of the Hebrew nation from a theocracy to a monarchy was not God's choice, it was approved. Now that Jesus had arrived and talked about something quite different from what many expected, they were not sure if it was what they wanted. His talk of the Kingdom brought into play a new element. And for Jews being hammered by the Romans, this turning-of-the-other-cheek did not get good play. But Jesus' Kingdom would not be bound up in charters, thrones, armies, and treaties, but in God ruling in the thoughts, intents, and actions of people. Christ's Kingdom would come by personal and inner rebirth. The role of God in life comes by means of inner power—Jesus told them that a person in control of him- or herself is greater than one who takes a city—something the disciples, after three years under Christ's tutorship, did not understand.

2. The Kingdom message includes all of life within its rule.

As Jesus stepped onto the pages of history and the Palestinian landscape, he brought an understanding that all of creation and history is part of the Kingdom. It was not necessary for Jesus to tell the listeners that. They knew it well.

Today, as inheritors of many forms of political theory and experience, it is important that we unwrap ourselves from all of that (at least in our attempt to understand what was implicit in the message of Christ's Kingdom) and try to hear the message as if we were standing alongside Christ in that day.

In Canada, our act of confederation, the British North America Act of 1867, referred to Psalm 72: 8: "He shall have dominion from sea to sea." As the domain of Canada's rule is everything between the declared boundaries, so Christ's Kingdom covers all that exists by Creation.

The Apostle Paul leaves no doubt about the territory of God's domain: "For by him all things were created: things in heaven and on earth, visible and invisible, whether thrones or powers or rulers or authorities; all things were created by him and for him. He is before all things, and in him all things hold together" (Col. 1: 16, 17).

Jesus said, "My kingdom is not of [a better translation is 'from'] this world" (John 18: 36). Some Christians interpret this to mean that the Kingdom has nothing to do with this world. Not so. Jesus is reminding Pilate that the source of authority for the Kingdom is not from the world. But he is not saying the Kingdom does not include this world. And that makes a world of difference.

Later, when Pilate said, "Do not you realize I have power either to free you or to crucify you?" Jesus replied, "You would have no power over me if it were not given to you from above" (19: 10, 11). The issue here concerns the source of authority and power. It is not about whether planet Earth is included under Christ's rule.

The lordship of Christ is affirmed over both heaven and earth. Not only are both God's creation, but in both places the observance of God's will is critical. "Your kingdom come, your will be done on earth as it is in heaven. ..." (Matt. 6: 10) is how Jesus instructs his disciples to pray.

The word "earth" is used in the New Testament in two ways: to describe physical reality—"heaven and earth will pass away" (Matt. 24: 35)—and social reality—"You are the salt of the earth" (Matt. 5: 13).

The territory of Christ's Kingdom goes beyond the physical planet and rulers or governments; it embraces all people. Jesus, replying to the Pharisees who wanted to know when the Kingdom would come, said, "The kingdom of God does not come with your careful observation, nor will people say, 'Here it is,' or 'There is it,' because the kingdom of God is within you" (Luke 17: 20, 21). What a turn of ideas. Those looking for release from their captors equated the domain of King Jesus with the land boundaries of Palestine.

That he said the Kingdom was "within" us was too radical in that it did not take into account the common assumption that a kingdom was primarily political, and therefore required the exercise of power. Jesus exploded that belief by saying that, beyond what is physical and obvious to us, there is a terrain that is as real as planet Earth. Speaking to the rich, young man, he challenged him to give up his riches and give the proceeds to the poor "and you will have treasure in heaven" (Mark 10: 21).

The Kingdom is outside the borders of time. Jesus understood that it was both a present and a future reality. Jesus stood in Israel during Rome's rule—a specific location and time. It is also a future reality. "When the Son of Man comes in his glory, and all the angels with him, he will sit on his throne in heavenly glory" (Matt. 25: 31).

The King, in arriving, brought the Kingdom. But the fulfilment and the full influence of the Kingdom are being held in suspension. Hope of what the Kingdom will be is still future. It is hope which drives the Christian community forward and gives us encouragement to live in the most difficult and debilitating of situations.

In its all-inclusiveness, the Kingdom extends beyond any particular group or race. Even though the sons and daughters of Abraham were very conscious of their lineage, Jesus made it clear that such ethnic attachment was not enough to guarantee a place in the Kingdom. In Jesus' opening message in Nazareth (Luke 4), he used illustrations of two non-Hebrews who responded to God's provisions: a widow in Sidon supplied with food during a famine, and Naaman, the Syrian general cured of leprosy. Jesus' message was unmistakable: membership in the Kingdom will not be limited to those of a particular clan or race.

As it was not reserved for those of a race, neither was it for those who maintained an outward purity, or even those who kept the law. For, if it was, surely the Pharisees would be the first to enter. Jesus reserved his deepest scorn for them: "Woe to you, teachers of the law and Pharisees, you hypocrites! You are like whitewashed tombs, which look beautiful on the outside but on the inside are full of dead men's bones and everything unclean" (Matt. 23: 27). Unsavoury people such as prostitutes, who seemingly had nothing to offer, were welcomed, while the teachers of the law were excluded (Matt. 5: 20).

Race, status, the meticulous keeping of the law—none of these qualifies one. Jesus' calling reverberates with what Isaiah heard God say: "When you come before me ... stop bringing meaningless offerings! ... They have become a burden to me. ... Stop doing wrong, learn to do right! Seek justice, encourage the oppressed. Defend the cause of the fatherless, plead the case of the widow" (Isa. 1: 12–17).

What could be more out of sync with a Roman-dominated society than the announcement that the new Kingdom would be made up of those who are meek and lowly: that its leader is willing to be the last in order to be first and one who models leadership by washing feet? He called the weary ones (Matt. 11: 28–30). The wealthy—well, they can come, but wealth is a hindrance, not an asset (Mark 10: 17–25). And thieves and prostitutes will make it to the entrance before the religiously upstanding people (Matt. 21: 31). This new Kingdom will be made up of the social rejects, patently irreligious, financially on the bottom rung: those who know they have nothing to bring but their failures, bankruptcies, broken dreams, and shattered hopes. Paul understood who comprised this strange Kingdom: "Think of what you were when you were called. Not many of you were wise by human standards; not many were influential; not many were of noble birth" (1 Cor. 1: 26).

This understanding is vital to our application of the relationship of the Kingdom to our notion of political/social leadership. Not only does the Kingdom hold all things under its rule, but Christ's concern for Kingdom rule encompasses groups we might otherwise exclude.

3. The Kingdom is transformational.

We most easily think of Kingdom power as a political, economic, or military power, but Jesus, as Creator, knows the heart and sets about to inaugurate that which will transform instead of adopting the human way—to dominate and control.

Members of the Kingdom are those who are ready and prepared to obey. Jesus did not use the law as the gate. He provided another point of entry. Paul described it this way: "Therefore no one will be declared righteous in his sight by observing the law; rather, through the law we become conscious of sin" (Rom. 3: 20). Obedience arises, not from a desire for religious perfection, but from a willingness to allow Christ to rule one's life—all of it.

The ensuing standards of life then are shaped by what Jesus expects his followers to obey. In the discourse on separating the sheep from the goats, Jesus leaves no doubt what is expected: "I was hungry and you gave me something to eat, I was thirsty and you gave me something to drink, I was a stranger and you invited me in, I needed clothes and you clothed me, I was sick and you looked after me, I was in prison and you came to visit me" (Matt. 25: 35, 36). Thus, although membership in the Kingdom does not require obedience to a series of laws, that does not exempt one from right living, or from obedience to the newly defined laws of the Kingdom.

Jesus' teaching is a window into the ways of his Kingdom. His primary form is storytelling: parables. When asked "Why do you speak to the people in parables?" he replied, "The knowledge of the secrets of the kingdom of heaven [Matthew used "heaven" rather than "God"] has been given to you" (Matt. 13: 10, 11).

His "sower" metaphor helps us see both Kingdom wisdom and Kingdom strategy. He was not depending on military force, or even calling on angelic assistance, but rather was using the power of the Word to call a willing belief and a faithful following. Rome or Ottawa can use its political levers to lead, but Christ's Kingdom begins at a more fundamental level: at the centre of inner reality, the heart.

Sowing is a gentle and seemingly harmless activity. A seed is dropped into the soil and, in time, brings a harvest. It is hidden from view; it takes time, makes no noise, competes with no one. Nothing threatening here.

It is not just that the words of Christ transform as do ideas of human thought. His words, as seed, are not only revolutionary (although that they are), but life-giving. The seed of the Word actually brings about a release from the chains of human sin and sets in process a new life which grows up within oneself and throughout one's relationships.

Jesus also demonstrated power over the physical realm by the authority of his words. In Capernaum, people "were amazed at his teaching, because his message had authority." When a man possessed by a demon recognized him as the Holy One of God, Jesus freed him (Luke 4: 32–36). In the region of the Gadarenes, when Jesus encountered a man with an evil spirit, there was an immediate recognition of Jesus' authority (Mark 5: 6, 7; cf. Matt. 8: 29; Luke 8: 28, 31).

The releasing of people from the control of the demonic struck people as evidence of messiahship. After Jesus had healed and delivered a man, "all the people were astonished and said, 'Could this be the Son of David?'" (Matt. 12: 23).

When the seventy-two of Jesus' disciples returned from their first mission, they told Jesus what they had seen. Jesus rejoiced with them and said, "I saw Satan fall like lightning from heaven" (Luke 10: 18). Satan had been defeated, and his power to subject people of God's Kingdom was curtailed.

It may seem strange to include Christ's miracles in a study of the social/political influence of his Kingdom, but they speak to the nature of the Kingdom. Nothing is left untouched by Christ's presence, even physical disabilities. One might say that, if Jesus is concerned about a storm in Galilee, certainly he is interested in the political powers that rule us.

We learn early in Jesus' ministry the strategic importance of miracles: "Jesus went through all the towns and villages, teaching in their synagogues, preaching the good news of the kingdom and healing every disease and sickness" (Matt. 9: 35).

The working of miracles existed alongside the casting-out of demons, and preaching as a means of announcing the Kingdom. Some people explain the miracles as only of that time, or as the workings of a primitive culture. John Bright disagrees: "He who regards them as an excrescence of the gospel story, an expression of the believers of a superstitious age which must be scaled away in order to get back to Jesus as he really was, may indeed recover a Jesus palatable to a rationalist intellect—but he may be assured that it will not be the Jesus of the New Testament faith."[3]

The raising of the dead is also important. The raising of the ruler's daughter (Matt 9: 18ff.) and Lazarus (John 11: 1ff.) serve not only to etch in the minds of the disciples Christ's true nature, but to identify the nature of the Kingdom. The ultimate expression of power is over death. The message is clear: this new Kingdom will deal with death in a revolutionary way.

As well as issuing searing words to religious leaders, Jesus cared for a dying woman. This coupling of care for the hurting, speaking to nature, and zeroing in on political strife is consistent with the nature of the Kingdom.

Jesus announced the Kingdom in the oral tradition of the Middle East—not "words, words and more words," but commands which transform. Luke the historian notes, "The Law and the Prophets were proclaimed until John. Since that time, the good news of the kingdom of God is being preached" (16: 16). The core message is that the Kingdom arrives in the preaching of the Gospel. "Gospel" and "good news" are used interchangeably. The word "gospel" literally means "joyful news."

Jesus' preaching is unlike others'. His words are beyond rhetoric. They are accompanied by power. He announces truth, which in and of itself is transforming. Jesus' healing of a paralytic, and then forgiving his sins, shows the relationship. After the healing, Jesus asked the Pharisees and teachers, "'Why are you thinking these things in your hearts? Which is easier to say, "Your sins are forgiven," or to say, "Get up and walk"? But that you may know that the Son of Man has authority on earth to forgive sins ...' He said to the paralysed man, 'I tell you, get up, take your mat and go home'" (Luke 5: 22). Miracles were one thing, but to actually forgive sin?

Because power and authority are clearly a function of Christ's being and mandate, the announced Kingdom is filled with all that Jesus is. Such a message is for all people in all times and places. For political leadership unaware of Christ's person, the good news is still a reality. For those of us in lands rich in the history of Christian political engagement, the need to speak again the good news is critical, not only for the benefit which accrues to the political enterprise, but because of the biblical call to speak the good news everywhere.

4. The Kingdom overturns our understanding of political power.

We assume that the words "political" and "power" go hand in hand. It is true, of course, that one cannot rule a nation without power. Power, in and of itself, is a gift. However, when we use the word "power," we do so with certain assumptions. We picture a king exercising power by requiring the subjects to obey. In our democratic society we visualize the prime minister deciding what will be done because the ruling party has sufficient power—that is, votes in the House of Commons—to make the decision for us all.

The practical question is, how are our political masters able to exercise political leadership? They can lead and exercise political power (meaning, influence) only when those over whom they rule give them the authority (meaning, office) to rule.

This plays out in everyday life. A teacher, though given the right and task to manage a class, can teach and lead only when the students are willing to recognize his or her authority to teach them. A minister, even though mandated to lead a church, can rule only as the people recognize that authority to lead.

Even in the most onerous of dictatorships, ultimately a ruthless ruler can continue only as long as the people allow it. All the military might in the world will not in the end hold the power to rule. Only the authority given by those ruled to those ruling will allow continuing leadership.

When we consider governance, we need not shun political parties or avoid giving leadership; rather, we need to remember that the source of authority is not in the process itself but in God's provision for leadership.

Those who argue that Jesus had no political concern assume that, because he did not specifically speak to the issue of Rome, his message was therefore not designed to bring about political change. Indeed, Jesus was a threat to the Roman Empire.

Jesus tells the story about the rich man who built more barns to store his wealth (Luke 12: 15–21). His message is not that he broke a law but that, in holding on to more possessions than he needs, he is a fool. Here, Jesus is attacking the social order of the powerful. Though this might not directly speak to Roman authority, it in effect does so by disturbing the social order—something Rome was concerned about. If such ideas got popular play in Israel, the ensuing upset would have been politically untenable. His call to the rich young man to sell everything was said in a land where many were poor and only a few were rich.

Jesus' treatment of the oppressed is often missed by some churches who react to a bias often associated with issues of the poor. But such misunderstanding fails to see Jesus' deep concern. When asked by John the

Baptist's friends if Jesus really was the Messiah, he said, "Go back and report to John what you have seen and heard: the blind receive sight, the lame walk ... and the good news is preached to the poor" (Luke 7: 22–23).

To a Messiah-awaiting people, the very idea that this Christ (Messiah) would die a death on the cross—the billboard of Roman power—was preposterous. "Just another pseudo-messiah," most would say. The hopes of the disciples and followers were smashed by the collusion of religious and political leaders and the dreaded and hated intruder, Rome. But the mighty Kingdom had come, and Rome's puny efforts could not bring it down. At the very time it seemed all had been lost, all had been won. The cross eventually became a symbol, not of tragedy and loss, but of victory and triumph: the power of evil was finally broken. The battle would continue for centuries, but the defeat of evil was certain.

◀●

This look at Christ's Kingdom sets in context our search for God's will about what is good for our nation, shaped and informed by what Christ meant about our role in fulfilling the prayer "Your will be done on earth." There are nine factors in this expressed will.

1. *Time-oriented*: Jesus came in time, which he both created and lived in. He does not trivialize this part of eternity, even though life on earth someday will wind up and be no more.

2. *Earth-concerned*: As Jesus came in time, he also graced this planet above all others with his body and life. We have no clue as to God's interaction with other planets, or whether life in some form exists there. We do know God's own-image creation in humanity is here. Earth is more than a vehicle: it is also an expression of God's own creation. Christ's Kingdom, launched here, works out its dynamics within societal living.

3. *Engaging darkness*: Jesus reminds us that evil is a reality working to disengage creation from its Creator. Jesus' Kingdom is about more than good ideas and integrative truths: it

strikes with power at Satan and his Kingdom. Facing Satan in the wilderness, the Kingdom is neither deceived by Satan's lies and seductions nor intimidated by his power.

4. *Enacting miracles*: The contamination of disease poses no formidable threat to the Creator. Jesus demonstrates to John the Baptist that the Kingdom, in facing physical disease and tragedy, brings about healing. In the eye of a storm, Jesus' words bring about atmospheric change. These miracles and others serve to remind us that, no matter the wonder or mystery of the physical Creation, the Kingdom envelops and has power over all.

5. *Redefining power*: It is here that we see most clearly the central force of Christ's Kingdom. Amid the expectation that any kingdom is really about the power to rule, Jesus redefines it. The Kingdom way to the throne goes by way of the cross. To rule, one must serve. To become fruitful, one must die; to receive, one must bestow.

6. *Encompassing politics*: Did Jesus expect Rome to live by his teaching? If he did not call on the disciples to rehabilitate society, then why should we try? The fact is he did, and that rule covers all of life; it is a rule that begins in the heart of the Creation, the human will. Transforming this centre, Christ's Kingdom-righteousness overflows to the surrounding world. Just because he did not tell us to build church buildings or run seminaries does not mean we should not do so; nor does it follow that just because he has not called us to be politicians or run grocery stores we should not be politicians or grocers.

7. *Recasting leadership*: Knowing Christ's recasting of power, we are impressed with the manner in which we are expected to lead. He shows us by example the Kingdom-understanding of "lord." We are called to remember the towel. As Messiah, Jesus will lead the people, but in ways that strike confusion in those who know only one way of leading—coercive power. As a servant, Jesus recasts our understanding of Kingdom-leading.

8. *Requiring ethics*: Jesus expected the disciples to take seriously the ethics of the Kingdom. While the Kingdom is the goal and the reward for those who follow Christ, it is also the means whereby we live out the good news. Our ethics, or moral requirements, are wrapped up in personal obedience to Christ as Lord and Saviour. His Gospel is not bifurcated, divided between personal and social, but rather is unified.

9. *Person-centred*: Though we want to avoid Enlightenment ideology of individualism, we see that Jesus gives focus to people. He asks blind Bartimaus, "What do you want?" He lovingly takes children in his arms. We more clearly understand his person-centredness when we read Paul's description: we are temples of God's Spirit. It is here God transforms and rewrites on the tablets—or micro-chips—of our hearts the eternal laws. At the same time, we live, not to ourselves, but with the community of God's people, the church.

The message of the Kingdom is political. It is not prescriptive in suggesting a political philosophy or structure, such as a monarchy or a democracy, but, in calling us to obey God's rule and to live in love with each other, Christ's message is political.

To decide what to do in relation to our political and social setting requires that we weave a garment out of the many threads of Jesus' life, teachings, and ministry. Avoiding formulas or specific instructions, Christ calls us to weave a garment which fits and serves us within the context of our life. By not giving us specifics, Kingdom-truth is not bound by era, situation, or political reality. The threads of the Kingdom are the same, but the pattern, shape, size, and purpose of the garment will be constructed so that Christ's will in relationship to political life is served.

CHAPTER 6

Thinking with a
Christian World-View

In the previous two chapters we examined the Old and New Testaments for clues as to what Christians might believe about their nation, and for insights to guide us in our response to social and political realities.

The Scriptures provide a window through which we look out onto life. In recent decades we have been subjected to a perspective or way of seeing: secularism has screened faith from our world-view. That's why it seems difficult to include a Christian point of view in discussions of public policy. For so long, faith has been excluded from such issues that it seems we must live without it. However, while this is at present the status quo of Canadian political and public life, it does not have to continue to be.

What is required is for Christians to live out their faith, be it in the classroom, in the House of Commons, or along the walk-ways of Canadian life, by framing all of life within a Christian understanding.

One summer, Lily and I spent a couple of weeks in Oxford. I was pleasantly surprised to see the number of colleges with religious names; Jesus College, Trinity College, Christ Church College. But we noted that much of their studies had little reference to their founding spiritual mandates. Their world-views were shaped by the secular; that is, God is ignored as a meaningful and knowable reality or object worthy of search.

Harry Blamires, author and colleague of C.S. Lewis, laments, "We Christians in the modern world accept, for the purpose of mental activity, a frame of reference constructed by the secular mind and a set of criteria reflecting secular evaluations."[1] To surrender to a non-Christian mind-set is to see through lenses that exclude a biblical vision of life.

Thinking Christianly has been discredited by both secularist and Christian sectarians. As secular thinking deprives one's world-view of faith as central to understanding life, Christian sectarianism assumes that, because the current world is temporary, Christ therefore has little interest in it.

Thinking Christianly is not as easy as it might seem. Contemporary public thought is often biased against a Christian world-view. This is Babel at its strongest. Surrounded by groups and communication systems, each broadcasting its own message, we unconsciously, or even consciously, accept their norms, putting on the glasses of our prevailing culture and seeing life through their lenses. The Apostle Paul urges us, "Do not conform any longer to the pattern of this world, but be transformed by the renewing of your mind" (Rom. 12: 2).

The prophet Elisha's assistant was frightened as he looked out onto the city and saw the surrounding foreign army. Elisha prayed, "'Oh Lord, open his eyes that he may see.' And the Lord opened the servant's eyes, and he saw; and behold, the mountain was full of horses and chariots of fire all around Elisha" (2 Kings 6: 17). Elisha didn't panic. Through eyes of faith, he saw more than what his associate saw. This window of faith gave him a broader perspective.

King David, wanting to know the strength of his army, instructed Commander Joab to number the people of Israel (2 Sam. 24: 10). Instead of relying on God, David trusted in the strength and size of his army. Turning from trusting God, David instead believed his strength was in the power of armaments and the size of the army. David later noted the futility of basing the idea of winning on his own strength: "Some boast in chariots, and some in horses; but we will boast in the name of the Lord, our God" (Ps. 20: 7, 8). "The king is not saved by a mighty army; a warrior is not delivered by great strength. A horse is a false hope for victory" (33: 16, 17). David learned in time that his window was too small.

Three Parts of a Christian World-View

In learning to think about life within a Christian world-view, we must be aware of three important elements in the framework through which to see life: creation, time, and humanity.

Planet Earth

God has not abandoned planet Earth. Creation includes this planet in the universe and, on this planet, humans are made in God's likeness. The physical creation, including distant planets, is part of the grander reality. While the whole universe will one day be made into a "new heaven and new earth," that does not mean that Earth is without meaning here and now. Indeed, the opposite is true. Created in God's likeness, we inhabit this earth. It was to planet Earth that God's Son came, and it is here that the eternal plan is being worked out. To minimize the importance of Earth is to marginalize the handiwork and plan of God.

David testifies to God's involvement with creation. "The earth is the Lord's and everything in it," he writes; "the world and all who live in it; for he founded it upon the seas and established it upon the waters" (Ps. 24). In Psalm 33, the Earth is God's expression of love: "The earth is full of the loving kindness of the Lord. By the word of the Lord the heavens were made, and by the breath of His mouth all their host." A Hebrew song describes God as the past, present, and future King of the Earth—not as an absentee landlord, or a spirit that we can know only after we die: "For God is King of all the earth. ... God reigns over the nations" (Ps. 47). This creation is under God's control. "It is I who made the earth, and created man upon it. I stretched out the heavens with My hands, and I ordained all their host" (Isa. 45: 12).

Earth's original human inhabitants received specific instruction in Earth management. After their disobedience, the instruction was to "cultivate the ground from which he was taken" (Gen. 3: 23). This was not punishment, but a continuation of the assignment given to them before the Fall (1: 28).

Jesus taught the disciples to pray: "Your kingdom come, your will be done on earth as it is in heaven" (Matt. 6: 10). The "on earth" of Jesus' prayer directly focuses our attention on God's concerns being worked out where we stand—on this geographical place of our existence. Jesus does not allow us to "spiritualize" his concern as being that of "in the sweet by and by," but holds us in the present tense and in the place where we live. Christians in the early church gave praise for the release of Peter and John. They prayed, "Sovereign Lord, you made the heaven and the earth and the sea and everything in them ..." (Acts 4: 24). We live with hope for our eternal existence, but, until then, as an integral part of the creation, we are called on to enjoy and care for this planet Earth.

Time

God has not abandoned time—it was created, and we are placed within it. We are not just putting in time, waiting until eternity wraps us up. Although we are to "set [our] hearts on things above" (Col. 3: 2) to establish right motivations, we are not to spend our days indolently dreaming of heaven. Rather, we are called to live out our days as a means of knowing and doing God's will and purposes. As a colleague said, time is when the genetic code for eternity is being written. Earth is not everything, and time is not all there is, but they are God's creation; they are both preparatory and preliminary to all of the very best there is and will be.

As we live from one millennium into the next, there is an enormous interest in "End Time" ideas. Jesus warned us not to be unduly preoccupied by the exact time of his return. Speaking of the coming of the "Son of Man," he warned, "No one knows about that day or hour, not even the angels in heaven, nor the Son, but only the Father. Be on guard! Be alert! You do not know when that time will come" (Mark 13: 32, 33).

Our life is not to be squandered; we are to use it both to manage the Earth and to prepare for Christ's return. Paul reminds us to use time well: "And do this, understanding the present time. The hour has come for you to wake up from your slumber, because our salvation is nearer now than when we first believed. The night is nearly over; the day is almost here. So let us put aside the deeds of darkness and put on the armour of light" (Rom. 13: 11, 12).

Humanity

In spite of sin, which spoils all creation, God has not abandoned us. Though Earth and time are part of creation, we are God's special creation. Made "in his image," humanity has the unique and awesome responsibility of bearing God's image in life. Even though humanity lives in rebellion, we have opportunity to know God. While the life of the Spirit and life of the world are in tension, Jesus gives us an opportunity to enter into life prepared for creation.

The entry of evil into earthly life changed the nature of creation and the workings of human motivations. This reality did not set aside God's interest or plan to have fellowship with the creation. For, in the midst of human history, with our failures and proclivity towards self-interest, God had a plan centred in Jesus Christ. Given that humans are a special creation, the freeing of humans from the bondage of evil was intrinsic to God's overall agenda.

Yes, people do matter. We are given the task of carrying on the Kingdom. What is astounding about and distinctive of Christian faith is that those who turn to Christ become the habitat of God's life. "Do you not know that your body is a temple of the Holy Spirit, who is in you, whom you have received from God?" the Apostle Paul asks. Why else would there be the constant reminder that our bodies are to be kept to honour God? Paul concludes, "You are not your own; you were bought at a price. Therefore honour God with your body" (1 Cor. 6: 19, 20).

Jesus' famous line leaves no doubt of his commitment to people: "For God so loved the world that he gave his one and only Son ..." (John 3: 16). Even in discipline, God's concern is shown. "When we are judged by the Lord," Paul writes, "we are being disciplined so that we will not be condemned with the world" (1 Cor. 11: 32). Even though evil works to destroy, it will never succeed, for it is God who protects and controls our destinies. Again Paul writes, "For by him all things were created: things in heaven and on earth, visible and invisible, whether thrones or powers or rulers and authorities; all things were created by him and for him" (Col. 1: 16). "For I am convinced that neither death nor life, neither angels nor demons, neither the present nor the future, nor any powers, neither height nor depth, nor anything else in all creation, will be able to separate us from the love of God that is in Christ Jesus our Lord" (Rom. 8: 38, 39). It is not possible to overstate our importance to God. While we do not know what exists on other planets of the galaxies, we do know that on planet Earth God invested the life of the Son so that by Christ's death and resurrection we too can know eternal life.

FINDING A NATIONHOOD VISION— DOES MY COUNTRY MATTER?

But does God's concern for humanity mean God has a particular concern for communities or nations? Does God care specifically about Canada or Ghana or Sri Lanka? Does the Bible say anywhere that God is concerned with a nation as such? To put it another way, does nationhood, as a category of human existence, have any place in the plans of God? Can there be for the Christian such a thing as a biblical vision for one's nation?

Some people are made nervous by such talk, and for good reason. Church and political leaders have too often used religion as a means of exercising power. Christians do not want to make national situations worse by embracing a simplistic or otherwise unsound biblical view of their country. Most Canadian Christians would reject the view that Canada has been especially chosen by God above other nations.

Overdramatization is not necessary. We examine the Scriptures to see what might be God's concern for a nation. But to develop an appropriate biblical model for Canada in our time, it is not enough to collect a few pithy Bible verses, mix them together with our religious past, and say, "Here's the answer."

The Bible does not let us get away with such narrow or shallow thinking. "The whole counsel of God" does not mean bits and pieces, "sound bites," or one-dimensional pictures. In approaching any controversial question, we need to "correctly handle the world of truth" (2 Tim. 2: 15). The Christian world-view is not made up of a series of slogans designed to address the problems of the day and posited as some sort of cure-all. It comes out of the Hebrew community's long struggle. It is epitomized in Jesus' teachings about his Kingdom. And it has been demonstrated in many forms through the continuing development of the church throughout its 2,000-year sojourn.

If we fail to look at the big picture, if we avoid struggling with the issues of Christian faith and action, the consequences could be monstrous. Working on the assumption that our nation and the way we relate to it are of concern to God, if we do not engage and show caring, we end up being unfaithful both to Canada and to the Lord we serve.

WHY SHOULD WE CARE?

For some Christians a nagging question remains: Given God's promise of eternity, is there any reason why a Christian world-view allows one to be concerned about the social and political structures of today? Often a person who asks me this assumes that aspects of Christ's Kingdom— including conversion, life in the Spirit, the coming of Christ, the future new heavens and earth—have nothing to do with our country. The question could be phrased another way: "Do our beliefs and actions have consequence only in so far as they affect eternal matters?" If the answer is yes, then any other concern about life is, at best, secondary, but not compelling. Such a view leads to four faulty conclusions.

First, the state exists without any legitimate essence of its own. It is not to bring glory to God but is only to be used by God for some purpose. But this runs against Paul's assertion that "by him all things were created: things in heaven and on earth, visible and invisible, whether thrones or powers or rulers or authorities; all things were created by him and for him" (Col. 1: 16, 17).

Second, if the state does not bring glory to God, it falls into the category of "necessary evil," without any legitimacy as a creation of God.

However, such a conclusion forces us to ignore the Scriptures, which speak of political concerns. Richard Mouw, president of Fuller Seminary, writes, "God's promise to bless the descendants of Abraham included references to their political well-being; when the Israelites were rescued out of Egypt, the bonds of their political oppression had to be broken; the Psalmists wrote political prayers; the prophets delivered messages about political policies; Jesus faced political temptations; apocalyptic visions include political scenarios."[2]

If the state is a necessary evil, it would follow that, not only would it be counter-productive for Christians to engage in any aspect of state activities—including teaching school or working as a forest ranger— but to care at all about our society or the environment would only serve the source of evil.

Third, by asserting that the state is without value, we end up saying that the significance of human institutions—and the individuals who work in them—can be determined only by what they will produce in eternity. It is as if our present life has nothing to do with our future; as though our inner life is disembodied from what is around us. Thus, as long as I am good on the "inside," this false view concludes, I have fulfilled my responsibilities as a Christian. James, a disciple and New Testament writer, had something to say about that: "What good is it, my brothers, if a man claims to have faith but has no deeds? Can such faith save him? Suppose a brother or sister is without clothes and daily food. If one of you says to him, 'Go, I wish you well; keep warm and well fed,' but does nothing about his physical needs, what good is it? In the same way, faith by itself, if it is not accompanied by action, is dead" (2: 14–17).

The false separation of Spirit life from life in Christ's creation leads to spiritual schizophrenia and the age-old heresy of Gnosticism. Some seeking inner spirituality discount the Earth as being of concern to God and deny material reality as a legitimate part of God's Kingdom.

Gnostic teachers made a distinction between the Demiurge (seen by ancient Greeks as an inferior deity, responsible for creating the material world) and the unknowable Divine Being. Into some humans entered the spark of Divine substance, and by means of "gnosis" (intuitive knowledge), they would be rescued from the material world and brought back into the world of the Divine. Material reality was therefore seen as evil. For them, Jesus Christ could not be incarnate, for that would have meant the combining of the Divine Being with the material. To a Gnostic, Jesus did not have a material body, but simply took the façade of a mortal. Those who opposed this teaching emphasized the actual hand of God in Creation; the goodness of material reality; and the literal physical existence, and the bodily life, death, and resurrection, of Jesus Christ.

Some Christians who deny that issues of public life are important to a Christian world-view are, on the other hand, successful in accumulating wealth or getting an education. Some who contend that their only concern is to prepare people for eternity build and maintain expensive buildings, and have salaried staff and large budgets to serve the many needs of their members, which in effect contradicts their view of God as being concerned only with eternity. At stake in this discussion is not whether these church activities are legitimate, but whether the importance invested in them is consistent with one's views of involvement in public life.

Fourth, by claiming that a nation is outside God's agenda, we unwittingly say that the ethics of Christ's Kingdom have no application to public affairs. This precludes anyone, Christian or a believer in another faith, from calling on government to be accountable to the Creator and to act in just and merciful ways. Truth, then, is relative, applying only to Christians. It denies that, if God is not God of all, he is not God at all.

These four conclusions point out the fallacy of assuming a nation has no place in Christ's concern. Also if we work outside of a rigorous biblical framework, we can be trapped by excessive nationalism—caught up in blindly believing that one's nation is closest to God's heart; by debilitating anxiety—fear that God has no concern for one's national habitation; or by corrosive cynicism—a complete discounting of any possibility of God's intervention into the affairs of state.

Israel: A Light to the Nations

The story of Israel is helpful in this context, for it speaks of God's mind for a nation. The Hebrews were called out as a people and given specific parameters within which to live. We can then take the stories, promises, and characters of their story and apply them to our lives. The proclivities of raw and ruthless characters such as Cain and Samson become warnings to our youth. David's songs became grist for sermons on hope. Prophetic thunderings become the stuff of cultural analysis. Dipping into this reservoir is too much to resist.

As we consider the shaping of our ideas for Canada, there are two dangers: to take God's promises to Israel and, without careful biblical study, make them promises to us; and to avoid Israel altogether for fear some misguided nationalist might apply God's treatment of Israel directly to Canada, claim "chosen" status for the country, and justify all sorts of power-mongering in the name of the will of God.

Such fears are well founded. Political errors have been made in the past. That does not mean we should give up searching for appropriate ways to apply these lessons. To keep us from that trap, there are a few "don'ts" to keep in mind:[3]

1. *Don't* pick up a promise from Israel, pull it into today's situation, and automatically assume the very same should, or will, apply today. Principles may be learned from the promise, but the promise may not be strictly applicable in the way it may first appear.
2. *Don't* assume that Canada is Israel, and that therefore what God did with that nation is true for ours. Our history is different, and so is our calling. God called the nation of Israel to a specific geographical area and promised certain things for them.
3. *Don't* assume that the Bible gives us a precise blueprint. The Bible describes what was said and what happened, and from that we learn principles of personal and national life. As we read of Israel's formation, its coming of age in the promised land, and God's use of surrounding nations to teach Israel lessons, a pattern gradually forms.

Two examples of abuse of national visions based on misinterpretations of the Scriptures come to mind. Central to the founding of the United States was the idea of "manifest destiny." There was an assumption that God had especially called America into being and had manifested a particular destiny for the nation—that is, to be the "Israel" of the new world. American sociologist Seymour Lipset, in analysing this fallacy, writes, "The United States is seen as the new Israel." Quoting Robert N. Bellah, he continues, "Europe is Egypt; America the promised land. God has led His people to establish a new sort of social order that shall be a light to all nations."[4]

It is healthy to hold one's own nation in high regard, but the use of God's call to Abraham and the subsequent forming of Israel as a parallel to the creation of the United States can lead to all sorts of excesses. For example, some defend the build-up of military power on the basis that, as God's chosen land, the United States is called to defend biblical values. While there may be sound reasons for a strong military, to base one's rationale on being the chosen nation to defend God's interests is a distortion, and very dangerous.

The Boers also abused their knowledge of God's covenant with Abraham in equating their takeover of South Africa with Israel's conquering of Palestine. The laws of apartheid rose out of this misapplication of the Hebraic model. South African church statesman Michael Cassidy describes the distorted nationalism that arose from those scriptural misinterpretations: "This leads us to what is perhaps the greatest problem which South African nationalisms raise for evangelism, namely the clash between the relative ethic of nationalism and the absolute ethic of Christianity. ... [S]ome African nationalisms, assuming a semi-religious dimension and defining their own ethical absolutes, begin to equate their own political process with the divine will."[5]

So, how do we fairly use Israel as a model or example? One helpful way is to see Israel as "a light to the nations." That light, as we know, almost went out. But we have a record of that light as a clue, a direction, an idea. We can learn from its history, its mistakes, failures, and successes. When we read the history of Israel, we are listening in on an extraordinary dialogue. The constant interplay between God and this people gives us an idea of what countries should and should not do, and shows us the concerns, expectations, and judgments of God.

In examining the history of Israel, there are guidelines to keep us from misapplying Israel's experience. First, Israel had a special place in the plan and economy of God. Abraham did not just happen to leave his homeland and venture into new territory. The design was to establish a nation through which God's salvation would come to the entire world. This semi-nomadic Semitic tribe was different from all other tribes and nations. Founders of new nations cannot assume that God will rubber-stamp their future plans just because of this promise to Abraham.

Second, the biblical record shows Israel growing into nationhood. For a good part of its history, Israel was an assembly of primitive Middle Eastern tribes travelling to Canaan, then wandering in the wilderness after their escape from Egypt—a far cry from most of today's nations, with their set boundaries. The story of its experience is just that—a story. We listen and watch as they fumble along, failing God, caught up in their own peculiar cultural problems, from time to time showing a flash of obedience and cultural genius. At the beginning, they had no land of their own. And, once they did claim what God had promised them, they were frequently invaded and carried off into other lands, forced to live as exiles.

As desert tribes with a relatively short history, they were, ethnically speaking, a homogeneous people who traced their roots to Abraham. They were instructed to protect their distinct language, history, and faith from contamination by other cultures and religions because they had a peculiar reason for being made a nation. No other nation would ever fall heir to the promise of being the cradle of God's Son; neither would any other nation ever be as clearly God-directed as Israel. Their history could not be written for any other peoples or nations. Their nation was unique, without parallel, and not to be seen again.

The Hebrews' understanding of God came from observing God at work. The Hebrews did not think in philosophical categories, as did the Greeks. They did not work from a plan or blueprint. They determined their future actions by remembering God's leading in the past and by recalling what God had done. We must, as Canadians, treat the historical record in this way as well, since it was written for that purpose.

WORLDLINESS

Now a word about a problem that has kept many Christians from seriously considering tackling concerns and issues in the broader society. The word most often used is "worldliness."

I was raised in a church community that defined certain behaviours as "worldly." One such behaviour was smoking. Because of its addictive properties (we did not then understand its relationship to one's health), smoking was associated with being unwilling to submit to the Lordship of Christ. Another "worldly" activity was drinking alcohol, which was seen as a cause for many of society's ills.

In much the same way, some Christians viewed engagement in public activity as a violation of the call to "come out from them and be separate, says the Lord. Touch no unclean thing, and I will receive you" (2 Cor. 6: 17). Concern for national/political issues was seen as wandering too close to worldliness.

We must take seriously this concern of "being in the world, but not of the world." To get at it, we need to see it through a Christian world-view. First, we must look at what "the world" does not mean, and then construct a working definition.

What It Is Not

"Worldliness" does not refer to the physical world. Planet Earth is God's creation. "The earth is full of the goodness of the Lord" (Ps. 33: 5). When it was created, God looked at it and said, "It is good." Subsequent to Creation, sin entered into all of human life, which includes the Earth. But that is not to say that the Earth and its products are "worldly."

"Worldliness" does not refer to the physical body. Made in God's image, the human body, though infected by sinfulness, is the handiwork of God's creation. John shocked those who believed the body was evil when he said, "The Word [Jesus] was made flesh and made his dwelling among us" (John 1: 14). Paul went so far as to remind us that our bodies are "temples" of God (1 Cor. 3: 16). God takes up residence in this physical construct.

Neither does "worldliness" mean the act of living in the world. It is in the world that we encounter the life of Jesus. The drama of God's re-creating life is played out on the stage of life, in this world.

Using one's gifts is not synonymous with "worldliness." Gifts and abilities are part of God's creation. At the very core of our being is a calling to live by making use of these gifts. To own and use our gifts is to fulfil our calling.

Thus, "worldliness" is not synonymous with the Earth, physical life, human experience, or abilities.

A Working Definition

So what do we mean by "worldliness"? It is giving preferred status to something other than God, setting up anything in life above devotion and obedience to God. When Moses was receiving the Ten Commandments and absent from the people, his brother Aaron crafted a golden calf, an object for the people to worship. The golden calf became a symbol for worship over the Creator, making it an idol.

"Worldliness" means allowing other concerns to overcome faith. It was "by faith" that Abraham heard and obeyed the voice of God. He understood this to be the most central aspect of walking with God. We are called to base all of life on the belief that God meant what he said and that our very lives are to be lived according to his Word.

"Worldliness" is also to live without regard to eternity, absorbed with storing wealth and gaining fame without any thought to how one will spend eternity. Because we are people of time, that is the only construct we really understand. Entering into adulthood, we chart a course that follows in line with whatever we believe is important. This is valid and appropriate. But it should not be all; we *will* live on into eternity. Not to compute eternity into the equation of what I do today is to miss a vital element of the Kingdom. If I do not respect my ultimate destination, life becomes worldly.

"Worldliness" is also to live outside of issues or matters that concern God. We don't have a simple listing, but the Scriptures faithfully record God's call. The Israelites were told what was required: "To do justice, to show mercy and to walk humbly before their God"—reinforced by Jesus in Matthew 23: 23. If, for example, in running a business our concerns are focused only on the "bottom line," and God's concerns—such as just treatment of employees—are ignored, that business is worldly.

Having a worldly spirit is to put oneself over others. The drive to be profitable, if it is at the expense of others, is "worldliness." Success is not the antithesis of a God-centred life. But, in all aspects of living, we are called to "love your enemies and pray for those who persecute you" (Matt. 5: 43). If getting ahead requires that I step on others, my profit has become rooted in worldliness.

"Worldliness" means preoccupation with religious correctness. In Jesus' day, it was the Pharisees who occupied this ground. Today, those of the religious left and right can be accused equally of having such a preoccupation. If holding onto my faith means intolerance of those with whom I disagree, that faith can itself be overcome by a worldly spirit. For example, a public stand on moral issues often leads to strongly expressed views by various sides. If, in the debate, a Christian is caught in personal recriminations, that is far from Christ's way. Firm convictions are important, and disagreement is expected, but the Spirit never bears the fruit of intolerance.

At its heart, "worldliness" overrides God's concern, which is the agenda of the King. The Sermon on the Mount is explicit, definitive, and all-encompassing. One just needs to ask oneself, "What would be the concern and action plan of Jesus in this situation?" If my attitudes, aspirations, behaviour, and relationships are not in line with the concerns of Christ's Kingdom, that is "worldliness."

WORLD-VIEW AS STRATEGY

A well-developed and thoughtful view is critical in developing a strategy for engaging our culture. By understanding that the Earth, time, people, and our work are part of God's concern, we can understand our activities to be spiritual in the deepest sense, which in turn reminds us that we are about eternal realities, and that our work is accountable to our Creator. We further understand that the political state is not necessarily in opposition to God's purposes, and that God's agenda can be furthered by Christian people's engaging in service to the state. This is in no way to give up the exclusive call to love only God, nor is it to assume that caring for our society means we buy into cultural assumptions. Our calling is not just to make this a better world in which to live. And neither should our politics determine our faith.

As disciples of Christ, we ask the tough questions and seek to honour Christ in all we do. Operating out of that biblical world-view, we are careful to employ the metaphor of Israel and seek to be guided by lessons and insights gained out of this unique calling.

PART III

KINGDOM LANGUAGE

CHAPTER 7

Lessons from the Past: Christians and Rome

This generation is not the first to wonder how their Christian faith relates to the ruling authorities. This conundrum has existed from the time of the earliest of Christian communities, and Canada has a strong history of both a formal and an informal relationship between the Christian community and the political order. The challenge for us, as Canadians, is made more complex by the fact that Canada has been greatly influenced by Christian faith, but our society in recent years has moved to exclude faith from the public square. Our very strong memory of the role of the Christian faith in shaping our nation, along with the sense of a secular marginalization of faith, has triggered a notable level of response from many Canadian Christians.

Beginning in Constantine's Rome, Christians have struggled with linking church to political reign. For 2,000 years, the church has tried to make sense of what relationship it should have with the political centre. In this chapter, working our way through the Holy Roman Empire to the Reformers and Radical Evangelicals, we examine the various models.

✝

Some Christians object to their colleagues getting involved in political leadership. They argue that, too easily, they can be drawn into a love for power or be subverted by worldly thinking. That, indeed, is a danger. History is replete with illustrations that underscore such concerns. The counterforce to the subtle and powerful magnet of wanting political power is to maintain a prophetic distance; that is, to be able to say, on any issue, "This is what God says." A tension between being engaged and retaining objectivity is essential.

The danger of being compromised by holding power does not, however, eliminate the importance of God's love for the whole world—"God so loved the world ..." Each human is imprinted with the image of God and is of such inestimable worth that God "gave his one and only Son ..." (John 3: 16). All of politics, notwithstanding its dangers, is subsumed under this reality.

As we explore the relationship of church and state, we note that, though individuals and governments are both part of God's creation, only people participate in the eternal Kingdom. Eternity is the privilege of the person, not of social systems.

Even so, while only the individual is made in the image of God (Gen. 1: 27), the government is also God's creation (Col. 1: 16). There is, as political scientist Glenn Tinder notes, an "ambiguity of our political obligations. If we recognize what God has done—so Christian principles imply—we shall be limitlessly respectful of human beings but wary of society."[1]

POLITICAL DISTINCTION

As God's special creation, we live in the world and its various social constructs. Yet we are wary of their inherent sinful inclinations. The political order, clearly designed to serve the social needs of humanity (Rom. 13), is maintained and influenced by humanity, the fallen. That is why we are to be wary. This wariness is the prophetic distance—not a barrier, but rather a perspective that reminds us of the tension between the knowledge of light and the knowledge of darkness. There is a difference between integrating faith with all of life—including politics—

and making it appear that one's particular political view is the only one which can be seen as "Christian."

The role of the prophet is to help us understand what it means to live as citizens of God's eternal Kingdom while being good citizens in Canada. We participate in public leadership, not because we believe that only Christ's followers have answers (for all truth is God's truth), but in response to the call to "occupy" (Luke 19: 13 KJV) until the master returns. (In this parable, the noble man, before he goes on a long journey, gave his servants money and told them to make good on this investment until he returned.) We offer our resources, not with the view that we have more than others, but with the knowledge that what we have under God's blessing is multiplied, as happened with the young lad who gave his meagre lunch, not to the crowds, but to Jesus, who in turn supplied the meal to the crowds. As distance is a characteristic of the prophet, so is humility.

There is an appropriate reserve that should characterize a Christian's relationship to societal activity. Uncritical nationalism wraps its flag around the Gospel. Emotional patriotism and chest-thumping confidence blind the eye to self-centred policies and activities. Paul, in reminding Christians in Corinth about the shortage of time, says, "For this world in its present form is passing away" (1 Cor. 7: 31). Take the world seriously, but not so seriously that it is seen as the only reality.

The prophetic stance also sees each political movement with a critical eye, looking down the road with a hope in what will be. In seeing beyond the current moment, we are reminded of God's promise. The Kingdom is here; it is at work; it will come in its fullness. Beyond the cyclical view of reincarnation or the hopelessness of nihilism, Christian engagement is reinforced by an understanding that God has both a plan and an order. For Christians in the first century, befuddled by the rampant worldliness of the church in Corinth, the Apostle John's revelation of the future gives hope (Rev. 1: 7, 8). Out of this conviction of God's current activity and hope in future reality, we work at bringing civility and goodness to our neighbours and society.

Some question that, if Jesus and the disciples showed such little interest in their surrounding social and political order, what business do we have in being concerned about our nation today? Jesus had a very specific focus; to announce the arrival of the Kingdom. His stated agenda lacked specifics, but the outworking of his message had enormous political impact. There were many things about which Jesus had little to say. For example, not much is said about the church. Only three times does Matthew record Jesus even using the word "church," and the other writers of the Gospels never mention it. Yet, Christ's coming founded the church. The point is that Jesus focused on setting out the essence and presence of the Kingdom and simply did not give details. However, this is not to say his life did not have profound political influence, as I'll note later.

THE RELATIONSHIP OF THE EARLY CHURCH AND ROME

During its early years, it seems the church authorities showed no interest in reforming Rome. They did hear the mandate of Christ to go into all the world and preach the Gospel, and did so to the point of death. It is evident they were making an impact: "Look at those who have turned the world upside down are come hither also" (Acts 17: 6 KJV). But there was no indication that the ruling powers were of any interest to them. It was not because the Romans were a defeated people; instead, there seemed to be joy in accepting the condemnation from their detractors. Stephen looked into the face of Jesus as he died. There was no sense of defeat or reluctance to go anywhere for their King.

The launching of Christ's Kingdom occurred in a time when Rome was at the apex of her political power, and the Greek culture of Hellenism was spread throughout the known world. A little band of people, known as Christians and considered to be members of a Jewish sect, were called on, by the nature of their faith, to live out their belief system in a world smug with its own military might and determined that those who lived under its political canopy were to give allegiance to none other than Caesar. Christians refused, and therein lies the essence of the story of the tragedy and heroism of Christians in Rome up to the fourth century A.D.

The politics of Rome was built on the view that the state was supreme. Increasingly the state was deified because Caesar, as its head, was seen as associated with deity. Within the pomp and ceremony of this nationalism, all were expected to put the veneration of the state above individual faith. Thus, allegiance to Rome was mandatory. For the Christian, such a view of the state was nothing less than idolatrous. It was at this point that the two kingdoms clashed.

In reflecting on the church of that era, keep in mind that, today, the church represents the status quo. In the European and North American communities, for hundreds of years the church was either close to or at the centre of power. But, in the early days of the church, it was revolutionary. The disciples were accused of "turning the world upside down." Christians were often seen as subversive to the Roman government because their allegiance to Christ was all-inclusive. Though Rome may have lumped Christians together with the many cults of that day, it is clear that Rome was offended, if not threatened, by the worshipping of Jesus of Nazareth.

The historian Tertullian, an African church father (160–225), in commenting on the way pagan Rome blamed them for all of its problems, said the pagans "take the Christians to be the cause of every disaster to the State, of every misfortune of the people. If the Tiber reaches the walls, if the Nile does not rise to the fields, if the sky doesn't move or the earth does, if there is famine, if there is plague, the cry is at once: 'The Christians to the lions.'"[2]

It was not so much a perceived Christian association with political unrest that seemed to confuse Rome as the way Christians lived, and their refusal to accept the primacy of Roman gods. The Christians could have had their own beliefs as well, but it was their exclusivity that affronted the Romans, who thought that their own gods were insulted. Rome was understandably confused by this religious sect.

An "Epistle to Diognetus," written by an unknown writer around A.D. 150, says: "The Christians are distinguished from other men neither by country, nor language, nor the customs which they observe. For they neither inhabit cities of their own, nor employ a peculiar form of speech, nor lead a life which is marked out by any singularity. ... They dwell in their own countries, but simply as sojourners. As citizens, they share in all things with others, and yet endure all things as sojourners. Every foreign land is to them as their native country, and every land of their birth as a land of strangers. ... They are in the flesh, but they do not live after the flesh. They pass their days on earth, but they are citizens of heaven. They obey the prescribed laws, and at the same time surpass the laws by their lives. They love all men, and are persecuted by all. ... They are poor, yet make many rich. ... To sum up all in one word—what the soul is in the body, that are Christians in the world."[3]

Christians felt the Bible called on them to give honour to the government as it acted under God's authority. Paul makes this assertion: "Everyone must submit himself to the governing authorities, for there is no authority except that which God has established. ... For this is God's servant to do you good (Rom. 13: 1, 4)."

Christians asserted they could not recognize Rome as supreme. So they were persecuted, not because they had a specific faith, but because they refused to say, "We have no king but Caesar."

Religion in Rome was not a private affair; it was intimately tied up with public life. Sacrifice, which was at the heart of ancient Roman ritual, was paid for by the state. The city, led by state officials, was absorbed by religious pagan celebrations. Note Acts 19, at Ephesus, in which the town clerk dismissed a rioting mob who thought the riot was some sort of meeting held in honour of a pagan god.

There was no consistent pattern of treatment of the Christians by the Romans during the first three centuries, but because Christians refused to be part of pagan worship, they were noticed. As well, by living a life which the Romans viewed as being unnecessarily puritanical, they stood out. They simply could not live their faith in a concealed way. While it seemed to others that they were being antisocial by avoiding the public celebrations and ceremonies, they stayed away because of the association with pagan gods. This was interpreted by the Romans as a boycott.

Although Christians avoided any kind of public involvement, their witness was not silenced. Celsus, the pagan pamphleteer, complained that Christian faith was showing up in pagan households. It also found its way into the army and into Caesar's household.[4] But what was its relationship to the state during this early period?

While there were periods in which martyrdom was the norm, Oxford scholar T.M. Parker warns us not to imagine that the tension between the Roman authorities and Christians was a conspiracy. "Rather it was a fight between the State on the one hand and, on the other, an organization which defended itself by endurance, by apologetic, by open challenge or by other public means short of armed resistance, going partially underground only when no other course was possible and never for long."[5]

Up to the time of Nero, Christianity was not seen as unlawful. Following the fire in Rome, Nero took out his vengeance on Christians, but their treatment was not consistent or continuous. They were a marked people, however, given the view of their refusal to participate in public religious ritual. Rumours quickly circulated, especially during times of difficulty, much as they did against Jews in Europe in the early twentieth century.

As well, Christians had no protection in law; that is, they did not have the right to live freely. Roman law did not operate on the premise that citizens could live freely as long as they observed what the law forbade. In Rome, the opposite was true: If apprehended by the authorities, an individual was held responsible for citing laws that supported his or her questioned behaviour or actions. Under this system, judges had wide discretionary powers. Thus, an anti-Christian, state-directed assault was possible, even though there was no law prohibiting Christian worship. It seemed that persecution was most often carried on by roving bands devoted to wreaking havoc on those who, by refusing to worship Roman gods, were seen as atheists.

So how did Christians respond? Parker notes two ways. First, they viewed political powers as being ordained by God. They saw the unfortunate mistakes of the Empire as attributable to Rome's failure to understand that Christians make the most loyal citizens. Even though, as Christians, they could not worship Caesar, they did pray for him and believed that the Roman Empire was a force for good. And, when persecuted, they prayed for the conversion of their persecutors. Parker refers to a passage in "Epistle to Diognetus," written in the Apostolic Age, which makes a comparison between the soul of the world and the Christian community. It holds high a view that respects human society, in which Christians are called to preserve natural morality. The writer acknowledges that "they are not of the world," but adds that their calling to exercise good influence on the world is their "highest order."[6]

The second way some Christians responded was by taking a more apocalyptic view: they saw the Roman Empire as demonic, opposing Christ's Kingdom. Parker suggests that this view was held primarily by Christians who were poor and less educated. Since most writers of this early period were better educated, the received wisdom reflected the view of Diognetus. However, Hermas did not concur with this view. A writer from the less-educated community, he took up the apocalyptic theme of the end of the age: "The black is this world in which ye dwell; and the fire and blood colour showeth that this world must perish by blood and fire; and the golden part are ye that have escaped from this world. ... But the white portion is the coming age, in which the elect of God shall dwell."[7]

Christians of both views shared a contempt for the pagan gods and rituals of Roman life. The pagan gods were not just fancy names for ceremony, but demonic personages who tricked people. An empire which worshipped such demons could only be an enemy of their God. Tertullian, grieved by the open paganism, prayed for the political leaders. His perception of Roman leadership was clear: "We must needs respect the Emperor as the chosen of the Lord, so that I might say Caesar is more ours than yours, appointed as he is by our God."[8]

Christians, in his view, had good reason for such prayers. If the Empire suffered, Christians in turn would suffer, so best pray for the emperors and the entire Empire. He offers this reason: "We know that the great force which threatens the whole world, the end of the age itself with its menace of hideous suffering, is delayed by the respite which the Roman Empire means for us. We do not want to experience all that; and when we pray for its postponement are helping forward the continuance of Rome."[9]

To Tertullian, Rome was just a moment in the plan of God, but a moment not to be seen as irrelevant. "A Christian is the enemy of no man, least of all the Emperor: knowing that he is set up by his own God, he must needs love him, reverence, honour and wish him well, together with the whole Roman Empire, as long as this age endures. For so long shall it endure."[10] Rome was God's means of holding society together until the End came.

The church, even under persecution, was making inroads into the Empire. Even before a new edict by Constantine in the fourth century, Christians owned buildings that housed their churches. Their leaders increasingly influenced the Roman community. As the third century drew to a close, the hostility and antagonism towards Christians by the Roman state was not strong.

CHRISTENDOM

In 306, in a Roman army outpost in Britain, Constantius Chlorus, chief emperor in the West, died, and his son, Constantine, was proclaimed successor. After a number of key battles, in 324 he became sole emperor of the Roman Empire.

This young Roman soldier, now emperor, brought enormous changes in the relationship of the church and the state. In the battle of the Milvian Bridge over the Tiber in Rome, in 312, on his way to becoming emperor, Constantine adopted the Christian insignia for his army. (Some suggest that, in a moment of anxiety before the battle, he called on the God of his Christian wife.) Under the aegis of the Edict of Milan, Christianity was given legal status and, in A.D. 381, made the official religion. The church, formally sanctioned by the political ruler, now received special privileges. This idea of a Christian state was new and radical to the experience of the early Christians.

This began the era in which the church would learn to use political power in inaugurating the Kingdom; it would last until Martin Luther nailed a set of propositions to the Wittenberg church door in Germany in 1517. Once the church had gained political influence, the longing for Christ to return and set up the Kingdom was modified because now the church had political power to bring in the Kingdom. The driving expectation of Christ's return faded. No longer did desperate life circumstances force Christians to rely on the hope of the immediate return of Christ. The blessings of martyrdom in the Coliseum in earlier times as a glorious entry into heaven were no more. The vision had changed. Now it was focused on the rule of all of society; the goal was to Christianize it and, by so doing, ensure that Christ's rule commanded all areas of society.

Constantine, in his leadership, was careful not to upset the pagan presence and rituals with this new Christian presence. In 313 a Roman medallion was struck. It portrayed the emperor in his helmet, the she-wolf of

Roman paganism on his shield, and a cruciform sceptre in his hands—an example of his skill in keeping all sides happy.

Constantine went beyond tolerance for the church, giving it legal freedom and equality. Bishops were given jurisdictional authority, as were civil magistrates. The clergy were not required to take part in civil duties, and Sunday was made a compulsory day of religious observance. In their prayers, soldiers were required to recognize Christian faith along with pagan rites. Constantine was caught up in various theological debates and, early in his rule, used the power of his office to decide on orthodoxy in the church. For example, he set up the Nicene Council to handle the controversy of Arianism, which stated that Jesus was not eternal but created. Although he gave the council freedom to debate, and even accepted the council's decision, which affirmed that Jesus was divine, it was evident that the hand of the emperor was now on the church.

He saw the state as responsible for regulating religion. Because the emperor had been responsible for overseeing pagan religions, it was a logical extension for him to also oversee Christianity. He was ex-officio head of the church as well as head of state.

The rule of Constantine was such a sudden change from the old ways that the church had no time to formulate its views. Whereas the state and church had been very distinct, now there was a mingling of the two, to the extent that the state saw as its role the Christianizing of society. It was Constantine's son Constantius who went further and is reported to have said, "What I will, let that be reckoned as canon."[11] Tearing down the remains of paganism, he made himself appear a Christian emperor.

The relationship of the church and the civil order underwent an important shift when the church was called on to take a larger role in the administration of local government. The Roman Empire, going through an increased crisis of management as a result of such matters as crop failure and barbarian invasions, consolidated its power by centralizing and eliminating municipal self-government. Because bishops were elected by their communities and more citizens were turning to Christian faith, bishops were seen as leaders and people of influence, and called on to judge disputes and care for widows and orphans. Gradually they came to take on local leadership in both religious and civil matters.

Constantine, in moving the centre of the Roman Empire to ancient

Byzantium (later renamed Constantinople, then Istanbul), made himself head of the Christian church in the eastern section of the Empire. He built elaborate structures and surrounded himself with spectacular and ostentatious religious celebrations in which people would prostrate themselves before him. In his public appearances, he expected people to greet him with shouts of "Holy! Holy! Holy!" A new feature had been introduced, called "Caesaropapism": the emperor of Rome now had power over the church. In the western centre of Rome, though distant from the spectacular developments in the eastern centre of Constantinople, Roman popes increased splendour and pomp in their ceremonies, even as Constantine was doing in the east.

In the wide-ranging Roman Empire, with its fragmented moral life, the church provided moral guidelines in areas such as marriage and family. As the church increased its influence, the lives of the citizens were shaped by the doctrine and teaching of the church. In this way, the church had a salutary impact on society.

The Christendom Model

Once Constantine made Christianity the official religion, the Christian church began to greatly influence, if not rule, society. Though church leaders considered the church and state two separate kingdoms, the church increasingly played a strong role. Referred to as "Christendom," church authorities more and more influenced society as well as church matters.

The church and state over time became almost inseparable. The church's message was mixed with concerns of exercising power. Constantine, even if well intentioned, failed to see the need for distance between state and church. Assuming the two to be one, he gave social dignity to Christians who frequently had been maligned and harassed, even to death. By taking over as head of the church, he effectively ended martyrdom, but he also muddied the waters of spiritual purity by adding in social and cultural self-interest.

This church under Rome is too different and distant to be a model for today. As emperor, Constantine was so steeped in running the religious and ceremonial life that for him not to take Christianity and guide it was unthinkable. In the end, the small, suffering church was changed suddenly into a community of politically and socially empowered people. To be a Christian had now become an advantage. Along with this rise in status came a loss of focus and commitment. The refiner's fire burned low in lives which had been lived out of love and devotion to God, not social standing or political power.

THE HOLY ROMAN EMPIRE

From A.D. 600 to 1000, a period known as "The Dark Ages," the western Roman Empire was assaulted by barbarians. In the early 800s, Charlemagne, a pious and yet powerful warrior, ruled as emperor over much of the old Roman Empire. On Christmas day, 800, he was crowned by Pope Leo III as emperor. His son Louis went to Rome in 816 to receive the crown from the Pope, a public admission that political authority could be finally given only by the church. This submitting to the Pope was an open acknowledgment that the church was a higher power than the state.

Throughout the Middle Ages, the growth of the church, and its increased hold on political life, led to its dominating the state. But, with its increased secular/political power, the church failed to provide effective spiritual leadership. Then, as the church lost its political hold, Christendom became more of a connection of various states. In 1302, Pope Boniface VIII was unequivocal about the absolute dominance of the papacy. In a quarrel with Philip of France, he wrote in the papal bull *Unam sanctam*: "It is altogether necessary to salvation for every human creature to be subject to the Roman pontiff."[12] However, the pontiff soon died; no ruler pursued this quarrel, and succeeding popes did not punish Philip. The monarchies had now gained too much power for Rome. However, it would be 200 years before the authority of Rome would crack from internal pressure.

THE REFORMATION

At the turn of the sixteenth century, Christendom still ruled most of Europe. But, within fifty years, that arrangement would be changed.

The relationship of the church's power and the state's power was about to alter radically.

For centuries it had been assumed that the state and church were to be intertwined. Changing views on the relationship of the two did not—even in the sixteenth and seventeenth centuries—lead to the assumption that the spiritual had no place in the temporal. That debate came out of the European Enlightenment of the early 1800s. However, at this time (the early 1500s), it was quite unthinkable for the state to be independent from the church. A close union of secular and religious life was assumed to be fitting and theologically acceptable.

Three church leaders, offering different views of the relationship of the church and state, emerged in the early 1500s: Martin Luther, John Calvin, and Menno Simons.

The Luther Model

Martin Luther, a teacher of theology, set loose the Protestant Reformation in 1517 with his famous Ninety-five Theses. He challenged papal authority, believing that faith alone, not the mediating work of the church, justifies. For him, redemptive faith was a gift of God; the church held a secondary role in salvation. The decrepit state of the Roman church only served to reinforce Luther's view that, as a human instrument, the church could be polluted. The final straw that broke his support of Rome was a scandal in which Pope Leo X allowed the buying of indulgences to help him pay for renovating St. Peter's in Rome. Tetzel, the German salesman of the indulgences, preached that a money payment would deliver a soul from purgatory. This proved too much for Luther.

As well, for Luther, a group of Christians meeting together constituted a church. The priesthood was not a special or privileged body, independent of the Christian community. In his view, faith rooted in one's relationship to God kept one from undue concern with world-centred issues, and the church was not to see itself as a competitor of the state.

That is not to say that, for Luther, the state was not important. Indeed, it was. It had plenty to do: "The world and greater number of men are and always will be unchristian, even if they are all baptized and called Christians."[13] Given his view of the depravity of the human person, the state—as God's provision—was a force with a duty to perform. The prime role of the state was to repress wickedness and inflict punishment on the evildoer. He viewed the two kingdoms as necessary but always looked forward to the final triumph of the church in the world.

In *On Secular Authority, And How Far One Owes Obedience to It*, he wrote: "Here we must divide the children of Adam and all men into two parts, the first belonging to the kingdom of God and the second to the kingdom of the world. Those who belong to the kingdom of God are all true believers in Christ, and are subject to Christ. For Christ is the King and Lord in the kingdom of God. ... The gospel should also be called a gospel of the kingdom of God, because it teaches, governs and maintains the kingdom of God. ... All who are not Christians belong to the kingdom of the world and are subject to the law."[14]

Although Luther divided the role of the two realms, as political and social disorder increased (the Anabaptist uprising in which tens of thousands were killed by both Luther's followers and Catholics, and the Catholic resistance against the Protestant reformation), he called on the state to re-establish order and rescue the church from what he saw as the tyranny of Rome. The irony is that, in the end, the church he initiated attached itself to the German state and, by so doing, became its subject.

The Calvin Model

Sixteenth-century reformer John Calvin was a remarkable thinker and leader. By age thirty, he had completed writing the massive *Institutes*, his commentary on his understanding of theology and the work of the church. Eventually, Calvin moved to Geneva, where later he ruled unopposed as a dictator and instituted his vision of the church as the ruler of society.

Like Luther, Calvin challenged the Christendom model by asserting that the state received its authority from God directly, and not from the church. The state did not have unlimited authority; its power was circumscribed by the authority given it by God. However, that did not restrain the church from influencing the state. Indeed, the work of the church was to reform the state. Calvin even went so far as to contend that the state was to be used in Christianizing the world but not converting it, for conversion was the sole work of God in the individual. But he did differ with Luther's view of the restoration of the created order. For Calvin, the world was not to be left on its own; God's people were called to engage it in renewal. In his view, being a disciple meant going beyond the Lutheran understanding of inward salvation to the believer as part of God's plan to bring renovation to all the world by ruling it.

For Calvin, God's will was the source of all life, be it the church, the individual, or the state. His vision for the church was as a redeeming factor at work as God was renewing the creation. This church was to extend its sway over the whole social order. The ruling of Geneva expressed that understanding. He once described the work of the reform movement in Poland as an effort to "establish the heavenly reign of God upon earth." As the gospel worked its way out into the world, those social and political structures which oppose the reign of God would eventually be destroyed, until the whole world came under the full and undisputed reign of Christ. Even though this reality was to be far in the future, that would not deter the people of God from pursuing God's reign as agents of Christ restoring the entire nations of the world to God's holy and final rule.

In the end, the influence of both Luther and Calvin linked the church and state, so much so that, throughout the eighteenth century, most Europeans who worshipped in a Protestant church did so in a church sanctioned by the state.

The "Otherworldly" Model

On the other side of the Reformed experiment was the Radical Reformation, or Anabaptists. Best known for one of its leaders, Menno Simons, the movement held a dualistic view of the world. Because the state was part of the world system, Anabaptists believed that Christians should separate themselves from it. Simons describes the two kingdoms: "The Scriptures teach us that there are two opposing princes and two opposing kingdoms: the one is the prince of peace, and the other is the prince of strife. Each of these princes has his particular kingdom and as the prince is, so is also the kingdom. The prince of peace is Christ Jesus; His kingdom is the kingdom of peace. ..."[15]

For Luther, the two kingdoms are interlinked in this age. For Simons, it was the opposite. He saw two distinct kingdoms, one ruled by God and the other by Satan. The separation was clear and absolute. The world is where the demonic rules, and it is nothing but a place of sin and corruption.

For Menno Simons, Christians were to obey the state, but not to hold office. The state had no final authority, and neither did the church have authority over the state. They were to remain separate.

John Calvin, Menno Simons, and Martin Luther were contemporaries. Coming out of a culture dominated by the church of Rome and its overwhelming power in ruling Europe, these three reformers sought a model they believed was faithful to the Scriptures, and yet spoke in practical ways to their situations.

Today, there are a variety of political theories rising out of these models. In North America there has been a revival of interest in finding one to counteract the ideology of individualistic materialism and the process of secularization. As we reflect on the Christendom, Lutheran, Calvinist, and Anabaptist models, the important question is, how are we to understand the relationship of Christ's Kingdom to the surrounding social and political realities?

LESSONS FROM THE EARLY CHRISTIANS

A Vision for Final Reality

The early church was driven by the expectation of being united with Christ. John the Apostle writes, "Now we are children of God, and what we will be has not yet been made known. But we know that when he appears, we shall be like him, for we shall see him as he is. Everyone who has this hope in him purifies himself ..." (1 John 3: 3). Two thousand years later, we know that such a moment of history has not come. Some Christians foolishly become so absorbed in predicting the future, examining dates, events, personalities, and national movements, that they discredit the central place the hope of Christ's return has in Christian living. But such abuse should not corrode or diminish our hope.

Why is the eschaton—the coming of Christ and the final triumph of his Kingdom—so neglected? Christians trapped by comfort and ease aren't compelled to expect Christ's coming. The accommodation we have made with the gods of this age—materialism, sciencism, and hedonism, just to note a few—camouflages the underlying imperative that, regardless of our own personal comfort, the new creation must take over the evil of this current age. A hostile Kingdom seems less threatening when we eat at its table. Those of us living in secure and materially satisfying circumstances are unwittingly caught by an underlying assumption that the final and triumphant reign of the King is no longer necessary. The heartbeat of the New Testament pulsates with the expectation of Jesus' coming: something that is lost in the clutter of today's material abundance.

The Work of the Kingdom

The early church keeps us from interpreting the Kingdom as being primarily concerned with the redemption of social systems. "Behold I make all things new" (Rev. 21: 5) does not contain the assumption that the transforming of social structures will usher in the Kingdom. John's reference is to the new heavens and new Earth that Christ will order at the end of history. It's not that social systems which shape our lives do not matter to the Gospel. But to confuse the redemption God expects of people with reforming systems is to misunderstand the nature of Christ's salvation.

(This is not to underplay the impact redemption can have on social realities. Indeed, it can make a difference. Human and social relationships, structures, and systems can be deeply affected by the way in which Christian disciples work out the meaning of their salvation in Christ.)

The Roles of Church and State

The early church made it clear that government is not to do the work of the church. Paul notes that the government has its own work to do:

it is to encourage social good and discourage social evil (Rom. 13: 1–7). But the call of the church is to serve Christ. The state, though it is Christ's creation and under his authority, is not designed to serve Christians any more than it is to serve those of other faiths. Living in a country with a Christian heritage, we too easily assume that our government is to be particularly supportive of the Christian church over other religious views. The New Testament gives no such indication.

That is not to say that Christians have no right or role in insisting that the government act in proper ways. Note Paul's sit-in (Acts 16): he would not move until the authorities came and apologized for what they had done. He insisted that the governing authorities act properly. He may have been making a point so that the church would be given fair treatment, reminding the state of its responsibility to properly treat the church and others. We do not know.

Neither do we ask the church to do the work of the government. The church has its own task: it calls into fellowship people who believe in Jesus Christ; in this community (body), members are nourished, discipled, and equipped to go back into the world as public evidence of God being at work in their lives. When the church tries to rule a nation, it is inevitably co-opted into using political power.

Judgment on All of Life

The early church also teaches us that the surrounding order is under God's judgment. Living in a nation in which Christians have had a profound influence on public institutions, we may be inclined to believe that what we have is good, and that a little tinkering will make it even better. Or that, if we could just construct a new system, then surely the Kingdom of Christ would be fulfilled. But all systems and organizations, be they religious or not, are under Christ's judgment. In his letter to the church at Rome, Paul analyses our rejection of God's truth: "The wrath of God is being revealed from heaven against all the godlessness and wickedness of men who suppress the truth by their wickedness" (Rom. 1: 18). Christ's Kingdom stands apart from all other kingdoms.

The Reality of Darkness

The corroding influence of our modern cultural and intellectual sophisti-cation desensitizes the contemporary church to what the early church faced head on: spiritual warfare. Out of our growing understanding of human personality, evil is downplayed and made to appear as an influence or force. Jesus had a different analysis. He defined evil as a living reality coming from Satan. In this world, in which the forces of good and evil do battle, we know that simply improving social systems or developing innovative political enterprises is not enough to undo the impact of evil.

Paul understood this: "For though we live in the world, we do not wage war as the world does. The weapons we fight with are not the weapons of the world. On the contrary, they have divine power to demolish strongholds. We demolish arguments and every pretension that sets itself up against the knowledge of God and we take captive every thought to make it obedient to Christ" (2 Cor. 10: 3–6). The early church also understood this.

The Test of Truth in Living

The early church also provided a model for living. It was not cowed by death. Today, too often it appears that the church cares more about its physical landscaping than the witness of truth. Such a church will not be drawn to the costly call of Christ and the Kingdom. It is so easy for a church that desires respect from the world to avoid conflict. Cloaked in this self-interest, the church is weak and without power, quite unable to deal with the tough moral issues of our time.

A Stand for Truth

In this age of religious pluralism, syncretism—a merging of religious faiths so that none is viewed as being truer than another—becomes the politically acceptable and preferred response. The early church thought otherwise. Peter declared, "Salvation is found in no one else, for there is no other name under heaven given to men by which we must be saved" (Acts 4: 12). This leaves no room for arrogance—regardless of how it may appear to others—but affirms that Christ's Kingdom is about Christ and none other.

✝

The church in its early years had little to do with the prevalent political arrangements. For good reason: Christians were trapped by a system which gave them no say. At the launching of the church on the day of Pentecost, it was a fragile and, at times, harassed religious sect. After A.D. 70, it dispersed throughout the Roman Empire. The history given in Acts deals only with the first few years of the church, a time when Christians were concerned primarily with doctrine and survival. We look to them and learn from their experiences, insights, and response to God's direction. In the absence of specific directives on a particular subject, we are reminded that, though this history is instructive, it does not spell out all that faith has to say about life around us. The underlying principles are set in place, but they are still to be applied in each time and culture.

It is good for us to be reminded that, when the early church did respond to a particular issue, it did so because it thought and believed what it did was best. And the Bible record is faithful and accurate in its recording. For example, Christians in Jerusalem sold their goods and lived in a communal economic relationship. Does that mean the church was right then, and does it mean we should use it as our model for today? Early Christians worked out of their understanding at that time, doing what they thought was appropriate and behaving according to what they believed was God's direction.

One could make the case that what they did was not necessarily appropriate. Paul later had to raise money to help Christians in Jerusalem. Could it be they bankrupted themselves by selling their capital items? Just because their experiences were faithfully recorded does not mean that what they did is always right for Christians today. We applaud their courage and learn from their mistakes, but we do not translate their experiences into doctrine (unless there is an explicit directive). We examine and learn, but we do not canonize their actions.

Living in a radically different age, we seek the call to be disciples of Christ, be that in relation to the community of faith or to the surrounding culture. We take clues given by Christ, the early church, and the church throughout history and use them as a guide, as we seek to do that which is faithful to the Gospel and, in Christian terms, shape our social and political life.

CHAPTER 8

Is Pluralism Just a Modern Babel?

While for many Christians the problems of newly arrived religious faiths seem at times to take precedence over the expression of Christianity, the essential challenge to Christians comes from a different source.

My experience with people from other faiths is that they don't want expressions of Christian faith to be lost in our culture. As one person said, the reason he came to Canada was because Christianity had created a framework of fairness and openness. His conclusion? Now that he was here, why would he want Canada to be less Christian? All religions share the desire for fair opportunities to live out their faith; even their differing goals do not usually explain the clashing of ideas.

The clash comes from another quarter: secularism. That is the challenge for Christians in this pluralistic world, and it is to gaining an understanding of pluralism that we now turn our attention.

✝

For some Christians, pluralism is a threat; for others, an opportunity. Some Christians who are alarmed by modern pluralism argue that, because of the history of Christianity in Canada, we should have the right to insist that society continue to adhere to the biblical principles and values within society, especially since all indicators show that a very large percentage of Canadians still consider themselves to be Christian.

As well, Christians threatened by our plural diversity ask what coexistence has to do with Christ's command to make disciples of all people. Inherent in the life of Christian faith is this inextinguishable light that seeks to illuminate the world. Such energy is not easily co-opted, and it is never satisfied with merely getting along.

What adds to this threat is the use of pluralism by authorities or institutions to prevent Christian faith from exercising influence in Canada's public life. When Christianity becomes just one among many world religions, it no longer is able to command any special place in Canadian life.

Yes, Canada is a plural society. While we have always been so, the difference now is that the plurality—the many different voices—has increased, and the laws rule that a majority view is no longer assured of holding prime position. Political theorist Paul Marshall writes, "Our challenge is how are we to live as Christians in this plural society? How do we live with our neighbours? How do we love our neighbours in the political realm? How do we live together justly with people of very different views?"[1]

To make sense of this issue, it is helpful to look at the primary ways pluralism is used. Here I distinguish between two of those ways: religious pluralism and cultural pluralism.

Religious pluralism is a view which asserts that, because many religions exist, no one faith (or world-view) can be truer than the others. This is itself a belief system, because it is something people believe to be true. Cultural pluralism is an arrangement whereby people of differing beliefs, ways, and backgrounds choose to live together. This is not a belief system, but a social arrangement.[2]

RELIGIOUS PLURALISM

Since religious pluralism is an assertion that one truth claim of faith is no truer than another, under this belief system, Jesus is seen as an important prophet, but no truer than another. Lesslie Newbigin, former bishop of the Church of South India, explains that, under religious pluralism, "the differences between the religions are not a matter of truth and falsehood, but of different perceptions of the one truth; that to speak of religious beliefs as true or false is inadmissible."[3]

Such a system of faith rejects even the possibility of a claim to truth—that one can say that something is true. The most that religious pluralism can say about truth is that it is relative. The implication, as Christian ethicist Max Stackhouse describes it, is that "no vision of God, humanity, or the world could be judged to be any more valid than any other view, and that what we have is some passing opinion or contextual eruption that has no claim on us and for which no warrants could be given."[4]

For a religious pluralist like theologian Ernst Troeltsch, there is no transcendent meaning in history; there is nothing above and over all, and nothing transcendent can or ever will intersect human life. For him, all religions or world-views are human expressions, each of which may be unique, but none of which is truer than the others. In that sense, all truth claims are relative and there is no authoritative standpoint. The resulting assumption is that no faith can ever make such a claim. And those who do are labelled intellectually fascist.[5]

Author Allan Bloom, in analysing the contemporary university scene, says, "Openness—and the relativism that makes it the only plausible stance in the face of various claims to truth and various ways of life and kinds of human beings—is the great insight of our times. The true believer is the real danger."[6]

Bloom, writing with tongue in cheek, says the tragedy is that people who are convinced that truth, as such, exists, are out of sync with prevailing thinking. The implication is that, because of the many choices, one cannot assert that something therefore is true. Increased choices create, not just more choices, but confusion. "If the typical condition of premodern man is one of religious certainty, it follows that of modern man is one of religious doubt."[7] This doubt, fuelled by multiple choices, philosophical argumentation, the mix of cultures, opportunity for travel, and the width and speed of the information highway, creates a superabundance of choices and a data overload that convinces people that, in light of all of these realities, it is quite impossible, and even irresponsible, for anyone to contend for a truth claim.

A follower of Jesus of Nazareth refutes such conclusions. The arrival of Christ's Kingdom dealt a death blow to denials of ultimate truth. In the mix of Hellenistic religious, cultural, political, philosophical, and mystical ideas and movements, Jesus announced his rule with no fuzziness over an exclusive truth claim. Jesus offered what no sect, military leader, Mother Earth religion, or great mind could: a way to understand all of life.

It was in those early days that the delusion of religious pluralism found its match. "In a fearful and capricious world, the gospel promised universal salvation in Jesus Christ; amidst cults of secrecy, the gospel was proclaimed openly in synagogues and market places; in a world searching for individual escape, the gospel took on the form of an organized church, a witnessing and sometimes suffering community of faith; and in an age when no way or truth was deemed compelling enough to demand the whole of human life, followers of Jesus Christ bore witness to their faith by the supreme sacrifice of martyrdom."[8]

Defending one's faith to the extent of martyrdom does not come from believing that all paths lead to the same gate. To respect the right of others to believe as they choose is one thing, but to believe that your faith is not qualitatively different from another, and then to die for your faith, is ludicrous. A professed Marxist, Professor Milan Machovec, commented, "I do not trust a Christian who isn't interested in converting me."[9] He understood Christian faith. He knew that, at the heart of the Gospel, is a voice that calls us away from all other voices. Truth compels us to tell others because it is restless until others know of it.

As well, the logic of religious pluralism in alleging that all truth claims are equally true breaks down. For, if each faith is said to be as valid as the others, it is called on to deny its own claim to truth.

Religious pluralism also confuses the very discussion of truth itself. Newbigin observes that the story of blindfolded people describing an elephant, often used to argue for religious pluralism, misses the point. One blindfolded person holding onto a leg describes the animal as a tree. Another, feeling the trunk, is sure it is the end of a fire hose. Each is convinced he has the truth. The conclusion? Nothing is really true; truth is only what one thinks is true, and each perception is equally true.

The telling point of the story, however, is that, as the blindfolded people fumble about in the dark, trying to decipher what they are touching, there is one person not blindfolded who knows the full truth about the animal. The sum total of life is not blindfolded people recounting their life experiences.

As a missionary in South India, Newbigin observed that, as he watched the acceptance of Jesus into the Hindu world, he was seduced. "Jesus had become just one figure in the endless cycle of karma and samsara, the wheel of being. ... He had been domesticated into the Hindu world-view." It was over time that Newbigin recognized that, by wanting a "reasonable Christianity," he had sought instead to explain the Gospel in his own terms. He concludes, "I, too, had been guilty of domesticating the gospel."[10] It is seductive to seek accommodation in order to avoid being seen as belligerent or insensitive. As well intentioned as this concern may be, it can lead to a modification of the message, a public posture of mutual acceptance, and the adoption of a world-view of religious pluralism. Newbigin sounds a clear warning: "As long as the Church is content to offer its beliefs modestly as simply one of the many brands available in the ideological supermarket, no offense is taken. But the affirmation that the truth revealed in the gospel ought to govern public life is offensive."[11]

Religious pluralism is an easy way out. But it blurs the Christian affirmation of Jesus: "I am the way and the truth and the life. No one comes to the Father except through me" (John 14: 6). Tough and exclusive, to be sure. But to skip over the assertion is to miss the point of Christ's coming.

Cultural Pluralism

At its centre, religious pluralism maintains that truth is relative. In the end, it is a belief system. Cultural pluralism is very different. It is not a belief system but rather a means of coexisting without resorting to legislative or physical war. It is an attitude which allows the constructing of social harmony, believing that people of differing ideologies, faith, cultures, and living standards can actually coexist. It does not mean that one group must give up their right to believe or assert that their faith is truth. In places such as Northern Ireland and Bosnia, sites of conflict between different religions or outright warfare or oppression by the ruling religion, cultural pluralism does not operate. Social commentator Don Posterski says that "a culture that is both 'principled' and 'pluralistic' invites people to be true to themselves, but also makes room for diversity."[12]

While religious pluralism is an enemy, cultural pluralism is an opportunity. The United States and Canada are both countries with many cultures. This was true from our very beginnings. But, with the arrival of an increasing number of visible minorities, our plurality is now more evident.

In our more recent past, as a nation we were more a single-coloured, single-ethnicity grouping. Even so, we were a country of people with various views—in short, a plurality. For example, in my father's Swedish community, assemble a hundred Swedes and you would find a mixture of liberals and conservatives, socialists and free-market advocates. This is cultural pluralism—various ideas, religions, and values living with respect for each other, even though at times in sharp disagreement.

Today we are a nation with an increasingly mixed national heritage. Canada no longer is made up primarily of aboriginal and European communities. Wars, famines, dictators, disease, education, and commerce have driven people from their native countries and, in their search for a homeland, many chose Canada, which in turn has increased our cultural mix and diversity. It is in this world of cultural pluralism that the Kingdom lives and Christ's people are called to live, minister, and affect all of life.

Newbigin defines cultural pluralism as an "attitude which welcomes the variety of different cultures and lifestyles within one society and believes that this is an enrichment of human life." He goes on to say that, though he accepts cultural pluralism, he wants to "qualify that acceptance with the obvious point that cultures are not morally neutral. There are good and bad elements in culture."[13] This point is critical, for if we fall into the trap of approving of other cultures out of our attempt to be cordial, we end up blind to moral flaws which are injurious to us all.

Cultural pluralism is a simple recognition of the many. It is not an affirmation of all aspects of culture, nor that cultures are the same. It is a descriptive label. It recognizes that cultures and faiths (or world-views) exist and that they have a right to exist. For example, I disagree with homosexuals on their view of what is biblically normative. I also disagree with many of their public policies. But I accept the fact that they exist as members of this society and they have a right to represent their concerns, to vote, to be employed, and to receive the same protection as all Canadian citizens.

Cultural pluralism, though, is not just an idea picked up as a social theory to help us all get along. It is a basic Christian affirmation that we—as God does—are to give space and allowance for people to think, believe, act, and hope with different assumptions. It is Jesus, with the unexpected directive to love others ("Love your enemies and pray for those who hurt you," Matt. 5: 44), who revolutionizes our way of treating others, including those who believe and act differently.

The Apostle Paul, in counselling Christians in Rome on how to live with others, built on Jesus' words: "Live in harmony with one another. Do not be proud, but be willing to associate with people of low position. Do not be conceited. Do not repay evil for evil. Be careful to do what is right in the eyes of everybody. If it is possible, as far as it depends on you, live at peace with everyone" (Rom. 12: 14–18).

Before the fourth century, Christians in Rome were a despised minority, living out a faith new to the culture. They had no privileged position. Indeed, they were persecuted and martyred. It is helpful to ask what life would be like in a country where Christian faith had no historical precedence or favoured position. If Christians in Rome were called to live in peace with others when they were a very small minority without any historically favoured position, how much more should that message be heard by Christians in Canada who live with the benefits of democracy and human rights?

The writer of Hebrews calls for Christians to "make every effort to live in peace with all men and to be holy" (Heb. 12: 14); Peter says, "Show proper respect to everyone: Love the brotherhood of believers, fear God, honour the king" (1 Peter 2: 17); Jesus, in the Sermon on the Mount, reminds us that goodness is extended to all: "He causes his sun to rise on the evil and the good, and sends rain on the righteous and the unrighteous." Jesus challenges their attitude to those outside of their circle of faith: "And if you greet only your brothers, what are you doing more than others? Do not even pagans do that?" (Matt. 5: 45).

The Scriptures leave no room for an end run. We are mandated to live at peace. No questions asked!

THE CANADIAN REALITY

Our educational system came out of a biblical vision. Educational curricula were developed with this Christian understanding and its corresponding expectations. In most provinces, the public-school system was Protestant, and the Roman Catholics had their own system. In Quebec, public schools were run by the Catholic Church. Both were Christian. This monolithic world-view was at the heart of our country. Today that singular view no longer rules. It has given way to a pluralistic model.

Even though social surveyors inform us that Canada is still very much Christian in its collective self-image, Christianity's majority position no longer gives it any more room to assert its view over another. The secularizing of faith by excluding it from public rule, and the proliferation of many cultures and beliefs, have made Canada an incredibly complex society.

As Christian faith was slowly but surely pushed out of the public square by the encroaching ideology of secularism, a variety of new religions worked their way into Canada, usually by means of immigration. The effect was to create a new kind of Canada. No longer was a biblical faith necessarily dominant. While it would be inaccurate and grossly unfair to say that the loss of a biblically based culture was the result of multiculturalism, it would be true to say that, as multiculturalism was reinforced by government policy and funding, the previous Canadian Christian claim to privilege was rejected.

This loss of a Judaeo-Christian presence was aided by a liberalized old-line Protestant Church, a reluctant Roman Catholic Church, and an uninterested evangelical Protestant Church. Fostered by secularists who sought to construct our culture out of an individualistic, anti-religious bias, this shift—away from a biblical vision—took advantage of a society in which Christians were caught up in narrow agendas, oblivious to what was going on around them.

Within a few decades, Canadians changed from being a religiously monolithic people—one to whom a biblical view was central—to being a pluralistic people in which no religion, no matter the size of its membership or the length of its history, is allowed a dominant place at the table. The old religious majoritarian position is gone.

The Charter of Rights and Freedoms

In 1982, Prime Minister Trudeau signed into law the Charter of Rights and Freedoms, which has fundamentally changed our nation. It has resulted in a series of court challenges as people use it as a lever to support claims that individual rights and freedoms have been violated. At the heart of the Charter is a defence of the individual (and groups) against unfair action by government. The Charter has affirmed that cultural pluralism is central to our way of living by assuring individuals of their right to be heard.

While there are deep concerns over the role and impact of the Charter on Canadian life, there are reasons why I accept the underlying reality of the freedom of our culture from the old Christendom.

First, it frees us from thinking in the old majoritarian ways in which the community was obliged to acknowledge Christian faith. The legal right for the church to dominate does nothing to advance the Kingdom. Some Christians prefer legislation to force the community to abide by a Christian view of life. A point of comparison is some Islamic states where the Koran is the final rule. For people raised in the West, such obligation is intolerable. Nevertheless, some Christians harbour a desire to obligate our society to set up rules and regulations solely according to our Christian heritage. Wanting your country to observe biblical truth and advocating the observance of biblical principles, which bring health to a people, has a place in modern life, but that is a far cry from religious domination, which does not.

To accept that our religious tradition does not rule by means of its long-standing tradition or history or because of its majority is not to say that Christians will not attempt to persuade Canadians. Neither will

Christians hesitate about influencing government. This is not majoritarianism at work, but rather Christians simply accessing their right to put forward their faith and views around the table of cultural pluralism.

Church of England pastor and teacher John Stott explains that "in social action ... we should neither try to impose Christian standards by force on an unwilling public, nor remain silent and inactive before the contemporary landslide, nor rely exclusively on the dogmatic assertion of biblical values, but rather reason with people about the benefits of Christian morality, commending God's law to them by rational arguments. We believe that God's laws are both good in themselves and universal in their application because, far from being arbitrary, they fit the human beings God has made."[14]

This understanding frees us from assuming that having the church at the centre of political power is the same thing as doing the work of the King. Often in countries where Christian faith is culturally dominant, while Christians are assured of a place in the political hierarchy, the church loses its spiritual edge. Lost is the need for people to live the Christ-like life of suffering, holiness, and love. The church, calloused by prestige and power, loses sight of the persistent reminder to make disciples. There is a purifying process in having to live out Christ's claims in an unbelieving world. Testing Christ's call in a hostile world has its own rewards. As Newbigin says, "Religious experience occurs in the sanctuary, but its claim to truth has to be tested in the public world ..."[15] Truth obliged is offensive, but truth defended is life.

IMPLICATIONS OF CULTURAL PLURALISM FOR CANADA

Cultural pluralism is different from religious pluralism in that it is not a faith system. Cultural pluralism recognizes the importance of public justice for all, without discrimination because of religion. A high-school student can know that, even if his or her faith is opposed by others in the class, he or she is assured of having the right to talk about it in school. The importance of understanding cultural pluralism is made clear by this very point. If the student is marginalized in the class or given a lower grade because his or her view does not align with that of the teacher, the teacher should be challenged. Cultural pluralism is a very strong defence against any ideological tyranny which might attempt to rule in our public schools and universities. It does not mean a loss of freedom, for Christians or for those of any other faith. It does mean that, if a church enjoyed special privileges because of its size or access to power in the past, it no longer does. Before the 1960s, evangelical churches in Quebec were attacked. Today, most of that overt intolerance is gone because the church that once had social dominance no longer does.

It is true that, sometimes in public life, cultural pluralism is used to prohibit Christians from having a voice. Some municipalities disallow nativity scenes, and some school districts eliminate any mention of Jesus Christ at Christmas. This is an exploitation of cultural pluralism. Instead, each faith represented in that community should have the right to show its symbols at special times of the year. The mistake is to assume that cultural pluralism eliminates expression. Political theorist Paul Marshall compares it to students gathering on the playground. The teacher asks what the children want to play. Someone calls out "Baseball," another "Skipping," another "Football," and another, "I don't want to play." "Well," the teacher responds, "since we cannot agree, we won't play at all." Cultural pluralism offers the opposite view: each person should have the right to public expression.

As well, cultural pluralism is not designed to thwart the ability of people to influence our society. Though the Christian faith is no longer accorded special status, cultural pluralism does provide the framework in which people and groups are able to put forward their concerns and ideas. It then becomes a forum of open debate, not a muzzle.

The problem for some Christians is that they assume that by acknowledging pluralism they are trapped by compromise. I believe the opposite. When, for example, a Christian argues against the widespread practice of abortion, compromise occurs when, for the sake of getting along, the other person responds, "I'll modify my belief so we can get along." This is the opposite of working cultural pluralism. Pluralism does not require people to change their views just to get along. Instead, we hold firmly to our commitments and learn to work with others, even though our views may be deeply divergent. Amid the differences, we seek a way for coexistence, with neither side giving up what it believes to be true.

For Christians who have known the central place of Christian faith in Canada, cultural pluralism is a shocking new reality. The religious majority no longer has preferred status, privilege, or the right to rule. Some Canadians feel this loss of a preferred position means that Christians now hold fewer rights than do minorities. But if an imbalance of rights does occur, it calls for a response. When people are given preferential treatment because of being in the majority or minority—unless both sides agree that, for particular reasons, that is good for a time—that treatment must be challenged.

Today, even while a large percentage of Canadians call themselves Christian, faith has little place in public debate. This Christians need to challenge. Cultural pluralism offers the right for people of faith to insist that media, governments, and school boards take seriously the right of people of faith to exercise their option to be at the table. Too often such opportunity is not allowed. I find this so with our national broadcaster, the CBC. Christians I know, employed by the corporation, admit that, if they press for the inclusion of a Christian voice or the reasoned comment from a Christian (especially a conservative Protestant), they are marginalized. To reverse that kind of faith discrimination, it is vital that we press our legitimate rights—as members of a pluralistic society—to have a voice.

The tragedy is that the church has caved in to the privatizing of faith and has left society to run as it chooses. But for Christians serious about having an impact on our nation, cultural pluralism opens the door to influence public life.

After a presentation to a federal parliamentary subcommittee, one MP said, "Yes, but are not you trying to get us to accept a religious opinion? After all this is a pluralistic world." He was right in what he said, but wrong in what that implied. Yes, I was expressing a definite Christian view. And yes, this is a pluralistic society. But he was wrong in his implied conclusion that, because it was a Christian view, it was therefore not legitimate. Canada offers people an opportunity to express views and make choices. When this is not allowed to happen, Christians need to contest the unfairness, not just for themselves but for others.

Cultural pluralism is a way of living with mutual respect, yet without basic compromise. Immigrants who come from lands where religious intolerance is the rule recognize that Canada is built on the

Christian view of the significance of the person and the right of people to make most choices without coercion. For Canadian Christians, especially those from a European or American background, this is an opportunity to unlink Christian faith from position and history as a means of imposing Christ's ministry on society. My hope is that Christians will move beyond racial biases or favouritism, ensuring that others also have a country to call their own.

THE WEAKNESSES OF CULTURAL PLURALISM

Any social arrangement for living together has its weaknesses: it may result in Canadians believing what Newbigin warns us against—that cultures are morally neutral. No culture is free of self-interests or destructive habits. Note our shameful treatment of aboriginal peoples. As wrong as that has been, it is also wrong to assume that their cultures are ideal. All cultures have flawed values and unacceptable behaviour, including attitudes—for example, of the Japanese towards the Koreans; Germans towards the Jews; and South African whites towards blacks. All of these attitudes rise out of cultures, none of which is morally neutral.

Another frailty of cultural pluralism is the effort to connect religious, cultural, and racial issues. It has been argued that cultural pluralism does not allow critique of a faith or culture, especially if the two are linked by way of racial origin. Sikhs wearing turbans in the RCMP was an explosive issue, especially for Canadians opposed to immigrants imposing their cultural patterns on existing traditions. It was also sensitive for Sikhs who saw this opposition to them wearing turbans while on duty as a racial or religious insult. Although some, in my view, did use this as an opportunity to let off racist steam, the right to critique another culture—even if it is closely identified with a particular race or religion—must be supported. Just because a person is a member of a visible minority, he or she is not guaranteed that his or her culture will not be examined and critiqued.

Cultural pluralism is also used as an argument that faith is private, and therefore has no place in the public sphere. Canadian public-broadcasting policies point this out. The rationale the Canadian Radio-television and Telecommunications Commisssion (CRTC) used in limiting religious broadcasting in the past was that to allow any single faith to run a station or channel would discriminate against another. What the commissioners conveniently ignored was that radio and television are always being used to sell materialistic ideologies, which, in real terms, are as religious as Christianity, Islam, or Hinduism. As one intervenor at a CRTC hearing asked, if commercials are not about promoting Mammon, what are they? There was no reply. The CRTC also failed to recognize or admit that to allow people of faith to support a broadcasting station is an expression of cultural pluralism. People are given the option to freely listen and support. If they don't like it, they can turn it off.

In public there is often a bias against Christian faith. The educational debate of evolution versus creation is a clear example. Evolution—a theory which says the strong survive over the weak, and that humanity rose out of an undefined past—advocates a world-view which holds no promise except the continual outworking of the principle of evolution. The biblical story of Creation, on the other hand, is set within an understanding of the source of life, the struggle of humankind, and the hope of Christ and the Kingdom.

Lesslie Newbigin says, "These are two different and incompatible stories. One is taught as fact; the other—if it is taught at all—is taught as a symbolic way of expressing certain values in which some people, but not all, believe. The first is taught as what we know; the second as what some people think."[16] Public schools tend to avoid the Bible story on the basis that it will violate the rights of those who hold other religious views. Actually the world-view or belief system called "materialistic evolution" has been allowed to stand as the "factual" rendering of the beginnings of human life (though there is certainly scientific doubt as to the veracity of the evolution theory), which violates the rights of other religious views.

PLURALISM AS AN OPPORTUNITY

My wife, Lily, and I, along with a few friends, were travelling in Jerusalem. Peter, our Israeli driver and guide, turned a corner into a narrow lane at the same time another driver entered from the opposite direction. There they sat, front bumpers almost touching, eyes glaring, voices raised. Then fists flailed the air. Someone had to move. But for both drivers, to give in was the worst of possible options. We sat there until Peter, muttering and shaking his head at such humiliation, moved. We cheered him. We told him he was the winner because of his willingness to get along. I am not sure if he believed us, but at least he appreciated our applause.

Learning to live in cultural pluralism calls us to learn to work with those with whom we are in conflict. By so doing, we work out how we can live in the same community without "going for each other's throats." An example of this is the Second World War story of Corrie Ten Boom from Haarlem in the Netherlands. The Nazis had invaded Holland, capturing Jews and any who would attempt to save them. Corrie tells of the time when a pastor refused to help a Jewish couple who needed someone to care for their child. "No. Definitely not," the pastor said. "We could lose our lives for that Jewish child." Corrie's father stepped forward and, taking the baby up in his arms, was heard to say, "You say we could lose our lives for this child? I would consider that the greatest honour that could come to my family."[17] In a world in which Christian faith was dominant, the oppressed minority was seen as worth saving, even if it meant the Ten Boom family might become victims.

Cultural pluralism, for a Christian, is not just coexistence or civility. It is a way of working out the Kingdom in real life. At the heart of living out Christ's Kingdom is a desire to be a faithful witness to the evangel of Jesus, the good news that Jesus has come; with the realization of Jesus' coming, we see all of life differently. Cultural pluralism is not something to fear; though there are dangers, there are also enormous opportunities. True, wherever one lives, in whatever culture, there are always opportunities for evangelism. But a culture that affirms the pluralistic ideal offers an opportunity for Christian interaction and influence which is missing in single-religion cultures.

"Occupying"

Jesus tells a story (Luke 19: 11–27 KJV) about caring for investments. The words he used were "occupy until I return." This stands in contradistinction to a withdrawing. In telling this story of a man of noble birth, Jesus makes it clear that the workers were to be diligent in managing investments entrusted to them by their master. And they were to manage in such a way that, on his return, those investments would have appreciated. He further reinforces the enormous responsibility each servant has in caring for what has been trusted to him. On his return, the master queries each on how well he has done. The first two are praised for their success. The third—who hid his talents in fear of the master—is handed out a most devastating judgment: "Take and throw him into hell fire." The tough consequences for disobedience meted out to the third servant are not a punishment for evil, but rather for failing to do what was requested.

To "occupy" in a culture of pluralism does not mean to just seek peace and harmony at the expense of truth-telling. Our calling is not to line up, as Lesslie Newbigin says, as if we are making contributions to a pot-luck supper. At the heart of our calling is a truth question which insists on a truth answer.

In Nazi Germany, a small group of Christian leaders found that their contribution to the debate on Jewry and nationalism was not enough. Led by German theologian and pastor Dietrich Bonhoeffer, they decided to reject the accommodation to the Nazis regime that some of their church colleagues had made. Some years later, at dawn on April 9, 1945, his young life was cut short by a Nazi hangman. He had risen up against the evils of Nazism and spoken in uncompromising terms, and, for that, his life was lost while others of his colleagues were drowned in a sea of compromise to the powerful Nazi machine.

Early in his life, Dietrich Bonhoeffer was interested in theology and faith. Beginning as a professor, he eventually saw his true calling to be a pastor. But a quiet pastoral life was not to be his. In a country caught up in the racist nationalism of Hitler, Bonhoeffer was called on to take a stand and to discern the evil of this rising empire within his own fatherland. He chose to voice strong opposition during a time in which most church leaders were knuckling under to the wishes of the Führer.

His concerns led him to join up with the Confessing Church, founded in 1933 by Pastor Martin Niemöller. Under the influence of Karl Barth, they wrote and signed the famous Barmen Declaration, which laid the basis for the resistance against the Nazis' attempt to make the Evangelical Churches an instrument of Nazi policy. In this document they outlined their deep opposition to extreme nationalism and the subverting of the Gospel of Christ to political power. Bonhoeffer eventually was forbidden by the Nazis to preach, and was removed from his teaching post.

When the war broke out, he was in America on a preaching tour. He knew what faced him if he returned, but he believed God was calling him back. He could not imagine staying away from his Christian colleagues when they were undergoing such oppression.

He did return, and in 1943 was arrested and imprisoned by the Gestapo at Flossenbürg. In 1945 he was hanged, but he left a legacy to all Christians, calling on us to occupy, even when deep personal sacrifice is required. His most powerful writings are contained in his book *The Cost of Discipleship*, much of which was written while he was in prison. I recall that, in university, his words caught my attention: when God calls you, he calls you to die.

The heartbeat of Christian service is to live one's life for truth. This is done within the framework of the one we serve: Jesus Christ made himself of no reputation, but became obedient, not to the power structures of Rome, but to the humiliating and deadening effect of the cross. The spirit that needs to cloak us as we work out our salvation and articulate a biblical vision of life "is not an imperial power, but the slain lamb."[18]

CHAPTER 9

Speaking a New Language

This final chapter is as close as I get to noting specific actions we can take. You'll have seen that my interest is in what it means to be disciples of Christ in a secular world, where the public sphere is often hostile to spiritual insights and understanding.

My vision is of Christians active in the public square. But what should be the nature of that action? How do I, as a citizen of Canada and a disciple of Christ, engage in public life?

As much as I love Canada, there is need here for a new vision. But that vision will come only as people filled with Christ's life speak a language of public discourse with truth and love.

May these final thoughts give hope for what Christ can do in our personal lives and in this nation. It is, after all, only by his empowerment that we can live out the Kingdom within the social and political framework of this great land called Canada.

✝

What Is To Be Our Attitude?

In looking from Babel to Parliament Hill, we've asked what a biblically informed nation looks like. Even deeper is the question of what Christians have to bring to enhance the qualities of Canada.

Christians who long for a more Christian Canada and insist on biblical principles as a right misunderstand Christ's Kingdom. For 2,000 years, Christians have struggled with finding the right relationship of faith to country. H. Richard Neibuhr, in *Christ and Culture*, suggests that Christians' attempts, in various times and circumstances, to meld their commitment to Christ with the political order can be described in five ways: Christ against culture, Christ of culture, Christ above culture, Christ and culture in paradox, and Christ the transformer of culture.[1]

I find Neibuhr's approaches helpful, but none of them is right for all times. Yes, the Kingdom has a transformative effect on society as "salt" and "light." Contemporary political events suggest it is so.

The revolution in Romania, which ended the oppressive Ceauşescu regime in the late 1980s, is an example of such transformative effects. One night, not long before this vicious government fell, Ceauşescu ordered soldiers to move in on a crowd protesting the regime. The people, carrying lighted candles, surrounded the church in the square to protect their pastor, who, as leader of the revolt, was hiding in the church. The next day, as the pastor was visiting the wounded in hospital, he met a young man whose leg had been mutilated by a bullet. After some words of encouragement, the man looked up at the pastor and said, "Don't feel sorry for me. You see, my candle was the first to be lit. Everyone got the flame from me. The price of my leg was worth it." This young man, along with thousands of others, faced a treacherous and violent government. By his faith and courage, the minister was a transforming influence in that country.

In South Africa in 1994, tension was running high as the spring election approached—the first in which blacks would have full democratic franchise. However, there was a rift between two major black factions. If the Inkatha Freedom Party, led by Zulu Mangosuthu Buthelezi, continued to refuse to participate in the election, blood might be shed among black factions. Professor Washington Okumu, a mediator with the Organization of African Unity from Kenya, and a practising Christian, was asked to assist in bringing about an agreement between Buthelezi and Nelson Mandela, head of the African National Party.

Michael Cassidy, of African Enterprise, had worked for years to bring about reconciliation among the races. He was present on April 15 when Okumu and Buthelezi were to meet at the Johannesburg airport. Okumu was late for the appointment, and so Buthelezi left to fly home, even though Cassidy tried to persuade him to wait. All Cassidy could do was pray. Buthelezi's plane taxied for take-off, but a malfunction forced it to return to the terminal. By then Okumu had arrived, and the meeting took place. Over time, the Inkatha Party agreed to participate in the elections, undoubtedly saving countless lives. Without political office, Cassidy exercised political influence by building relationships and supporting leaders through encouragement and prayer. The *Durban Daily News* carried the headline "How God stepped in to save South Africa." They quoted Buthelezi: "It was [as] though God had prevented me from leaving [the airport] and I was there like Jonah, brought back. ... My forced return was a God-send."

The church is part of a bipolarity: it stands against world-centred ideologies. Christians have a reforming presence by opposing those powers which run contrary to biblical values. Here are five different ways Christians can relate to the public order: through personal involvement, through institutional engagement, as the alternative community, as the "arm's-length" community, and through withdrawal.

Personal Involvement

This view is that the mission of each Christian is to engage personally in public life: because this is God's world, we are called to engage. There is an awakening among Christians to the critical importance that decisions on public policy have for us all. To ignore them is to jeopardize our future and the well-being of Canada.

Since the early 1980s I've served as a national spokesperson for a part of the Canadian evangelical Protestant community: it comprises more than 10 per cent of the Canadian population. There has been a remarkable rise of interest in public-policy issues, and an increased personal commitment to take action. This commitment makes itself known on issues such as abortion, euthanasia, violence in the home and in the media, attempts to redefine marriage, and the role of parents in education. These issues have galvanized people into forming groups and associations in local, provincial, and national communities.

From an urgent sense of needing to "do something about it," Christians from both Protestant and Catholic faiths have run for office at provincial and federal levels, as well as at the local level of school boards. At an even more grass-roots level—by attending meetings, writing letters, and raising money—the Canadian Christian electorate has expressed this profound desire to make a difference.

Institutional Engagement

This view is built on the approach that institutions and organizations are the most effective forum for dealing with issues of public concern. New organizations—including new political movements—often rise out of this view. Problems are seen as being more societal than individual. The Social Gospel movement of the early twentieth century and the formation of the Co-operative Commonwealth Federation (now the New Democratic Party) symbolize this approach.

Once the shift was made from the historic view that sin was personal to the perception that sin is social, institutions became the primary issues of concern. Christians shaped by this understanding formed protest groups, which led to political action and organization. Under the auspices of the Canadian Council of Churches, a variety of ecumenical task forces have sought to interact with government on issues ranging from refugees to poverty.

The Alternative Community

This view asserts that Christians are called to transform culture. Christian Reformed communities (mostly of Dutch origin) have built alternative structures in politics, education, and labour. They set up

Christian organizations shaped by their theological tradition in order to influence the mainstream.

For example, they pioneered the Christian school movement. Even at great personal cost—having to pay tuition for their children as well as public-school taxes—the majority of them send their children to private Christian schools at the primary, secondary, and university levels. King's University, in Edmonton; Redeemer College, in Ancaster, Ontario; and the postgraduate Institute of Christian Studies in Toronto are expressions of their commitment. For many Christians, Trinity Western University (Langley, British Columbia) is the university of choice as an alternative to the publicly funded universities.

Another example of an alternative organization is Citizens for Public Justice. It is a non-partisan political, research, and advocacy group financed by its members, a large percentage of whom belong to the Christian Reformed community, that seeks to confront public-policy issues and propose alternatives. The Christian Labour Association of Canada (CLAC) is a labour union, separate but working much like other unions, organizing workers in a variety of workplaces.

The Arm's-Length Community

Not to be confused with the withdrawal approach, an arm's-length approach seeks to build a church community that is distinct from the world. The purpose is not only to avoid worldly enterprise, but to model a very different community. Anabaptists (better known in Canada as Mennonites) have provided us with this model.

This is different from the alternative-organization model in that the goal is to be faithful to the Gospel on a community level, rather than to transform culture. The fear inherent in this model is that, by engaging the ruling powers, there is the temptation to use the same levers of influence as those who make no confession of Kingdom faith. Adherents of the arm's-length approach believe that Christians are to live for Christ without resorting to political power. Yet, at the same time, by setting up a purer biblical and Christ-like model, they will be able to influence the wider culture. John Howard Yoder, a political writer in the Mennonite community, puts it this way: "The key to the ultimate relevance and to the triumph of the good is not any calculation at all, paradoxical or otherwise, of efficacy, but rather simple obedience. Obedience means not keeping verbally enshrined rules but reflecting the character of the love of God. The cross is not a recipe for resurrection. Suffering is not a tool to make people come around, nor a good in itself. But the kind of faithfulness that is willing to accept evident defeat rather than complicity with evil is, by virtue of its conformity with what happens to God when he works among men, aligned with the ultimate triumph of the Lamb."[2]

Withdrawal

This was very much the guiding view of many evangelicals during the early and mid-twentieth century. This view was fuelled by a heightened expectation that, because the return of Christ was seen to be imminent, the only right way to serve Christ was to have as little to do with the systems of the world as possible, and instead get ready for eternity. Some even refused to allow their members to vote.

Within each of the above approaches there is a wide continuum. The withdrawal view, for example, includes a curious assortment: on one side there is the Hutterite community, who choose to live alone on their own farming settlements; on the other side is my own Pentecostal tradition. Up to the late 1950s, although part of the social mainstream, Pentecostals interpreted the Bible's call as requiring a withdrawal from social and political life. It was assumed that, with the Lord's return just around the corner—and God's obvious lack of interest in an impermanent world—we were to live apart. This is an example of recent shifts within many Christian groupings in moving from the social fringe to a more aggressive stance in taking their place at the table of social concern. Today it is the largest of evangelical Protestant churches.

So which approach to Christian living is most biblical? Each has a legitimate case to make, depending on times and circumstance. Indeed, each approach can seem to be appropriate at different times. The problem is that responses tend to be institutionalized and take on bureaucratic structures, becoming entrenched in church life.

Working out of these models developed through the centuries, each generation must decide which approach or synthesis is appropriate, based on what they understand of the call of Christ, the needs of society, and the political and social structures of the time. That said, an increasing number of Canadian Christians agree that the Scriptures and the Spirit are calling Christians to engage and participate in public discourse and leadership. The very well-being of this country is dependent on Christians who will engage in public leadership so that biblical values of truth, integrity, and justice pervade the legislative agenda. We should not be duped into believing that such engagement will completely reform our land. Neither should we see it as a mandate to reimpose the Christendom model. Rather, it is a call to live out the Gospel in a redemptive way, with an eye to Jesus' return and with a heart of obedience.

Not to take hold of the many tough and challenging issues our nation faces is to fail both Christ's call and our country.

THE TASK OF A NATION

Paul notes that the task of the political state and public servants is to serve: "For he [the ruler] is God's servant to do you good" (Rom. 13: 4).

So what do we do with the growing resentment against the high cost of government? While government must always be carefully critiqued, the Bible views public employees as servants. At the same time, government employees need reminding of what such a calling requires of them. As Christians living in a liberal democracy, what can we expect from our nation and what is it to do? I suggest the following.

To Organize

People need organization, whether they live in the wilderness or in congested urban sprawl. People thrown together in refugee camps or prisons end up organizing themselves into working groups. No one tells them they must; they just do. Moses learned that the only way he could function was to divide the people into groups and appoint leadership. You cannot get food, arrange for accommodation, resolve disputes, and care for sanitation without organization. For people to fulfil God's will, a place of relative calm is required. Nations have the structures to provide that. (That is not to say that Christians living in less favourable situations aren't effective in working out their Christian commitment.)

Organization implies agreed-upon rules. People need to understand the common ground in the group. The development of rules happens through the struggles and interplay of the community; they arise democratically through process or are imposed by a ruling body or person.

The strength of a nation is its people, and the strength of a people grows as they are encouraged to use their gifts. An organized community, by a responsible and fair division of labour, builds up the strength of the nation. As well, people are given freedom to work in an environment without fear that they will be overtaken by an enemy, by anarchy, or by fellow citizens who violate societal rules.

To Protect

Members of the Hebrew nation expected their king to protect them from foreign enemies. Guards were constantly on the alert in case of attack. Such protective measures were essential to the survival of the nation during its wanderings and once it was established in Canaan.

An unprotected people, caught up in the struggle for survival, lacks the freedom to progress. An unprotected society is fearful and unproductive. The crucible in which life issues are tested needs to be secure. A good nation then becomes the place in which people are allowed to live out the purposes of God.

We pride ourselves on our relatively low incidence of violence, especially in relation to the American scene. But the daily news, and statistics related not only to domestic but also to organized crime, remind us that, for all of our supposed disposition to be irenic, peace-loving, we too are a country of increased violence.

While we agree that the government's role is to protect and administer justice, a caution is appropriate. To simply remind government of its task and then to walk away is to misunderstand the nature and call of government as only one factor in the Christian life. If there is one mission field calling for Kingdom ingenuity and presence, it is the field of justice and criminal reform. The hearts of criminals, often battered and abused in childhood, need spiritual reconstruction. Correction and rehabilitation ought to be at the heart of our mandate: the insight and power of Christian faith ought to be a force acting against the tragic realities of crime and abuse.

To Care for Its People

One cannot read Old Testament prophets and not be impressed with their focus on the needs of the fatherless, widows, refugees, the physically violated, the hurting, the sick, and the impoverished. They reminded the nation that God judged, not on political arrangements or military might, but on how the people treated the needy, marginalized, and hurting.

The people of Israel, including some landowners who were exploiting their workers while professing their own piety, had so distorted the meaning of religious fasting that Isaiah rebuked them strongly, then offered this definition of a true fast: "Is this not the kind of fasting I have chosen: to loose the chains of injustice and untie the cords of the yoke, to set the oppressed free and break every yoke? Is it not to share your food with the hungry and to provide the poor wanderer with shelter—when you see the naked, to clothe him, and not to turn away from your own flesh and blood?" (Isa. 58: 6, 7).

Prior to the modern state, many of our charitable efforts were made at the instigation of the church. Today, the complexity of life, the diminishing role of the church, and the growing role of state reinforce our interdependence: the poor are more in need of help than ever. How we care for our citizens in need is a measurement of the quality of our nation. This is not to give *carte blanche* approval to all government bureaucracies, nor is it to say that government departments are the most effective means of serving people's needs. (A legitimate concern is that the charitable nature of Canada's social safety net may be exploited and, in the end, create a preference in some of its users for social support over work.) Yet, a fundamental task of the state is to care for those most adversely affected by poverty and injustice.

To Be a Model of Justice and Mercy

Policies and legislation of a government not only resolve issues, but serve to signal to the society what it believes is best. Some assume that government doesn't legislate morality. But the truth is that each government bill, be it on abortion, taxation, or money, is a legislation imposing a moral view of life. Morality—defined as what a people believe is right—is always at stake in rules that define how people ought to act. While spirituality cannot be legislated, governments do set moral guidelines, whether they know it or not.

Too often people with deeply held religious convictions want governments to legislate laws supportive of their own views. The call to government is to be just—that is, to be fair and not to implement legislation that favours one group over another. For a government to force people to live by the beliefs of any religion would be unjust, even if the citizens accepted these beliefs as basic for national life. There is no biblical mandate that suggests government should enforce any religious beliefs. The government is not called on to do the work of the church. Jesus did not call the government to go into all the world and preach the Gospel. The requirement of government is to support a fair and just environment so its citizens can live in an orderly, peaceful way, free from an arbitrary imposition of values and beliefs.

Justice also includes respect for ethnic diversity. Racial animosity is fuel to many wars. A lack of respect for other races is often a manifestation of fear or arrogance. Canada's multiracial strains can, in moments of national disunity, become targets of abuse.

Canada is a nation inhabited by immigrants: Native peoples who migrated thousands of years ago; Europeans over the past 500 years; newcomers from Africa, Asia, the Caribbean, and South America over the past few decades. It is a complex picture. And, in this setting, is there a Christian response? Yes, there is. With Christ as Creator, all humanity is God's expression. While cultures will clash, our witness of Christ is measured by how we speak and treat others. Christians are called to live so that our witness expresses Christ's rule.

To Choose Its Political System

Reinhold Neibuhr commented that democracy is that child of which Christianity need never be ashamed. Even so, there is no one biblical political system. Neither democracy nor any other political formula is noted in the Bible as an appropriate political model.

Canada has been blessed because our political ideals, and even our political parties, have been influenced by Christian thought and leaders. In 1981, during discussions on Canada's heritage, former prime minister Pierre Trudeau reminded Canadians that "the golden thread of faith is woven throughout the history of Canada from its earliest beginnings up to the present time. Faith was more important than commerce in the minds of many of the European explorers and settlers, and over the centuries, as successive waves of people came to this country, many in search of religious liberty, they brought with them a great wealth and variety of religious traditions and values. Those values have shaped our laws and our lives, and have added enormous strength to the foundation of freedom and justice upon which this country was built. ... It was in acknowledgment of that debt that the Parliament of Canada later gave its approval during the Constitutional debate to the statement that Canada is founded upon principles that recognize the supremacy of God and the rule of law. Faith played a large part in the lives of so many men and women who have created in this land a society which places a high value on commitment, integrity, generosity and, above all, freedom. To pass on that heritage strong and intact is a challenge worthy of all of us who are privileged to call ourselves Canadians."

To that the Rt. Hon. Joe Clark added: "I ask that we never forget the faith and the vision of the people who originally brought this country together, the Fathers of Confederation, who from the depths of their own profound faith took as their guide a verse from the Psalms of David, the verse that has since become the motto for our nation: 'He shall have dominion also from sea to sea, and from the rivers to the ends of the earth.' We pray that God's sovereignty over our Canada continues to bless and to guide us."[3]

During the Great Depression and a harsh prairie drought, two political parties were founded by Canadian Christian ministers: one by J.S. Woodsworth (later taken up by the Reverend Tommy Douglas) and the second by "Bible" Bill Aberhart (later led by E.C. Manning, who also was a preacher). Though their responses to the difficulties were different, both emerged out of a personal biblical vision. Their different interpretations of the Bible and its application to public life serve as recent reminders that people of Christian faith will interpret the Scriptures, and from that, work out the political system they see as faithful to their Christian calling. In other words, there is not one political philosophy which has a biblical endorsement. A nation will choose from those who stand for leadership. But to "baptize" one ideology or person as being more "Christian" than another is dangerous. However, we are obliged to evaluate a party's policies and politicians by biblical standards.

To Act with Economic Fairness

Economics is part of God's concern for his creation. During the rise of the Social Gospel movement in the 1930s and 1940s, some argued that the country's economy was outside biblical concerns.

Old Testament theology disagrees. There was to be an integration of money management with God's redemption. The exodus from Egypt included a plan God had for the people: politically, they were freed from a tyrant; socially, they were lifted from outside interference in family life; spiritually, they were called to leave aside foreign gods and enter into a full covenant with God; economically, they were unchained from forced labour.

In the promised land, there was an equitable distribution of acreages but, given the variability of the terrain, "it did not mean that every family should have the same, but that every family should have enough for economic viability."[4] After receiving land, families varied in how successfully they managed their enterprises. Some became wealthy, while others ended up selling themselves into service in other households just to survive. For those who lost out on economic well-being, there was special concern and protection, along with other groups such as widows, orphans, immigrant aliens, and Levites (Exod. 21: 2–6; Deut. 15: 12–18).

Overriding it all was a long-term vision and hope that there would be a day when "every man will sit under his own vine and under his own fig tree" (Micah 4: 4). Ezekiel holds out the promise that aliens with no land will be given secure tenure and will be able to share in the inheritance given by God.

There are obligations and responsibilities placed on people, but these only support the inclusive nature of economics in the ordering of God's good creation.

The Task of Christian Citizens

Christians are called to alert government to fulfil its mandate. A secular state, insensitive to God's rule, will miss warnings which a Christian, sensitive to biblical values, it is hoped, see and understand.

To Remind the Nation It Is under God

What a challenge in a secular, materialistic world. If Christian faith is relegated to the private enclaves of personal living and church life, how can a Christian remind the nation of where it sits in relationship to God's creation? It can't. And that's why Christians are called to live out the life of Christ, reminding the nation that the sovereign Lord is Lord of Canada too. These reminders take place in hospital operating rooms, union halls, day-care centres, courtrooms, cabs of tractor-trailers, fishing trawlers, factories, and election-campaign headquarters—yes, in every part of life. Our lives speak of Christ's lordship wherever we are.

To Remind the Nation That It Is Not For Ever

People ask if I believe Quebec should stay in Canada. Personally I say yes; my wife, Lily, and I have lived in Quebec, have great affection for the French-Canadian culture and its people, and very much want Quebec to remain within this confederation. But that is not to say I find the Bible says it should. There are sound arguments for remaining: one, Quebec in Canada provides greater strength as we live alongside our powerful neighbour to the south; it also provides the economies of scale so we can operate internationally.

As well, I am unwilling to forget the long history and the intermingling of peoples in Canada over the centuries. For such a large land mass and number of people to remove themselves from the national union could create a tidal wave with profound, even devastating, effects for all of Canada. But is that to say that it is God's will for Canada to remain as it is?

Nations have their history. They travel far from their early beginnings. Compared with our early years, today we live in a very different national climate. Amid deep fragmentation and hostilities, various groups have made new political, social, and economic arrangements. Canada, now in closer economic union with the United States, continues to change. What will that do to our future political and social arrangements? We do not know.

But we do know that God uses nations as he does people. Canada has been a "spiritual bread basket" for the church worldwide. Canadians have been characterized by their generosity. Canada's image and presence as a mediator and peacekeeper is one that I wish to maintain. Our effectiveness is appreciated by nations the world over.

But, again, this is not categorical evidence of God's will; it is merely what I believe. However, God's will is not detached from what Christians do. We do not live our lives without regard for our feelings and beliefs. If enough Christians have the will to keep this country together, I believe that is what will happen. The unfolding of Canada, to that degree, is in our hands.

To Remind Canada That It Is Part of Something Larger

Jonah learned that his nation, Israel, was not all there was to God's world. The real story of Jonah is not the large fish. Jonah refused to go to Nineveh because he did not believe God should have any interest in a nation so evil. To Noah's chagrin, God not only was interested in Nineveh, but spared it from punishment.

Nationalism has its down-side. It can create a preoccupation with one's own nation to the exclusion of others. This leads to wars, disputes, and flagrant disregard for the fact that we are all on this planet together. Canada, as a smaller, less significant nation than its southern neighbour, tends to be more conscious of other nations. Being small by standards of population, and given our history and the development of our national character, in spirit we tend to be more like the Swedes and Swiss: not big enough to seriously offend or hurt others. While we end up with an inferiority complex, it does help us see beyond our own borders.

To Remind Its People That Political Service Is a High Calling

A group that is unfortunately constantly put down and derided is politicians and government staff. Some say politicians bring it on themselves. We hear the Opposition accusing the ruling party of using its power for personal benefit; after the next election, if the Opposition wins, it is accused in turn of doing what the former government did. This only feeds our cynicism. It is here the Christian community can act.

What can be done to restore the high office of political leadership to credibility and effectiveness? First, the church must believe that public leadership is a calling from God and requires the most skilled and prepared people. Cynicism about political leadership (which I hear too often from Christians) will not encourage gifted Christians to offer themselves for political service. It is important that we see the profound need there is for Christians to view such a task as worthy of their lives and commitment.

Once Christians are elected, they don't need rebuke, but encouragement, as they learn what it means to be faithful to the Gospel in the cut and thrust of political life. Churches offer training courses, manuals, and refresher courses on missionary service, but where do you ever see courses in preparing leaders to serve in political life? To guide this country, we need to prepare people for public service. We think missionary service is a priority, and I don't know of a more needy "mission field" than Ottawa or our provincial capitals.

I find people in political life are deeply committed to serve and to be effective and honest in their dealings. Our current parliamentary system makes it difficult for members to hold publicly to their personal views. Party solidarity, enforced by our entrenched party-caucus system, expects its members to abide by party policy, whether or not that policy accords with the personal beliefs of the parliamentarian.

During the political term, our MPPs, MLAs, and MPs need encouragement. Once elected, most are startled by what happens. One MP said, "When I was running for office, people encouraged me, but when I got to Ottawa, not only did they forget I was here, but they seemed to forget I, too, was human and needed encouragement. They only called me when they were angry or wanted something."

To Remind the Nation That There Are Consequences

We cannot blind ourselves to our national failures and sins. As God has a purpose for a nation, it is not exempt from the law that sin will inevitably be found out.

Our current massive national debt is a clear and frightening example. Regardless of which government we blame, as citizens we are finally responsible. We elected the governments. And the money was spent on us. From time to time there is an attempt to curtail the spending, but too often those affected by a cutback cry out, "Not in my backyard." That sin we will pay for, either in this generation or in the next.

Our punishment may come from an internal backlash or something external. On the issue of debt, the consequences may come from other nations who, in managing their own finances, simply ignore our predicament and push us out of our traditional export markets.

This prophetic role of examining a society's weaknesses and sins and speaking with power and conviction is important for Christians. Without this insight, a nation can quickly become absorbed in its immediate self-interests, blinded to the consequences of its sins.

Is a Christian Political Party Needed?

Even after being with Jesus for three years, the disciples quarrelled as to who would rule in the future Kingdom. After Constantine, the church was enmeshed in the business of running the political order. The reformers—Luther, Calvin, and Menno Simons—worked out their own views of the relationship between church and state. European countries from time to time have had parties called

Christian, Christian Democrat, or some variation. Today, in North America, especially since the rise of the Religious Right in the United States, the debate has taken on a North American flavour. The issue in Canada, however, is not whether the church as an institution should be involved in running our nation, but rather what relationship Christians should have to our political systems. The question is, does a nation such as Canada need a party designated as Christian?

The question is not a new one for Canada. Early this century, two parties rose out of explicitly Christian thought, led by people with clearly reasoned Christian convictions and views. The Co-operative Commonwealth Federation (CCF) had its genesis in the Christian concerns of minister and politician J.S. Woodsworth and formed its first government in Saskatchewan in 1944 under Baptist minister Tommy Douglas. Influenced by the Social Gospel Movement, the CCF espoused a Christian vision of Canada within the socialist tradition.

During the same period, in the adjoining province of Alberta, another party was formed. William Aberhart, a school principal and radio preacher, built the Social Credit Party in an attempt to find a way out of the economic malaise of the Great Depression, to overcome eastern Canadian banker dominance, and to develop a political understanding shaped by Bible prophecy.

Today, the CCF has become the New Democratic Party and has seemingly set aside its biblical agenda. The Social Credit Party, now almost extinct, has removed any specific reference to its biblical roots.

In more recent years, the Christian Heritage Party has attempted to gain a national presence but has failed to elect a single MPP, MLA, or MP. Its narrow self-definition limits its membership to people who are willing to abide by a particular theology. In Canada that does not provide enough of a base to mount an effective political drive. Its activities, however, have given experience to a growing number of people at the grass-roots level.

The Reform Party, led by Preston Manning (who is open about his Christian convictions), has become a significant force in national Canadian political life. In the 1993 federal election, it was estimated that 40 per cent of Reform's MPs were evangelical Protestants. Though some people argue that Reform's social/economic/political views are merely conservative, and therefore a narrow representation of what many Christians believe, its success has radically changed the perceptions of many evangelicals with regard to Christian involvement in political life. This party reflects a determination by many Christians, within both the Roman Catholic and the evangelical Protestant communities, to no longer be trapped outside a political process that has patently ignored conservative Christian values. It is not, however, a Christian party.

The concept of such an entity as a "Christian" party is not without difficulties. Who defines what it means to be Christian? Will such a party be Roman Catholic or Protestant, liberal or conservative? Who decides the biblical economic policy? Will it be socialist, as promoted by Tommy Douglas, or free enterprise, as was the view of E.C. Manning of the Social Credit Party? Is there even a single biblical view of economics, child care, or the military? Or do Christians hold many views on all of these subjects, each of them claimed to originate in biblical principles?

Another concern is the use of the label "Christian" either to define a party or to name it. In effect, such a label makes an explicit claim on all that such a party does. Inevitably the party—notwithstanding the good intent of its people to be Christian—will do something that dishonours the name of Christ.

There is also a danger that Christians will feel obligated to join that party. Party leaders will experience an involuntary antagonism from Christians who do not share their political vision and views. But the question of whether we need a designated "Christian" political party continues to call for answers.

Does the Bible Call for Such a Party?

The simple answer is no. Nowhere in the teachings of Jesus, the history of the early church, or the texts of any of the New Testament writers is there even an oblique reference to the need or the call for a political party or a ruling government that is Christian.

In the Old Testament, God first established a theocracy from which society was ruled, then a monarchy whereby rule was undertaken by a designated king. Though everything Jesus says is in a sense political, there is no call for the people of God to set up political parties. That is not to say they should not. (Neither did Jesus tell us to build schools or church buildings.) There is no implicit or explicit command or instruction in the New Testament that mandates a "Christian" political party.

Will Having a "Christian" Party Do Any Good?

There are several reasons which justify establishing a Christian party. First, it would bring together Christians from various church denominations, including those who might normally interact only with those of their own Christian group. As well, it would provide a political setting for people gifted and interested in thinking through their independent philosophy.

It is much like the Christian school movement. The goal of alternative Christians schools is to provide an environment in which children can learn about life and develop skills, nurtured by a Christian worldview. The assumption is that, once trained, graduates will be equipped to move into the marketplace with a solid view of their faith. The same argument could be made for a "Christian" political party. If the intent is to nurture people in the specific field of public leadership and to equip them to serve Christ and the church in the political world, then the forming of such an enterprise may prove to be of value.

A Christian party has another benefit as well: it would alert the political system that there are citizens whose policies rise out of different values and objectives. Our political caucus system makes it difficult for elected members to speak publicly on anything but the party line. A separate party would permit the public expression of a point of view that not even Christians in other parties can speak to.

But there is a pragmatic side to this question. People have only so much time and money, and they want to know whether or not such an investment will bear any fruit. In Canada, given our diversity, it would be very difficult for such a party to win an election. Provincially, electoral success would depend on the demography of the population and its inclination to move to non-mainline parties, or the presence of a strong, Christian community who believes that separating from the mainstream parties is a more faithful witness of their faith.

The creation of a Christian political party might have benefits to both the Christian community and the society, but there is no call from the Scriptures for such.

Building a Vision for Canada

Given our history, our Christian heritage, and a desire to bless this nation with Christian ideals, how does a Christian, recognizing the varied political, regional, and religious points of view, construct a vision for Canada? In using the phrase "the nation of Canada," I mean a political entity created by a people (one nation) or peoples (more than one nation) and recognized by others as a *bona fide* political state.

In developing a vision for Canada, there are two prime considerations: that God is honoured by the activities of the nation, and that people within the nation are enabled to fulfil their calling. This is not to imply that all will become Christian, or that the nation is synonymous with Christ's Kingdom. It is to recognize that there is an accrued blessing to a nation whose understanding of creation and life is shaped and guided by a Christian world-view. The psalmist said, "Blessed is the nation whose God is the Lord."

Government, as a creation of God, is the means for a nation to operate. Therefore, those who have the task to govern do so by the authority given by God.

Joseph was given the task of governing Egypt following his spectacular rise to power. Years later, Moses was called to oversee, lead, and govern the Hebrews trapped by slavery in Egypt. Moses, in leading his collection of tribes, appointed "capable men from all Israel and made them leaders of the people, officials over thousands, hundreds, fifties and tens. They served as judges for the people at all times" (Exod. 18: 25–26). As they moved out to Canaan, Moses wrote laws and regulations under which this nation, now wandering but soon to be in residence, would operate.

A brief overview of the history of Israel makes clear the importance of a governmental system. The names of many leaders come to mind: Joshua, who followed Moses and settled the Hebrews into their new land; Gideon, who, although frightened by the enemy, responded to the need for protection of his people, defeated the enemy, and went on to give leadership; Deborah, a wise and motivating leader; various kings, the best known being David, under whose rule the country was unified and Jerusalem became the centre in which Jehovah was worshipped. The anointing ceremony under the instituted monarchy was a public statement that God had established the lines of authority to ensure the possibility of harmony.

Paul makes it clear that the role of government is part of God's creation and social order. "The authority that exists have been established by God ... For he is God's servant to do you good" (Rom. 13: 1, 4). And, "for by him all things were created: ... whether thrones or powers or rulers or authorities; all things were created by him and for him" (Col. 1: 16).

THE KINGDOM

The last of the beatitudes is: "Blessed [privileged or happy] are you when men revile you and persecute you and utter all kinds of evil against you falsely on my account. Rejoice and be glad for your reward is great in heaven, for so men persecuted the prophets who were before you."

In the first eight beatitudes, Jesus creates an understanding of what his Kingdom is by showing us its construct: the poor receive the Kingdom; mourners are comforted; the meek inherit the earth; those who hunger for righteousness will be filled; the merciful are shown mercy; the pure in heart see God; the peacemakers are called the sons of God; and the persecuted inherit the Kingdom.

In this final one, Christ shifts by calling us to be part of the agony of the Kingdom in this world. First, Jesus told us what the Kingdom is. Now he tells us how we are expected to behave by staying in the world and not escaping from it. This is radical. Jesus calls the church to think and behave in ways that are out of sync with the prevailing culture.

Observe the interests that essentially preoccupy Canadians. Then set them alongside Christ's Kingdom and ask what they have in common. Do our personal and public attitudes towards leadership and people in need match the guidelines given by Jesus?

This Kingdom of heaven is not that which will come only in the future. Christ has already come. The coming of the King at the end of the age does not imply that the Kingdom is not alive and active today. Robert Bellah, known for his critique of society in *Habits of the Heart*, said, "If we do not recover the language and practice of Christianity, if we do not discover that the Kingdom of heaven is our only true home, the place that defines our most essential identity, then not only can we not contribute to a genuine pluralism, but we will be lost in the wilderness of decayed traditions and vulnerable to the combination of modernity's suicidal infatuation with power, the exact opposite of the Gospel message."[5]

At the heart of the matter is a need for Christians to be radical in their understanding and in the outworking of the Gospel of Jesus. Canadians do not need Christians spouting more political theories. They need to hear the language of the Gospel. The Gospel offers a radical presence that is not merely words on paper but the way of life of Jesus of Nazareth.

Fear or anger at a society adrift from biblical truth will do little to renew it, and for certain will not bring a witness of Christ's creative and restorative power. Instead, I suggest that we must seek a new understanding and strategy of engagement.

Assumptions of Engagement

As we seek to be change agents in this pluralistic world, there are assumptions we bring to the task: spiritual weapons; being a neighbour; a sacrificial spirit; learning from the Spirit of Truth; seeing widely and with a courageous spirit. The Apostle Paul sets the context of our witness by reminding us we are temples of God (1 Cor. 6: 19). We do not engage our culture equipped only with our talents, education, personality, and personal goals. We are not to live as if we are accountable only to ourselves. We are Christ's by the offering of salvation and we live in a community which calls on us to be accountable to other Christians. We are united with Christ in our witness. As we begin the witness, we are anointed with the Spirit.

Consider these gifts of his Spirit: love, joy, peace, patience, kindness, goodness, faithfulness, gentleness, and self-control (Gal. 5: 22). They are like a mantle. They speak to how we are to conduct ourselves, how our attitudes are to rule us, and how they might modify our style as we give witness of Christ.

As we engage our world, we are to be ruled by Christ's loving spirit. Jesus travelled through the community, preaching the Good News with mercy: "When he saw the crowds, he had compassion on them, because they were harassed and helpless, like sheep without a shepherd" (Matt. 9: 39). It is too easy to be caught in anger against those who are destructive and confrontational. I understand that only too well. But an instinctive reaction of anger is not right, as the next story reminds us.

A small group from the Social Action Commission of the Evangelical Fellowship of Canada was asked to appear before a parliamentary committee on abortion. I knew our views would antagonize some. As we prayed before the meeting, one of our members asked the Lord to give us the spirit of gentleness and humility. As the meeting progressed, tough questions were asked. I could feel the heat rise. But, in the answer we gave, I noted a gentle spirit. At the close, an MP opposed to our views said, "I never knew evangelicals cared so much about the well-being of both women and the unborn." I suppose he had heard only our strident expression of concern about the lives of the unborn, and not that of our deep love and concern for mothers as well. Paul wrote, "By the meekness and gentleness of Christ, I appeal to you ..." (2 Cor. 10: 1).

At the same time, being fair, just, and compassionate does not imply simply accepting other views without examination. Social commentator Don Posterski puts it well: "Pluralism without discernment can lead to a convictionless culture."[6] Determining to find a way to live peaceably should lead to a tough critique of the public positions put forward by others. For example, homosexual groups lobbying for what they regard as their rights requires from Christians more than either an outright rejection in the name of truth or a wholesale acceptance in the name of compassion. The call for "fairness" from an opposing position in any argument does not mean that the logic of that position is unassailable. What is required is to discern the difference between treating homosexuals fairly and opening the door to a profoundly unbiblical view of sexuality, resulting in the breaking down of our understanding of marriage and family. Discerning the difference is key to being both fair and helpful in developing public policy.

To the public arena we bring weapons, but weapons not common to the world. "For though we live in the world, we do not wage war as the world does. The weapons we fight with are not the weapons of the world" (2 Cor. 10: 3, 4). The Spirit places into our hands God's weapons. How quick we are to fight words with words or political power with political power. Those who led the Social Gospel Movement of the early twentieth century, while concerned about bringing in the Kingdom, resorted to the same implements of political warfare used by those they opposed. Public protest and strikes, electing politicians, and eventually starting their own party were the only means they saw of instituting Kingdom principles. Although some of them surely did, little does one read of them praying and seeking God's will. In the end, we are called to acknowledge that our ways are not God's ways.

We also live in the Spirit by being a neighbour. When I come in contact with a neighbour (the story of the Good Samaritan reminds us that a neighbour is anyone we meet), I am compelled by the great commandment to love my neighbour as myself (Luke 10: 27). Neighbour Link, established by World Vision Canada, is a means whereby churches and Christians can give love in such a way as to help people in need. The Mennonite Central Committee has been at the forefront of caring for people in need and calling on their members to be loving in substantial ways.

Central to Christ is the sacrificial spirit. Discomfort and inconvenience are not to be seen as evidence that we are out of sync with the Spirit. Indeed, the opposite may be true. The Apostle Peter put it this way: "Dear friends, do not be surprised at the painful trial you are suffering, as though something strange were happening to you. But rejoice that you participate in the sufferings of Christ ..." (1 Peter 4: 12). Our culture is so antiseptic in its ways that suffering is seen as something to be avoided. Too easily we connect our culture's fear of suffering to personal living, and so construe our experiences so that discomfort or pain in our Christian lives is to be avoided.

We are linked to the church. As members of the household of faith, we do not live to ourselves. Luke notes Peter's first defence on the day of Pentecost: "Then Peter stood up with the eleven ..." (Acts 2: 14). An individualistic spirit does not fit. We are in community, accountable to each other. Not only does that give us encouragement, but it refines our words and actions. None of us is a John Wayne, striding off across the prairies, gun in hand, epitomizing the ideal of individualism. We do not live in isolation. What we do or say affects the rest of the church. And, because it does, we are accountable.

The Spirit of Truth is one name for the Holy Spirit (John 14: 17). Learning the facts and truth is indispensable. Misinformation is unacceptable. Our arguments, community, and the one we serve are discredited by untruth.

Germans have a wonderfully descriptive word, *Weltanschauung*, meaning "comprehensive philosophy of life." It reminds me of Jesus, who noted that his disciples were caught up in their own narrow and self-serving issues. "Open your eyes and look at the fields! They are ripe for harvest" (John 4: 35). In other words, don't be caught up in just looking at the field around you. Take a look beyond your fences! An issue is not isolated. It is part of a larger reality. For example, Francis Schaeffer, along with then surgeon general of the United States Dr. Everett Koop, warned that abortion was just the beginning of the life issue. Soon would come euthanasia and "mercy killing," he warned. This is a world-seeing Spirit in which we perceive how life is interconnected. They noted that, once you start on the slippery slope of caring more for the mother than for the unborn, it's not far to the assumption that the elderly or severely handicapped also have little in life and so why not end their lives too.

The Holy Spirit is world-seeing and end-seeing. Writer Stephen R. Covey suggests that, in analysing the importance of today's work, you should visualize standing at your own funeral, hearing your own eulogy. What would I want to be said at that time? This helps me more carefully decide what I do today as I live today with the end in view. For a Christian, the end is a certain and joyous reality. This can keep us from being caught up in or consumed by a single issue, without regard for how it might play out in the future.

A key assumption of our approach is humility. But our driving concern for self neutralizes our efforts. Pride, more quickly than almost any other contrary spirit, will destroy effective Kingdom work. I learned that, even when I believed my views were consistent with the Scriptures, my attitude was wrong, keeping me from doing good.

One day I was invited by the late Barbara Frum, host of the CBC television program *The Journal*, to participate in a public debate on AIDS. Around the table were a number of medical and social-welfare professionals. My role was to ask the religious questions. Across the table was Al, a schoolteacher dying from AIDS. I knew my calling was to speak truth into this debate. But I was not ready for what occurred.

During the early part of the round-table discussion, I looked at Al.

Instead of seeing his failings, it was as if the Spirit used his eyes as a mirror and I saw myself. What I saw was not attractive: pride, hatred, revulsion, self-righteousness. I struggled through the taping. I knew I had been found out. I had brought no humility to the discussion. Spiritual pride ruled. After the taping, I walked around the table, put my arms around Al, and told him I loved him. It was my way of confessing my sin of pride and restoring a spirit of humility. Without that spirit, our works and words become clashing cymbals in the culture. I continue to affirm a biblical sexuality, because it is best for our country and because I believe such an understanding is true. But my heart has been changed.

The spirit of fear and the desire to dominate will also destroy effective Kingdom work. Henri Nouwen has good things to say about this in *The Way of the Heart* .[7] We "become conspirators with the darkness" when we give in to our dependence on the "responses of our social milieu." Having the comfort of knowing we fit in and are approved of by the majority can become a "compulsion." When we feel that we no longer fit in, when we no longer have society's approval, we become angry and afraid because we are being deprived of that which we have become dependent on.

The Spirit of Christ is also a courageous spirit. In resisting the status quo, we refuse to be intimidated by opposing forces. "For God did not give us a spirit of timidity, but a spirit of power, love and of self-discipline. So do not be ashamed to testify about our Lord or ashamed of me his prisoner" (2 Tim. 1: 7, 8). The very act of courage will bring others out of hiding. It will model to Christians how to give a public witness.

How To Work

Mindful that we are surrounded by the Spirit and his truth, we don't need to back away from engaging our culture. But to engage there are some principles to help us on the way. Some of those principles I first learned through open-line radio and television shows. In one early program it was with Henry Morgentaler, the doctor who has become well known for promoting abortion on demand. The Toronto radio station linked me in Calgary with Dr. Morgentaler, who was sitting in the Toronto studio.

As I waited for the phone link-up, I silently asked for wisdom. I was impressed with three ideas: (1) Be kind. Railing against him discredits the one we serve and ends up making my counterpart into a hero. (2) Do not try to win the entire argument today. Critique the foundational arguments and show their inconsistencies. (3) Do not use Bible verses in this public forum. Yes, I believe in the Bible, but to use it with those who do not believe is to invite their scorn and repudiation of the Bible. Instead, use biblical ideas expressed in non-biblical language.

As I take calls on radio or television, I visualize being at a round table with people from various faiths and insights: some hostile to Christian faith, some ignorant, most uninterested, and a few open to ideas. My task is to engage them in a thoughtful, interesting, and challenging debate on the meaning of Christian faith. It is a round-table expression of public opinion. My call is to present ideas in such a way as to alert people to Christ, to challenge their false assumptions and remind them of the cultural gods they serve. There are many tables around which our culture sits to organize: in education, economic enterprises, and medical and legal programs, to name just a few. With the image of the table in mind, there are basic steps in making a public witness.

STEPS IN BEING AT THE TABLE

1. Get your facts straight.

For a number of years, gullible Christians have been hoodwinked into writing to the U.S. Federal Commission on Communication, calling on the government to reject Madalyn O'Hair's alleged attempt to push Christian radio off the air. First, she has never worked to do this. Though it sounds like something she might have done, akin to her objection to the Lord's Prayer in public schools, she has not. And, even if she had, Canadians cannot do anything about it. That is an American issue. Well-meaning people copy petitions in the effort to do something good, often all to waste, for one reason: they have not checked out the facts. This is an enormous waste of time and energy. The Gospel is discredited when, in arguing for even a good idea, one works with the wrong set of facts.

2. Decide what is the real issue.

If you are asking for parental involvement in the education of your child, do not allow yourself to get caught up in an argument over something like sex education. If the issue is to permit parents to have a say in what is done in the classroom, stick with that issue. Raising other issues distracts and pushes up the wall of resistance. Deal with other issues at another time.

3. Digest other arguments and views.

Take time to know and understand the other points of view. It will surprise opponents to know that you have taken time to understand their concerns. Knowing the essence of their view not only forces you to come to grips with what they believe, but provides you with a basis for response.

4. Test your approach with others.

It is easy to assume that you know the arguments and have captured the essence of the debate; then, in the actual encounter, the arguments seem weak. What has gone wrong? You have not sufficiently refined your arguments in advance to test out your rationale and logic in public.

5. Meet the major players.

If your presentation is before the city council, meet the councillors earlier. If the issue is with a teacher, find out who that teacher is as a person.

6. Learn how the system works.

Often Canadians, because of our familiarity with the American political system (a function of the enormous amount of American television we consume), assume that that system works in Canada. Each community, governmental, or political entity has its own way of functioning. Get to know how the municipal, provincial, or national system operates.

7. Be at the table.

Decisions are made at places and meetings. If there is occasion for input, or if there is opportunity for membership or participation, you must find the time and place and get permission to attend. Often a Christian voice is lost because the logistics have been neglected.

8. Build coalitions.

Policy makers make decisions within certain deadlines. The variety of interests, views, and opinions must be analysed and a decision made; from the varied positions, a final position will be hammered out. The issue may not be as much one of truth as of process. There will be pressures on the decision makers to come up with answers and solutions that best fit the majority of views. In expressing your views, seek ways of developing liaisons with others. Don't compromise on the fundamental issues, but combine strengths in order to influence the decision in the right direction.

9. Learn the appropriate role of compromise.

We have scrambled away from interaction with those of opposing views because of the fear of compromise. But we all live in marriages and personal relationships because we are prepared to reduce our demands or expectations. Likewise, in public life one must modify expectations and demands in dealing in public matters. The line to draw is not whether or not to compromise, but on what grounds.

During the debate on Bill C-43 (tabled on November 3, 1989), the abortion bill, some pro-life organizations opposed it because in their view it did not go far enough in protecting the unborn. I saw it another way. There were essentially three approaches the government could take on abortion legislation. The first was based on gestation: that is, abortion could be allowed up to a certain number of weeks. This was a mechanical view of life. And how would the law decide at what week to disallow abortions? The second approach was to permit no abortions, which was unacceptable to the majority of Canadians and stood no chance of being approved. The third approach, which was adopted in Bill C-43, affirmed life as existing from the point of conception, but it did allow abortion in a number of exceptional circumstances.

Although the bill allowed too many exceptions, I supported it on the basis that it was public policy pointed in the right direction and, over time, the number of exceptions could be reduced. The right principle was in place, even if some of the specifics were flawed.

Here the principle of the right of the unborn was affirmed. There was no compromise of principles. The conviction was retained. In the end, the bill was defeated in the Senate by one vote. And so, today, Canada is the only country in the Western world that has no legal restrictions on abortion—at least in part because those who wanted to do right failed to understand the legitimate place of compromise in the writing of public policy.

10. Finally, do not be weary in well-doing.

The shaping of an idea and then the moving of it into the laws and policies of our society does not happen overnight. Remember that the takeover by ruling ideologies occurred over many years. If your concern is worth the effort, then use the opportunity and structure to pursue your agenda and goal.

WHAT WILL NOT WORK

I am called to follow Christ in all of life. This I bring to any discussion. Sitting around the table of pluralism, it is a challenge to remain faithful to the Gospel and yet work in a cordial manner. Given that a dominant Christian presence is gone, we are called, regardless of the setting, to be faithful. So, in this new setting, what will not work to advance a biblical vision? I suggest there are three positions that will not work.

1. Imposing

The first is to try to impose the values of a Christian faith on an uninterested, hostile, or non-believing public. Christians often ask, "Why must we always give in to others when our country was founded on Christian principles? Do we not have the right to insist that these be retained?"

There are two responses. First, in the Charter of Rights and Freedoms, Canada has codified protection so that people's religious rights, along with others, may not be violated. We cannot turn back the clock.

But, more basic to our spiritual calling, there is the tough question "What would Jesus do? Is that the way of Christ?" Even though we have experienced centuries of the dominance of Christendom in the Western and European communities, does that give us the right to insist that people live the way we have known? I hardly think that conforms to either the Spirit or the ways of Christ.

2. Doing nothing

It is difficult to engage with those who are indifferent or hostile to our views or concerns. How easy it is to back away and live my spiritual life within the confines and protection of those who believe as I do. This carries with it two hazards. First, it simply allows the forces that have already displaced Christian faith to continue without resistance. If the reshaping of our society holds any interest—even within the belief that the return of Christ is near—then the cost of influencing the direction of our society is high. Beyond the issue of cause/effect there is one of obedience to Christ. He calls us to be "in the world," even though we are not to be "of the world."

3. Building barriers

Another response is to build barriers against those you oppose. This does create a certain comfort by excluding opposing views from your domain. But it accomplishes nothing. We live in a nation in which public policies are written and decided by people within an environment of secularism. This we must not forget. To access that decision-making process and to achieve public policies that reflect a biblical vision for life requires, not the building of barriers, but the tearing down of walls.

CALLED TO SPEAK GOD'S LANGUAGE

Language is the essential means whereby beliefs and feelings are expressed. In the Christian tradition, words are of great importance. God spoke and Creation became a reality. God spoke to Moses and gave the Ten Commandments. The prophets spoke God's word and people were expected to understand and obey. Jesus Christ is called "The Word." The Bible is a written document that conveys truth. For Christians, the notion of words as the conveyors of truth is critical.

When people who confess Christ speak about Canada, its leadership, or its people in the language of resentment, bitterness, and cynicism, two languages are in conflict. One may not be surprised when a person hostile to Christian faith expresses cynical views of Canada. What is surprising and dismaying is the language coming from the mouths of those who should know what Christ expects of his followers.

Listen to what is said, be it about taxation, bilingualism, Quebec, "the rest of Canada," multiculturalism, immigration, free trade, Native demands, partisan politics, or the multiple layers of governmental bureaucracy. What is lacking is a language that expresses a biblical vision of what God would have for this country. From the right wing, there will be complaints about taxation and about the incessant demands by unions. From the left wing, the complaint may be over the unfair advantage business has over the worker. From the West, the control of Canada by Ontario and Quebec. From Quebec, the lack of understanding the rest of Canada shows to their cultural needs. The variations of complaints are limited only by the topics and points of view.

Within these many discussions, one wonders, does Christ make any difference in the way we view our nation? Are our self-interests so overriding as to exclude the fundamental question of what Christ expects of us? Have the resentments gone so deep in our lives as to cut us off from any ability to think and ask the biblical questions?

When we wistfully long for a renewal of the kind of society we had when "Canada was Christian," we must ask, what is there about the life of the church in Canada which would attract our society to ask it for guidance? Does the church have something of substance to say to the culture, or has it become just another noisy group within a society that wants more and more?

Responding to the questions of our culture requires a new orientation. Now that the overriding assumptions and evident Christian influences within our nation are a thing of the past, today we at times feel like foreigners, struggling to live in this land. We are like the exiled Hebrews trying to sing in Babylon. In exile they were asked to sing the songs of Zion—that is, Jerusalem. The psalmist wrote: "By the rivers of Babylon, there we sat down and wept, when we remembered Zion. Upon the willows in the midst of it we hung our harps. For there our captors demanded of us songs, and our tormentors' mirth, saying, 'Sing us one of the songs of Zion.'" The singer asked, "How can we sing the songs of Zion in a foreign land?" (Psa. 137: 1–4).

The answer? You can't.

Exiled from Israel, missing the familiar sounds of the homeland and the great celebrations and feasts of the Jewish calendar, the psalmist found it impossible to sing the songs of Zion in Babylon. To sing the songs of the past in a culture paganized by its rejection of the transcendent and secularized by its laws and policies is impossible.

The poet could not sing the songs of his past culture, that is, Zion or Jerusalem. But he could have sung the songs of the King. You can sing the songs of faith anywhere. Could it be that in our longing for the seemingly pleasant days of the past, in which the common song of faith could be sung in the public square of this nation, we are trying to sing the cultural songs of Zion instead of the liberating songs of the King?

We can rail against the incompetence of leaders in all spheres of public life; we can decry the moral bankruptcy of their policies and plans; we can go so far as to call for their downfall. But is that song any different from what we hear in the roads and squares of the Babylons of this nation? The songs of the cultural past, as nice as they seem in memory, will not be listened to today. Does that mean that the message of God is irrelevant today? No. But the song must be that of faith and truth. It must come from the heart of the King, and not from the culture. The culture of the church is often irrelevant to the message of the Kingdom of Christ and becomes a barrier, preventing people from understanding and entering the Kingdom.

And who will sing the songs of the King? Will they be heard in the arena of political sniping? Will the melody line be heard in the harsh sounds of anti-this and anti-that? If people who claim to be of the King do not sing the King's songs, then who will?

The tragedy of Canada is not primarily our political fragmentation or the disagreements over Native land claims, forms of taxation, or even public leadership. It is that the church has stopped singing the song of biblical faith and life in the public square. Or do we sing off key? By not saying that only the truth will set you free, we have a society that hopes life will get better. We have layered our message with so much of the world that our tune is neither distinctive nor noticed.

We know that Christian faith has profoundly shaped our language, vision, institutions, and policies. But, with the radical shift in cultural assumptions, many Christians wonder if there is any value in expending effort in attempting to reinstate Christian norms. Some will ask, "Is it possible?" Others, "Is it worthwhile?" And still others, "Does Christ even call for it?"

These questions are vital. The Bible gives us the mandate to care for all of creation. Many people will care about Canada without any reference to the biblical call, but that does not exclude me from being obedient to biblical faith. Furthermore, in being a citizen, I have legitimate concerns that require me to respond.

This smacks hard against the pervasive attitude of this age. Indeed, when we read the Bible carefully—without the filters of overfamiliarity and our many cultural excuses—it is troubling to note what we are called to be. But that is the song we are called to sing. It is time for us to return to that song.

A rabbi in Britain supported Christianity as the predominant religion in the public schools in England. It was his conviction that it would be better to be a Jew in a Christian country than to be a Jew in a secular country. Then he added a proviso, "provided it is a Christian country."

He went on to tell the story of a rabbi who gained an audience with the czar and the czarina to ask their assistance about the problem of anti-Semitism in nineteenth-century Russia. The czarina rudely commented, "If they want peace, then let the Jews become Christians."

The rabbi thought for a moment and replied, "No, let the Christians become Christians, then we shall all have peace."

What we have to offer is Jesus Christ, not a mimicry of the surrounding culture. He calls us to see life through the lens of eternity and not the demands of time. We must hear the language of his creation and his redeeming call, and not the surrounding noise.

The Unity of Many Tongues

On the day of Pentecost, the Gospel was preached in the many tongues to those who had gathered in Jerusalem for the Hebrew celebration. The message of Christ was not tied to the immediate culture, nor heard only in the Greek language. It was for all people, within the sphere of their own languages. What a spectacular display of God's will that his message was heard by every culture. God is not against culture; it serves as a vehicle of life. The dividing line we too often cross over is making the culture the final word on truth. All cultures are circumscribed by both space and time. Canada has many wonderful ideas and views to offer the world. Could it be that we have been so shaped by the size and difficulties of our land that our thinking has been stunted, and our language curtailed?

Over all that I love and appreciate about being a Canadian, I know that Christ calls me to understand the language of God's Word. That language calls me to rise above the spirit of the age and be guided by the Spirit of the Ages.

Notes

Chapter 1: The Babel Syndrome: A Country Fragmented

1. Andrew H. Malcolm, *The Canadians* (Markham, ON: Fitzhenry & Whiteside, 1985), p. 10.
2. Throughout this book the term "nation" is used loosely to mean in most instances a country or state. Technically "nation" means a people with a common language, culture, history, and vision of life, whereas "country" or "state" refers to a geographically defined area in which a governing body rules. Canada, for example, is made up of many nations. "First Nations" is a designation used by aboriginal peoples to denote an arrangement whereby a number of aboriginal nations cooperate. At the core of this is the clear identity they have with their particular "nation" even though they live within the country or state called Canada.
3. The term "mosaic madness" was first used by Canadian sociologist Reginald Bibby in his *Mosaic Madness* (Toronto: Stoddart, 1990) to describe the radical alteration of the Canadian cultural landscape by many cultures and the increased fragmentation of Canada by the multicultural policies of government.
4. Seymour Lipset, *Continental Divide* (New York: Routledge, 1990), p. 9.
5. Angus Reid polling results as reported in *Maclean's*, April 12, 1993: "God Is Alive." pp. 32–50.
6. F. Underhill, *In Search of Canadian Liberalism* (Toronto: Macmillan of Canada, 1960), p. 222.

Chapter 2: Was Canada Ever Christian?

1. John S. Moir, "The Search for a Christian Canada," *Arc* 20 (1992), 19.
2. Mark Noll, Nathan Hatch, and George Marsden, *The Search for Christian America* (Colorado Springs: Helmers & Howard, 1989), p. 31.
3. H.P. Biggar, ed., *Works of Samuel de Champlain* (Toronto: Champlain Society, 1922–36) pp. 16–17.
4. George Rawlyk, *Champions of the Truth: Fundamentalism, Modernism and the Maritime Baptists* (Montreal: McGill–Queen's University Press, 1990), p. 26.
5. Maurice W. Armstrong, "Neutrality and Religion in Revolutionary Nova

Scotia," in *Historical Essays on the Atlantic Provinces*, ed. George A. Rawlyk (Toronto: McClelland & Stewart, 1967), p. 34.

6. John Webster Grant, *A Profusion of Spires* (Toronto: University of Toronto Press, 1988), p. 95.

7. J.L.H. Henderson, ed., *Strachan: Documents and Opinions* (Toronto: McClelland & Stewart, 1969), p. 94.

8. Egerton Ryerson, *Letters from the Reverend Egerton Ryerson to the Hon. and Reverend Doctor Strachan* (Kingston, 1828), p. 17.

9. John Webster Grant, *The Church in the Canadian Era* (Burlington, ON: Welch, 1988).

10. John Webster Grant, *Moon of Wintertime* (Toronto: University of Toronto Press, 1984), p. 205.

11. Census figures for 1981 show that 92 per cent of Canada's aboriginal population claims Christian affiliation. Of these, the largest groups are those which expended the most effort on missions during the nineteenth century: Catholic (53 per cent), Anglican (20 per cent), and United Church (9 per cent). Those indicating "No religious preference" comprised 6 per cent.

12. C.E. Silcox, *Church Union in Canada: Its Causes and Consequences* (New York: Institute of Social and Religious Research, 1933).

13. John W. Grant, *The Canadian Experience of Church Union* (London: Lutterworth, 1967), p. 23.

14. Ibid., pp. 28–29.

15. John G. Stackhouse, Jr., "Whose Dominion? Christianity and Canadian Culture Historically Considered," *CRUX* 28/2 (June 1992), 29–35.

Chapter 3: How Did We Lose a Biblical Centre?

1. John Webster Grant, *The Church in the Canadian Era* (Burlington, ON: Welch, 1988), p. 240.

2. Ibid., p. 26.

3. David B. Marshall, *Secularizing the Faith: Canadian Protestant Clergy and the Crisis of Belief, 1850–1940* (Toronto: University of Toronto Press, 1992), p. 4.

4. S.D. Clark, *The Developing Canadian Community* (Toronto: University of Toronto Press, 1962), p. 168.

5. William Westfall, *Two Worlds: The Protestant Culture of Nineteenth-Century Ontario* (Montreal: McGill–Queen's University Press, 1989), pp. 107–111.

6. J. Donald Wilson, "Religion and Education: The Other Side of Pluralism," in *Canadian Education in the 1980s* (Calgary: Detselig Enterprises, 1981), p. 99.

7. Douglas Lawr and Robert D. Gidney, eds., *Educating Canadians: A Documentary History of Public Education* (Toronto: Van Nostrand Reinhold, 1973), pp. 69–70.

8. Bruce Curtis, *Building the Educational State: Canada West, 1936–1871* (London:

Althouse Press, 1988), pp. 110–11.

9. Carl Berger, *Science, God and Nature in Victorian Canada* (Toronto: University of Toronto Press, 1983), pp. 54–55.

10. Os Guinness, *The Dust of Death* (Downers Grove, IL: InterVarsity, 1973), p. 8.

11. Marshall, *Secularizing the Faith*, p. 57.

12. Ibid.

13. Michael Gauvreau, *The Evangelical Century* (Montreal & Kingston: McGill–Queen's University Press, 1991), p. 147.

14. Marshall, *Secularizing the Faith*, p. 71.

15. Grant, *The Church in the Canadian Era*, pp. 102–103.

16. Richard Allen, *The Social Passion: Religion and Social Reform in Canada, 1914–28* (Toronto: University of Toronto Press, 1973), p. 8.

17. George Grant, *Technology and Empire* (Toronto: Anansi, 1969), p. 114.

18. *Equality for All: Report of the Parliamentary Committee on Equality Rights* (Ottawa: Supply and Services, 1985), p. 29.

19. Gregory Baum, "Catholicism and Secularization in Quebec," in *The Church in Quebec* (Montreal: Novalis, 1991), p. 16.

20. Ibid., p. 33.

21. Gregory Baum, "A Church's Response to Secularization: Analysis of a Response," *The Ecumenist*, September/December 1994, p. 99.

22. Marshall, *Secularizing the Faith*, p. 3.

23. Grant, *The Church in the Canadian Era*, p. 68.

24. Marshall, *Secularizing the Faith*, p. 189.

Chapter 4: Windows on Nation Building

1. These three windows or hermeneutical methods through which the Old Testament can be interpreted come from the writings of Christopher J.W. Wright, *An Eye for an Eye* (Downers Grove, IL: InterVarsity, 1983). Note Chapter 4, "Economics and the Land," especially pp. 88–102.

2. See Revelation 12: 7 and Ezekiel 28. "Lucifer" is a Latin word referring to the Hebrew word for "morning star," used by Isaiah: "How you have fallen from heaven, O morning star, son of the dawn! You have been cast down to the earth, you who once laid low the nations" (Isa. 14: 12).

3. Wright, *An Eye for An Eye*, p. 72.

4. *Baker Encyclopedia of the Bible*, ed.Walter A. Elwell (Grand Rapids, MI: Baker Book House, 1988), vol. 1, p. 243.

5. Wright, *An Eye for an Eye*, p. 106.

6. Genesis 25: 12–18 lists Ishmael's descendants. "North Arab genealogists trace their ancestry back to Ishmael," *Baker Encyclopedia of the Bible*, vol. 1, p. 145.

Chapter 5: Jesus and Politics

1. John Stott, *Decisive Issues Facing Christians Today* (Old Tappan, NJ: Fleming H. Revell, 1990), p. 11.
2. John Bright, *The Kingdom of God* (Nashville: Abingdon, 1953), p. 18.
3. Ibid., p. 217.

Chapter 6: Thinking with a Christian World-View

1. Harry Blamires, *The Christian Mind* (Ann Arbor: Servant Books, 1963), p. 4.
2. Richard J. Mouw, *Politics and the Biblical Drama* (Grand Rapids, MI: Eerdmans, 1976), p. 10.
3. For help on this question of the use of Israel as metaphor for nationhood, be advised of the cautions expressed in Mark Noll, Nathan Hatch, and George Marsden, *The Search for Christian America* (Colorado Springs: Helmers & Howard, 1989).
4. Seymour Lipset, *Continental Divide* (New York: Routledge, 1990), p. 77.
5. Michael Cassidy, *The Passing Summer* (London: Hodder & Stoughton, 1989), p. 101.

Chapter 7: Lessons from the Past: Christians and Rome

1. Glenn Tinder, *The Political Meaning of Christianity* (New York: HarperCollins, 1991). Note the prologue on the prophetic role of the church.
2. Richard A. Todd, *God and Caesar*, ed. R.A. Linder, Proceedings of the Conference on Faith and History (Longview, TX, 1971), p. 18.
3. Os Guiness, *The Dust of Death* (Downers Grove, IL: InterVarsity, 1973), p. 364.
4. T.M. Parker, *Christianity and the State in the Light of History* (London: A. & C. Black, 1955). p. 28.
5. Ibid.
6. Ibid., p. 36.
7. Ibid., p. 37.
8. Ibid., p. 39.
9. Ibid., pp. 38-39.
10. Ibid., p. 40.
11. Ibid., p. 59.
12. Robert G. Clouse, Richard V. Pierard, and Edwin M. Yamauchi, *Two Kingdoms: The Church and Culture through the Ages* (Chicago: Moody, 1993), p. 223.
13. Parker, *Christianity and the State in the Light of History*, p. 149.
14. *Luther's Works*, vol. 45 (Philadelphia: Fortress, 1962), pp. 88–92.
15. John Tonkin, *The Church and the Secular Order in Reformation Thought* (New York: Columbia University Press, 1971), p. 145.

Chapter 8: Is Pluralism Just a Modern Babel?

1. Paul Marshall, Secularity and Pluralism Conference, Camp Couchiching, Ontario, 1991.

2. Lesslie Newbigin, *The Gospel in a Pluralist Society* (Grand Rapids, MI: Eerdmans, 1989). The distinction between religious and cultural pluralism comes from this book.

3. Ibid., p. 14.

4. Max L. Stackhouse, *Public Theology and Political Economy: Christian Stewardship in Modern Society* (Grand Rapids, MI: Eerdmans, 1987), p. 159.

5. See Carl F.H. Henry, *Revelation and Authority*, vol. 1 (Waco, TX: Word, 1976), pp. 216ff.

6. Allan Bloom, *The Closing of the American Mind* (New York: Simon & Schuster, 1987), p. 26.

7. Peter Berger, *The Heretical Imperative* (New York: Anchor/Doubleday, 1979), p. 25.

8. Allen C. Guelzo, "Intellectual Sources of Pluralism," in *The Challenge of Religious Pluralism: An Evangelical Analysis and Response*, Proceedings of the Wheaton Theology Conference (Wheaton: Wheaton Graduate School, 1992), p. 89.

9. Ibid., p. 93.

10. Lesslie Newbigin, *Foolishness to the Greeks* (Grand Rapids, MI: Eerdmans, 1986), p. 3.

11. Ibid., p. 7.

12. Donald C. Posterski, *True to You* (Winfield, BC: Wood Lake, 1995), p.161.

13. Newbigin, *Foolishness to the Greeks*, p. 14.

14. John Stott, *Involvement* (Old Tappan, NJ: Fleming H. Revell, 1984), p. 82.

15. Newbigin, *Foolishness to the Greeks*, p. 18.

16. Newbigin, *The Gospel in a Pluralist Society*, p. 17.

17. Corrie Ten Boom, with John and Elizabeth Sherrill, *The Hiding Place* (New York: Chosen, 1971), p. 94.

18. Newbigin, *The Gospel in a Pluralist Society*, p. 159

Chapter 9: Speaking a New Language

1. H. Richard Neibuhr, *Christ and Culture* (New York: Harper & Row, 1951).

2. John Howard Yoder, *The Politics of Jesus* (Grand Rapids, MI: Eerdmans, 1972), p. 245.

3. Global Network Broadcast, "Salute to Canada," June 20, 1981.

4. Christopher J.H. Wright, *An Eye for an Eye* (Downers Grove, IL: InterVarsity, 1983), p. 77.

5. Robert Bellah, "Christian Faithfulness in a Pluralist World," in *Postmodern Theology,* ed. Frederic B. Burnham (San Francisco: Harper & Row, 1989), p. 91.

6. Don Posterski, *True to You* (Winfield, BC: Wood Lake, 1995), p. 168.

7. Henri Nouwen, *The Way of the Heart* (New York: Ballantine, 1981), pp. 10–12.

Bibliographic Notes

Like most writers, my ideas are not that original. They are either a reworking (conscious or unconscious) of thoughts and ideas of others or a synthesis arrived at by a point of view out of the past bombarded by a new one. To cite a source for each idea here would have cluttered up the page. In cases of direct quotation, I've tried to show the source. However, I want to acknowledge that, while the idea of examining what it means to be a Christian in Canada within a social/political context came out of my own interest in the subject, I am indebted to many writers in Canada and abroad for their enormous help.

Chapter 1: The Babel Syndrome: A Country Fragmented

I find it ironic but often true that those with the clearest perspective of who we are are born, and sometimes raised, outside of Canada. This is so with Andrew H. Malcolm, *The Canadians* (Markham, ON: Fitzhenry & Whiteside, 1985), and Seymour Lipset, *Continental Divide* (New York: Routledge, 1990).

Sociologist Reginald Bibby was particularly helpful to me in my early search. His first book, *Fragmented Gods: The Poverty and Potential of Religion in Canada* (Toronto: Irwin, 1987), outlines the changing religious Canadian scene. *In Mosaic Madness* (Toronto: Stoddart, 1990), he points out the confusion which comes from a culture aided by government largesse in reinforcing cultural bits and pieces, leading to cultural fragmentation. As well, his demographic studies have helped me more carefully note the real numbers of church attendance and religious affiliation.

Senior VP Andrew Grenville of the Canadian pollster organization Angus Reid has been helpful in providing me with data from their monthly research, especially on the religious nature of Canadians. His research made the cover of *Maclean's* magazine in April 1993, where the high percentages of Canadians who rated faith important surprised the editorial board. Grenville's research was prompted by his father-in-law, the well-known Canadian church historian of Queen's University, the late George Rawlyk.

Historian and professor of religion (University of Manitoba) John G. Stackhouse provides helpful insights in *Canadian Evangelicalism in the Twentieth Century* (Toronto: University of Toronto Press, 1993), and in "Whose Dominion? Christianity and Canadian Culture Historically Considered," *CRUX* 28/2, (June 1992).

Chapter 2: Was Canada Ever Christian?

There has been little research devoted to this subject. My hope is that this brief treatment will encourage scholars to give more attention to this important issue. I refer to a number of sources in this chapter. Note especially John S. Moir, "The Search for a Christian Canada," *Arc* 20 (1992), and work by three American scholars, Mark Noll, Nathan Hatch, and George Marsden, *The Search for Christian America* (Colorado Springs: Helmers & Howard, 1989).

It would be quite impossible to deal with the matter of faith and culture without referencing the classic by H. Richard Niebuhr, *Christ and Culture* (New York: Harper & Row, 1951). I refer to his five possibilities in chapter 9; however, his framework has been part of my thinking since I first read him in my undergraduate studies.

There is no one with a better understanding of the Canadian church than Ian Rennie, past dean of Ontario Theological Seminary. Note "Was Canada Ever Christian?" *Faith Today*, May/June 1986.

While my personal history is within the Protestant Church, the central role of the Roman Catholic Church in founding Canada needs much more attention. On this, note Cornelius J. Jaenen, *The Role of the Church in New France* (Toronto: McGraw-Hill Ryerson, 1976), *Works of Samuel de Champlain*, ed. H.P. Biggar (Toronto: Champlain Society, 1922–36) , and H.H. Walsh, *The Church in the French Era* (Toronto: Ryerson, 1966).

A period of religious revival quite unknown is the New Light Movement in the Maritimes at the turn of the nineteenth century. The specialist on this period is the late George Rawlyk. Note Nancy Christie, "'In These Times of Democratic Rage and Delusion': Popular Religion and the Challenge to the Established Order, 1760–1815," in *The Canadian Protestant Experience, 1760–1990*, ed. George Rawlyk (Burlington, ON: Welch, 1990); George Rawlyk, *Champions of the Truth: Fundamentalism, Modernism and the Maritime Baptists* (Montreal: McGill–Queen's University Press, 1990); and Maurice W. Armstrong, "Neutrality and Religion in Revolutionary Nova Scotia," in *Historical Essays on the Atlantic Provinces*, ed. George A. Rawlyk (Toronto: McClelland & Stewart, 1967).

Rawlyk's writing spreads from the East Coast into central Canada in *Canada Fire: Radical Evangelicalism in British North America, 1775–1812* (Montreal: McGill–Queen's University Press, 1994), and George A. Rawlyk, ed., *Revolution Rejected, 1775–1776* (Montreal: McGill–Queen's University Press, 1969).

The role of the church in Ontario is described by William Westfall in *Two Worlds: The Protestant Culture of Nineteenth-Century Ontario* (Montreal: McGill–Queen's University Press, 1989), where he identifies these two world-views: the religion of order and the religion of experience; John Webster Grant, *A Profusion of Spires*

(Toronto: University of Toronto Press, 1988); J.L.H. Henderson, ed., *Strachan: Documents and Opinions* (Toronto: McClelland & Stewart Limited, 1969), and Egerton Ryerson, *Letters from the Reverend Egerton Ryerson to the Hon. and Reverend Doctor Strachan* (Kingston, 1828).

John Webster Grant, *The Church in the Canadian Era* (Burlington, ON: Welch, 1988), gives an overview of the expansion of the church in the twentieth century.

The issue of missionary work with North American Indians is problematic. For help on this, see Cornelius J. Jaenen, "Amerindian Responses to French Missionary Intrusion, 1611–1760: A Categorization," in *Prophets, Priests and Prodigals: Readings in Canadian Religious History, 1608 to Present*, ed. Mark G. McGowan and David B. Marshall (Toronto: McGraw-Hill Ryerson, 1992), and John Webster Grant, *Moon of Wintertime* (Toronto: University of Toronto Press, 1984).

Volunteerism was central to the influence of the evangelical Protestant world. Note Phyllis Airhart, "Ordering a New Nation and Reordering Protestantism, 1867–1914," in *The Canadian Protestant Experience, 1760–1990*, ed. George Rawlyk (Burlington, ON: Welch, 1990); a complete list of Howland's numerous associations can be found in Ronald Sawatsky, "Looking for that Blessed Hope: The Roots of Fundamentalism in Canada, 1878–1914," PhD diss. University of Toronto, 1986. Even a partial list of Howland's business accomplishments is staggering: at age twenty-five he was director of a trust company and president of two insurance companies, a bank, and the Toronto Board of Underwriters: Lindsay Reynolds, *Footprints: The Beginning of the Christian and Missionary Alliance in Canada* (Toronto: Christian & Missionary Alliance, 1981). Among other endeavours, Howland became chair of the Toronto Mission Union and founding chair of the Mimico Boys' Industrial School; founder and first president of the Toronto Willard Tract Depository, the Prisoners' Aid Association, and the International Christian Workers' Association; superintendent of the central Prison Mission School; chair of the Ontario branch of the Dominion Alliance (temperance); a worker in the Prison Gate Mission and Haven (a home for unwed mothers), the Hillcrest Convalescent Home, and the Toronto branch of the YMCA; and a noted Sunday-school teacher and frequent church speaker.

The creation of a national church (the United Church of Canada in 1925) was an important juncture in the life of Canada. Note C.E. Silcox, "Church Union," in *Canada: Its Causes and Consequences* (New York: Institute of Social and Religious Research, 1933); John W. Grant, *The Canadian Experience of Church Union* (London: Lutterworth, 1967); John Webster Grant, *The Church in the Canadian Era* (Burlington, ON: Welch, 1988); N. Keith Clifford, *The Resistance to Church Union in Canada, 1904–1939* (Vancouver: University of British Columbia Press, 1985). Clifford points out that both those favouring union and those resisting it saw it as their Christian duty to do so. The main issues were whether denominational competition strengthened or weakened the cause of Christianity in Canada, whether religious pluralism was a good or bad thing, how to combat rising secularism in Canadian society, and how to be most faithful to the Christian gospel.

Timothy L. Smith charts the rise of the Social Gospel and the connection between evangelical faith and social reform in *Revivalism and Social Reform in Mid-Nineteenth-Century America* (New York: Abingdon, 1955). According to Smith, revivalism and the quest for Christian perfection were crucial, characterized by lay leadership, a drive to interdenominational fellowship, and the primacy of ethics over dogma. Much the same can be said of the Canadian experience. The prime Canadian authority is Richard Allen, *The Social Passion: Religion and Social Reform in Canada, 1914–1928* (Toronto: University of Toronto Press, 1971).

There is a debate on the extent to which Canada really was Christianized. On this see John G. Stackhouse, Jr., "Whose Dominion? Christianity and Canadian Culture Historically Considered," *CRUX* 28/2, (June 1992); and the data presented by Reginald Bibby, *Fragmented Gods: The Poverty and Potential of Religion in Canada* (Toronto: Irwin, 1987). It shows the pervasive overlapping of attitudes and behaviours between the groups he calls religiously "committed" and "uncommitted"; Michael Gauvreau, *The Evangelical Century* (Montreal & Kingston: McGill–Queen's University Press, 1991).

Chapter 3: How Did We Lose a Biblical Centre?

A primary resource to this topic is David B. Marshall, *Secularizing the Faith: Canadian Protestant Clergy and the Crisis of Belief, 1850–1940* (Toronto: University of Toronto Press, 1992). He provides the most comprehensive reasons why Protestant Church leaders (at that time mostly evangelical in theology) shifted from their orthodox stand on the Scriptures to a more liberal view. Also note John Webster Grant, *The Church in the Canadian Era* (Burlington, ON: Welch, 1988), and Phyllis D. Airhart, "Ordering a New Nation and Reordering Protestantism, 1867–1914," in *The Canadian Protestant Experience, 1760–1990*, ed. George A. Rawlyk (Burlington, ON: Welch, 1990).

Historian Michael Gauvreau, *The Evangelical Century* (Montreal & Kingston: McGill–Queen's University Press, 1991), argues that the nineteenth century was greatly shaped by the evangelical leadership and community. He says that investigating "the process that dislodged Protestant religion from its central place in English-Canadian society and culture provides one of the most compelling questions for Canadian intellectual historians" (p. 4).

Peter Berger provides a definition of "secularization" as "the process by which sectors of society and culture are removed from the domination of religious institutions and symbols" in *The Sacred Canopy: Elements of a Sociological Theory of Religion* (Garden City, NY: Doubleday/Anchor, 1969). The term should not be confused with "secularism," which refers to a world-view that actively seeks to promote indifference, or even hostility, towards religion and is devoid of any beliefs in the supernatural. Though they are not synonymous, secularism often does accompany the process of secularization. See the discussion in Elmer J. Thiessen, *Teaching for Commitment: Liberal Education, Indoctrination and Christian Nurture* (Montreal: McGill–Queen's University Press, 1993). Note definitions in David Lyon, *The Steeple's Shadow: On the Myths and Realities of Secularization* (Grand Rapids, MI: Eerdmans, 1985).

The turning of the century and westward expansion generated excitement for church growth, as noted by Keith Clifford, "His Dominion: A Vision in Crisis," in *Studies in Religion* 2/4 (1973).

Education was critical to the church. Note J. Donald Wilson, "Religion and Education: The Other Side of Pluralism," in *Canadian Education in the 1980s* (Calgary: Detselig Enterprises, 1981); Lynda Parker, "A History of Protestant Schools in Ontario," PhD diss., Regent College, 1982; William Westfall, *Two Worlds: The Protestant Culture of Nineteenth-Century Ontario* (Montreal: McGill–Queen's University Press, 1989); Douglas Lawr and Robert D. Gidney, eds., *Educating Canadians: A Documentary History of Public Education* (Toronto: Van Nostrand Reinhold, 1989). It is not simply a coincidence that the groups like the Baptists, Congregationalists, Methodists, and "Free Kirk" Presbyterians, who believed that the state should be responsible for public education and the church should be responsible for Christian education, were also the ones involved in the formation of Sunday schools: Bruce Curtis, *Building the Educational State: Canada West, 1936–1971* (London: Althouse Press, 1988); Bruce Curtis, *True Government by Choice Men? Inspection, Education and State Formation in Canada West* (Toronto: University of Toronto Press, 1992); David B. Marshall, *Canadian Historians, Secularization and the Problem of the Nineteenth Century*, Canadian Catholic Historical Association, *Historical Studies* 60 (1993–1994), pp. 57–81; Harro Van Brummelen, "The World Portrayed in Texts: An Analysis of the Content of Elementary School Textbooks," *Journal of Educational Thought*, December 1991; John S. Moir, *The Church in the British Era* (Toronto: McGraw-Hill Ryerson, 1972), notes that Horton College was formed by a group of Anglicans who had seceded from St. Paul's Church in Halifax.

New ideas reshaped the church at the turn of the century. Owen Chadwick, in *The Victorian Church, Part I* (London: A.&C. Black, 1973), suggests that "Darwin was only a sign of a movement bigger than Darwin, bigger than biological science, bigger than intellectual inquiry"; Carl Berger, *Science, God and Nature in Victorian Canada* (Toronto:

University of Toronto Press, 1983); Os Guinness, *The Dust of Death* (Downers Grove, IL: InterVarsity, 1973).

While the historic churches were declining, others were not. By the end of the century, any one of several relatively small Protestant denominations, including the Christian and Missionary Alliance, the Christian Brethren, or even the Associated Gospel Churches (only 14,000 members), sent out more missionaries than did the United, Anglican, and Presbyterian churches combined: Bruce Guenther, "Canadian Evangelicalism in the 1980s," a paper presented at the Religion in North America Conference, November 1991, Plymouth State College, New Hampshire.

On the Social Gospel Movement see Richard Allen, *The Social Passion: Religion and Social Reform in Canada, 1914–1928* (Toronto: University of Toronto Press, 1973). Opinions vary regarding the contribution of the Social Gospel to the process of secularization. For example, Richard Allen claims that the movement "Christianized" Canadian society by providing a religious underpinning for an indigenous tradition of democratic socialism, thereby stemming the advance of secularization (*The Social Passion*, pp. 350–356). Also note Walter Rauschenbusch's works, which include *Christianity and the Social Crisis* (1907), *Christianizing the Social Order* (1914), and *A Theology for the Social Gospel* (1917). The last was an attempt to provide a systematic theology to undergird the Christian social emphasis. One of his most popular books was *The Social Principles of Jesus* (1916), a study book for college students.

Foundational reading for Canadian nationalism is the work of George P. Grant, including his most important book, *Lament for a Nation* (Ottawa; Carleton University Press, 1965), *Technology and Empire* (Toronto: Anansi, 1969), and *English-Speaking Justice* (Toronto: Anansi, 1974).

One of the most important influences in my study has been political theorist Paul Marshall. The three points of liberalism I refer to in this chapter come from his work "Liberalism, Pluralism and Christianity," *Fideset Historia* 21/3 (October 1989). On the subject of liberalism and its relationship to the French, see Eric Voegelin, "Liberalism and Its History," *Review of Politics* 37 (1974,) and Alasdair MacIntyre, *Whose Justice? Which Rationality?* (South Bend: University of Notre Dame Press, 1988).

On the issue role of the 1982 Charter of Rights and Freedoms, note Paul Marshall, "'Temples of an Incrusted Faith': An Inquiry into the Question of Secularization from Within," Robert Nadeau, "The Charter of Rights and Freedoms: An Overview for Christians," an unpublished commentary available from the office of the Evangelical Fellowship of Canada.

American Fundamentalism and its accompanying issues have washed up into Canada. For a background look at this important early-twentieth-century religious movement, see James Davison Hunter in *Piety and Politics*, "The Evangelical World View Since 1890," eds. Richard John Neuhaus and Michael Cromartie (Washington, DC: Ethics and Public Policy Center, 1987), especially Chapter 2.

A critical doctrinal shift within the American and Canadian evangelical (earlier called "fundamentalist") movements was led by Plymouth Brethren preacher and writer J.N. Darby, and his theory of "Dispensationalism" made it seem that Christ was about to return immediately. This idea is described in Paul Boyer, *When Time Shall Be No More: Prophecy and Belief in Modern American Culture* (Cambridge, MA: Harvard University Press, 1992).

The growth of twentieth-century denominations was first drawn to my attention by seminary professor and Presbyterian minister Dennis M. Oliver, who in 1979 delivered a paper, "The New Canadian Religious Pluralism," at the Canadian Society of Church History. He did so on the basis of membership and attendance statistics compiled for the year 1977. These numbers are supported by a more thorough compilation done by Arnell Motz in 1988 in *Reclaiming a Nation* (OC Ministries, 1990).

On the enormous influence of the Roman Catholic Church, I found the following instructive: Nive Voisine, "L'ultramontanisme canadien-français au XIXe siècle," in *Les Ultramontains canadien-français*, eds. Nive Voisine and Jean Hamelin (Montreal: Boréal Express, 1985); Grant, *The Church in the Canadian Era;* Gregory Baum, "Catholicism and Secularization in Quebec," in *The Church in Quebec* (Montreal: Novalis, 1991); Raymond Lemieux, "Les Catholiques," *Le Devoir*, April 8, 1982; Gregory Baum, "A Church's Response to Secularization: Analysis of a Response," *The Ecumenist*, September/December 1994.

A central factor in the process of secularization was consumption and the hold it had on the most fervent of Christians. These books are a beginning in this analysis: in the United States, R.W. Fox and J.J. Jackson Lears, *The Culture of Consumption: Critical Essays in American History, 1880–1980* (New York: Pantheon, 1983), and, in Canada, George Rawlyk, *Wrapped Up in God* (Burlington, ON: Welch, 1988); It also becomes most clear in the recent literature on immigration: see Bruce Elliott, *Irish Migrants in the Canadas: A New Approach* (Montreal: McGill–Queen's University Press, 1988); Cecil Houston and William Smyth, *Irish Emigration and Canadian Settlements: Patterns, Links, and Letters* (Toronto: University of Toronto Press, 1990); and Marianne McLean, *The People of Glengarry: Highlanders in Transition, 1745–1820* (Montreal: McGill–Queen's University Press, 1991). The literature on settlement also stresses the overwhelming concern for material well-being and progress; see especially David Gagan, *Hopeful Travellers: Families, Land, and Social Change in Mid-Victorian Peel County, Canada West* (Toronto: University of Toronto Press, 1981); and Donald Akenson, *The Irish in Ontario: A Study in Rural History* (Montreal: McGill–Queen's University Press, 1984).

Chapter 4: Windows on Nation Building

There is less need for notation on these next few chapters as much of the material came more from my lifelong search and study, and thus many of the ideas were either more or less original or from sources I've simply lost over time.

Important texts for the Old Testament studies, in searching for roots of New Testament Kingdom material, came from Christopher J.W. Wright, *An Eye for an Eye* (Downers Grove, IL: InterVarsity, 1983). I especially found Chapter 4, "Economics and the Land," to be helpful. Note also John Bright, *The Kingdom of God* (Nashville: Abingdon, 1953), and Herman Ridderbos, *The Coming of the Kingdom* (Philadelphia: The Presbyterian and Reformed Publishing Company, 1962).

Chapter 5: Jesus and Politics

Some books to assist in study include John Stott, *Decisive Issues Facing Christians Today* (Old Tappan, NJ: Fleming H. Revell, 1990); John Bright, *The Kingdom of God* (Nashville: Abingdon, 1953); Herman Ridderbos, *The Coming of the Kingdom* (Philadelphia: The Presbyterian and Reformed Publishing Company, 1962); Glenn Tinder, *The Political Meaning of Christianity* (New York: HarperCollins, 1991).

Chapter 6: Thinking with a Christian World-View

We are assisted in thinking Christianly by the following: Harry Blamires, *The Christian Mind* (Ann Arbor: Servant, 1963); Vinay K. Samuel, "A Christian Attitude to the State—An Indian Perspective," *Transformation* April/June, 1991; Richard J. Mouw, *Politics and the Biblical Drama* (Grand Rapids, MI: Baker Book House, 1967).

The use of Israel as metaphor for nationhood is loaded with danger. Mark Noll, Nathan Hatch, and George Marsden, *The Search for Christian America* (Colorado Springs: Helmers & Howard, 1989), and Seymour Lipset, *Continental Divide* (New York: Routledge, 1990), deal with America, while Michael Cassidy, *The Passing Summer* (London: Hodder & Stoughton, 1989), speaks of South Africa.

Chapter 7: Lessons from the Past: Christians and Rome

The relationship of the church and state over the centuries is fascinating and instructive. Of the countless numbers of reference and history books, I found these to be helpful: Glenn Tinder, *The Political Meaning of Christianity* (New York: HarperCollins, 1991); Richard A. Todd, *God and Caesar*, ed. R.A. Linder, Proceedings of the Conference on Faith and History (Longview, TX, 1971); T.M. Parker, *Christianity and the State in the Light of History* (London: A. & C. Black, 1955); Carroll V. Newsom, *The Roots of Christianity* (Englewood Cliffs, NJ: Prentice-Hall, 1979); Robert G.

Clouse, Richard V. Pierard, and Edwin M. Yamauchi, *Two Kingdoms: The Church and Culture through the Ages* (Chicago: Moody, 1993); John Tonkin, *The Church and the Secular Order in Reformation Thought* (New York: Columbia University Press, 1971); Jon Butler, *Awash in a Sea of Faith* (Cambridge, MA: Harvard University Press, 1990).

Chapter 8: Is Pluralism Just a Modern Babel?

The distinction between religious pluralism and cultural pluralism comes from Lesslie Newbigin, *The Gospel in a Pluralist Society* (Grand Rapids, MI: Eerdmans, 1989). Other books on pluralism include Richard Mouw and Sander Griffioen, *Pluralism and Horizons* (Grand Rapids, MI: Eerdmans, 1993), a more theoretical treatment that supplies a background to the thought-shaping by contemporary pluralism, and *The Challenge of Religious Pluralism: An Evangelical Analysis and Response,* ed. Allen C. Guelzo, Proceedings of the Wheaton Theology Conference (Wheaton: Wheaton Graduate School, 1992). The lectures begin with a discussion of Ernst Troeltsch, then analyse John Hick's approach and offer suggestions to the church on how it might respond. Also Max L. Stackhouse, *Public Theology and Political Economy: Christian Stewardship in Modern Society* (Grand Rapids, MI: Eerdmans, 1987): Allen C. Guelzo, "Intellectual Sources of Pluralism," *The Challenge of Religious Pluralism: An Evangelical Analysis and Response*, Proceedings of the Wheaton Theology Conference (Wheaton: Wheaton Graduate School, 1992): Allan Bloom, *The Closing of the American Mind* (New York: Simon & Schuster, 1987); Peter Berger, *The Heretical Imperative* (New York: Anchor/Doubleday, 1979): Lesslie Newbigin, *Foolishness to the Greeks* (Grand Rapids, MI: Eerdmans, 1986).

Chapter 9: Speaking a New Language

No study of the church and culture is complete without a look at the classic work, H. Richard Neibuhr, *Christ and Culture* (New York: Harper & Row, 1951). For the Anabaptist view, see John Howard Yoder, *The Politics of Jesus* (Grand Rapids, MI: Eerdmans, 1972). Christopher J.H Wright, *An Eye for an Eye* (Downers Grove, IL: InterVarsity, 1983), brings together the Old and New of the Scriptures and points the way to a better way of serving out Christ's Kingdom. I've been especially encouraged by Richard Mouw's book, *Uncommon Decency* (Downers Grove, IL: InterVarsity, 1991). See especially chapter 3, "Defending Christian Civility." Canadian colleague Don Posterski's *True to You* (Winfield, BC: Wood Lake, 1995), is a call to careful and thoughtful Christian attitude and living. And in the end, it is Christians like Henri Nouwen, author of *The Way of the Heart* (New York: Ballantine, 1981), who call us to first love God and then, out of that, love our neighbour.

Index